YOUTH AC'
AND TH
ENVIRONMENT

GW00854158

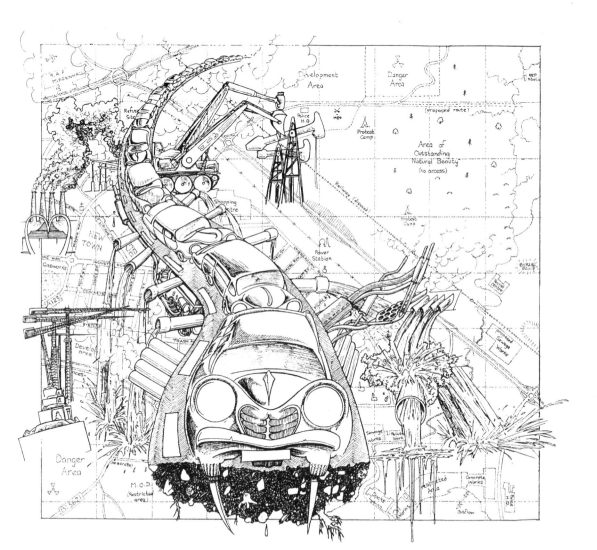

ALAN DEARLING
WITH HOWIE ARMSTRONG
ILLUSTRATIONS BY GUBBY, KATE EVANS
AND OTHER FRIENDS

First published in 1997 by Russell House Publishing Ltd in collaboration with the Council for Environmental Education

Russell House Publishing Limited
4 St. George's House
The Business Park
Uplyme Road
Lyme Regis
Dorset DT7 3LS

Council for Environmental Education
University of Reading
London Road
Reading RG1 5AQ

Photocopying Permission
Permission is given by the authors and the publishers for photocopying material in the games and exercises, as indicated in the text, by organisations purchasing the book.

British Library Cataloguing-in-Publication Data:
A Catalogue record for this book is available from the British Library.

ISBN 1-898924-07-4

The Council for Environmental Education (CEE) and Russell House Publishing (RHP) are delighted to have been associated with this publication and are confident that it will make a significant contribution to the field of environmental work with young people. The views expressed in the book are those of the authors, Alan Dearling and Howie Armstrong, and the many other people who have contributed material, and are not necessarily the views of either CEE or RHP.

This book has been printed on paper derived from sustainable forests.

Printed by Hobbs the Printers, Totton, Hants.

CONTENTS

Ancient Tombstone Melrose Abbey

•Alan D. 1996•

ACKNOWLEDGEMENTS

Literally hundreds of people have contributed to this book. As authors of the collection of ideas, reports, exercises and information we are very much custodians and reporters. As you work your way through the rich tapestry of environmental material you will hear the voices of many young people themselves, youth workers, teachers, outdoor and adventure educators, environmentalists, agriculturalists, travellers, DiY activists. For the very reason that there are so many, we have tried to acknowledge all the people who have helped us in the text rather than producing a two page list in unreadable small type. Anyway, you know who you are – please accept a Big Thanks!

Most of all we'd like to express our appreciation of all the efforts that young people and those who are working with them are making on the environmental front. It can never be too much, otherwise it will be just too late to stop our country and our planet being destroyed by our own avarice. This book contains accounts and ideas from many, many individuals and organisations. Some are involved in youth work and education; others are active in the 'green' and environmental worlds.

Our particular thanks go to our friends and colleagues at the Council for Environmental Education and Russell House Publishing for helping all the way along the sometimes twisting path towards publication. Thanks also to the photographers and artists who have enlivened the words.

Walk softly on the Earth and enjoy its splendours

Alan + Howie

Alan and Howie

INTRODUCTION: The How, the Why and the What

The How

"This came up in the pub! I'm interested in exploring a book that looks at how youth workers can introduce young people to, and get them involved in, some of the following: energy use; recycling; organic food; the local environment."

The above is a much shortened version of the memo Alan's colleague, Geoffrey Mann, who is the boss at Russell House Publishing (RHP), sent to Alan. Alan then talked to his mate, Howie Armstrong, who works for NCH Action For Children about whether they fancied embarking on writing yet another practical book about work with young people. At this time they were still busy writing the *New Youth Arts and Crafts Book,* which was published in May 1996. Meanwhile, Geoffrey contacted the Council for Environmental Education (CEE) to see whether they would be interested in being partners in the project.

And, just less than eighteen months later, you are looking at the outcome. The process in between has been one of making connections. At the outset, Howie and Alan brainstormed a possible 'shopping list' of topic areas that might go into the book. Following discussion with Bud Simpkin, Libby Grundy and Margaret Feneley at CEE, this list was refined. Finally, over about eight months, various modified versions of the possible contents of the book and an invitation to get involved, were circulated through CEE networks; Alan's own contact list, and a number of publications such as *Youth Action, School's Out, Youth Clubs, Young People Now, EARTHlines, Living Green, SQUALL and The Business.*

During the process of interviewing, researching, visiting, editing and talking which led to this book, literally hundreds of individuals and projects were in some way involved. It was during this time that Alan found himself in the driving seat as key writer. Howie had many other work commitments, but was still able to work with a few projects, primarily in his home area of Scotland. Alan enlisted his environmentally-friendly illustrator, Gubby, to the project, and contacted a diverse spectrum of young people and organisations working in a wide assortment of environmental arenas.

In the final stages of putting the book 'to bed', CEE has supplemented the material collected by the authors with a resource list section and a couple of sections, such as the National Young People's Environment Network (NYPEN), which are very much examples of CEE's direct involvement with young people in creating fora for young people's participation.

The Why

Back in 1990, CEE had published their *EARTHworks* packs. These had proved very successful, but some parts had drifted out of date. There was also a feeling that there was a need for something which described activities which young people could initiate or get involved in, which were across a wider frame of reference than the original CEE publication. The difficulty for Alan and Howie was that the environmental themepark is a very big place indeed! Once responses started to come in to the original outline and letter, it quickly became obvious that the contents would have to be allowed to have a life of their own, rather than trying (it would have been hopeless!), to slot the exciting and challenging material into the pre-determined contents framework.

The raison d 'etre changed somewhat in the writing and compiling. Instead of simply being a book of games and activities which could be used by youth workers, teachers and the like to introduce environmental issues to young people, the motivation of the groups who were submitting the material became a major part of the driving force. For the authors, this was at once very challenging and rewarding. The respondents who were keen to have their practice and experiences included in the book were from a much wider constituency than the CEE membership organisations. They were drawn from a far wider constituency than the world known as Youth Work. To describe them is, in itself, quite difficult. In addition to the youth organisations and Agenda 21 groups, there are conservationists, naturalists, environmental groups, single interest groups; some are involved in human rights work, some are community artists, some are international and global campaigners, and some are young people involved in direct action. Together they provide a rich diorama.

The authors found that the material they were creating and collating showed that young people are increasingly angry at the way they see both the natural and human environment being treated. Yet they desperately want a chance to celebrate. For increasing numbers, getting involved in environmental action and activities offers a chance to do something 'real' – celebrating cultural and environmental diversity and at the same time engaging in environmental activities which can lead to effective change. Green Activities and participation in youth councils, Local Agenda 21, local conservation and clean-up schemes and the like, are one element of the opportunities available to young people. But, this book takes both debate and practice one stage further, and *doesn't* dodge the difficult and controversial problems facing those working with young people. Should youth work stick to the 'safe' areas of environmental work such as recycling and tree planting, or can empowerment embrace the DiY culture of the road and tree protesters?

The What

Instead of a neat collection of programming material, we found ourselves, especially Alan, getting involved in what was a complex series of journalistic investigations. And that determined the style of presentation. What you have in this book is a series of 'snapshots' of environmental action which *has* or *could* involve young people. We feel strongly that this is more empowering than keeping strictly to the safe areas of environmental youth work.

As a resource for working with young people, this book provides a unique and highly diverse range of examples and case studies:
- Agenda 21 initiatives;
- conservation and reclamation projects;
- arts, drama and animation work;
- human rights issues: homelessness, unemployment, war, poverty and discrimination, and a range of potential responses;
- problems and solutions regarding sustainability, pollution, food and other resources, power and transport;
- options for participation and involvement;
- games and activities;
- the most popular elements of CEE's *EARTHworks;*
- global and international issues and action; and
- taking direct action.

The authors have collected the material in the book from youth projects, organisations and individuals throughout the UK, beyond into Europe, and even Bombay, Kenya and Colombia. Examples of innovative practice in the natural and built environment, which can be easily adapted for use in local communities, rub shoulders with calls to action from human rights organisations such as Homeless International and Children's Aid Direct. The range includes the work of Friends of the Earth, RSPB, Common Ground, the Development Education Association, the Adventure and Environmental Awareness Group, the Duke of Edinburgh's Award Scheme, the National Trust, the British Trust for Conservation Volunteers, and the Quakers through to Earth First! and Road Alert, and, of course, the Council for Environmental Education itself!

Finally, and perhaps slightly tongue in cheek, we offer users of this book one of the many disclaimers which are printed each week in *SchNEWS,*

> *"The SchNEWS warns all its readers not to attend any illegal gatherings or take part in any criminal activities. Always stay within the law. In fact, please sit at home, watch TV, and go on endless shopping sprees filling your lives with endless consumer crap...you will then feel content. Honest."*

Alan and Howie

THE BUZZ WORDS
SUSTAINABILITY, BIODIVERSITY, ECOSYSTEMS, GAIA, SHADES OF GREENNESS AND CHAOS!

Some of the theory
There are a number of 'buzz' or jargon words which inhabit the Green and ecology movement. The problem is that such words are a turn-off for many people, the young included. It all sounds too complicated and unrelated to their own worlds and communities. However, unless we have some understanding of the more common environmental terms we can't really come to grips with the problems we, and young people, have to tackle. Given that this is a book primarily for people working informally with young people, we are not advocating you holding environmental theory lessons. That said, this next bit does have some important ideas in it – honest!

Biodiversity
Everything on the Earth is interconnected. The problem as we move into the new millennium is people's avarice. Our consumption of resources and the growing population across the world threatens to destroy many of the lifeforms with whom we co-exist. Biodiversity is the word which describes the rich variety of living organisms: insects, plants, trees and shrubs, birds, fish, animals. Unfortunately, humans are rapidly destroying that diversity in many different ways. Pollution, factory farming, chemicals and fertilisers, deforestation, desertification, industrialisation, and over-fishing are all culprits. The result of all this is that, of perhaps 10-15 million species on Earth (the majority of which have still not been described), it is estimated that around 20 per cent could be lost before we are very far into the new millennium. Because of the interconnectedness of species, the loss of one species can lead to the disappearance of many others which cannot survive without it.

One branch of scientific study has evolved what is called the **chaos theory.** This contends that since everything in nature is so finely balanced and inter-dependent, then the effect of one action (for instance, the destruction of a species of life) has a chaotic, unpredictable effect on everything else.

Ecosystems
The study of the interconnectedness of life forms and the environment is called

ecology. An ecosystem is any single community of life forms in a particular physical environment which co-exists in balance. Disruption of the balance through drought, pollution or other changes can destroy an ecosystem. All of us live in complex ecosystems. To help understand how an ecosystem works, you might like to try introducing the following experiment.

A Bottle Ecosystem

The idea is to build a living ecosystem. The model we offer gives an idea of how diverse species exist together and depend on one another as well as light and water for sustenance and growth. To get a group of young people started you need certain materials:

- clean, two litre plastic bottles with their tops, and with labels removed (two or three per group);
- scissors;
- a strong, large sized safety pin or compass points;
- a craft knife;
- permanent marker pen;
- waterproof tape;
- silicone sealant to waterproof joints between bottles.

A useful hint is that labels and plastic bottle bottoms can often be removed using a hair dryer, but take care, it is easy to melt and warp plastic bottles!

In our drawing you'll see the basic idea for the bottle ecosystem – but encourage your groups to experiment. There are no right or wrong ways to build up the system. The size of the ecosystem can be varied to accommodate different species and environments.

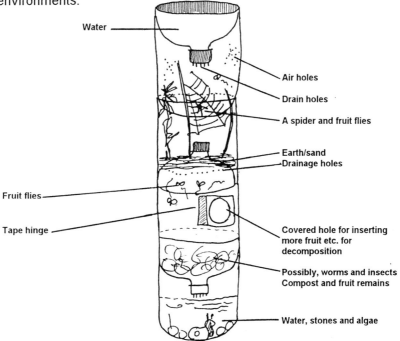

Water

Air holes

Drain holes

A spider and fruit flies

Earth/sand
Drainage holes

Fruit flies

Tape hinge

Covered hole for inserting more fruit etc. for decomposition

Possibly, worms and insects
Compost and fruit remains

Water, stones and algae

A few points worth making to the participants:
- make plenty of appropriately sized air holes for the living creatures inside;
- construct a drainage system which enables water to pass down through each level of the system;
- make sure that adequate, regular water is provided;
- top up the decomposition section with small fresh amounts of fruit and vegetables;
- avoid exposing to full sunlight;
- the bottle structure can be hard to balance and will need support from string, Velcro or rubber bands.

The experimental ecosystem can be kept going for as long as your group wish. Once finished with, return the inhabitants of the ecosystem back to their natural habitats.

A Few Key Learning Outcomes
Through building and nurturing the ecosystem, young people can learn about water and food cycles, decomposition, life cycles and the various life forms that have lived in the ecosystem. Young people are trying to duplicate a natural process. It is important therefore that the review of the activity should emphasise how complex even a simple ecosystem like the Bottle Ecosystem is.

There is also an opportunity here to introduce animal rights. What does the group think about experimenting with live 'animals' in this way? Not only can this view point raise an interesting discussion it also ensures that some care is taken in returning the insects to their habitat.

And finally....if the principle of incarcerating insects in plastic bottles is not for you then why not go on a **'mini-beast safari'**. Although these activities are often aimed at a younger age group, as with many children's activities, young adults can take them on quite successfully. A simple activity would be the building of a pitfall trap. Dig a small hole in the ground and place a yoghurt pot in it so it is flush with the ground. Place some bait in the 'trap' like a piece of meat or fruit, leave it for 24 hours and then inspect the 'trap' and see what you have caught.

Using one of the many reference books like *The Usborne Book of Insect Watching* by Ruth Thompson, get the group to identify the insects and find out a little bit about them and their habitat. This simple activity helps to introduce young people to both the richness and the complexity of the ecosystem.

Sustainability.
Sustainability has been defined as,
> "...development that meets the needs of the future without compromising the ability of future generations to meet their own needs" (the Brundtland Report, *Our Common Future*, 1987).

A sustainable planet, like a sustainable lifestyle, is one which:
- tries to use renewable energy sources;
- divides up resources based on need rather than greed;

- protects rather than squanders its non-renewable resources;
- manages to limit its consumption and waste;
- plans for the future rather than just living for today.

However the reality of 'sustainability' depends on the actions of humans to put a stop to activities which jeopardise the balance between many aspects of life on planet Earth. Some people believe that the Earth will protect itself and that sustainability is a continually changing concept. For instance, the death of dinosaurs allowed the evolution of mammals.

One of the key outcomes of the Rio Earth Summit in 1992 was *Agenda 21, an 'action plan for the 21st century'*. Agenda 21 set out a strategy for working towards sustainable development, which includes and involves all sectors of society. Chapter 25 of Agenda 21 explained that:
- young people across the world make up about a third of the total world population and in some communities up to half of the population;
- children and young people's concerns on environmental issues should be canvassed at local, regional, national and international levels;
- governments should provide ways in which young people can participate actively in decision making about the environment, social and economic development.

A good access point to the ideas of Agenda 21 (since the original is a rather weighty 700 page document!) is *Rescue Mission Planet Earth: a children's edition of Agenda 21*, which presents Agenda 21 in a style highly accessible to young people, highlighting their concerns and perceptions and is full of ideas and illustrations to inspire others.

Agenda 21 also encourages local authorities to develop local action plans for sustainability, entitled not too surprisingly, Local Agenda 21s. UK local authorities have been particularly proactive on this, and many are actively working to ensure that young people are involved and represented in this process. The Local Government Management Board's guideline document, *Local Agenda 21 and Young People*, produced as a result of a roundtable co-ordinated by CEE, and with 50 per cent of its participants being young people, gives ideas and examples for how to achieve this (more about this is included later in the section, 'CEE/LGMB roundtable: young people and Local Agenda 21').

The *Rescue Mission: Planet Earth Indicators* pack and the children's edition of Agenda 21 are really useful resources for involving young people in project activities to investigate their own environments and assess how 'sustainable' they are. They are available from: Rescue Mission Headquarters, Peace Child International, The White House, Buntingford, Herts, England SG9 9AH.

Gaia theory
Some years ago James Lovelock introduced the 'Gaia theory', which in simple terms suggests that,
> "...the entire range of living matter on Earth, from whales to viruses, can be regarded as a single entity, capable of manipulating the environment to suit its needs."

In his most recent work, James Lovelock has been conducting experiments which have shown that the richer the diversity of lifeforms in an ecosystem the more adaptable the system is to change, such as rainfall levels, temperature or carbon dioxide levels. The problem is that no-one knows if the harmony of Gaia can continue given that the elements of Gaia – energy, water, air, land and climate are abundant but not infinite. What responses we will or should make, as individuals and on a global scale, depend to some extent on our level of optimism or pessimism. This is sometimes described in terms of 'shades of greenness.'

Shades of Greenness

Those of us working with young people have a responsibility to offer information which informs those young people about how they can make their own lives more Gaia friendly – more sustainable. A 'light green' response anticipates the Earth being able to protect its own ecosystem, meaning that it will remain in balance with just a little help from humans; a 'deep green' vision is of the apocalypse unless drastic remedial action is taken. At the individual level young people can have effects on the future of the environment by:

- arming themselves with knowledge and information about the environment;
- joining together with friends and taking local action on issues such as: conservation; pollution; recycling, packaging, consumerism, re-using and repairing of materials; and rights issues;
- joining existing environmental groups ranging from the RSPB, Greenpeace, Friends of the Earth, World Wide Fund for Nature through to Earth First!; or forming their own new groups and organisations;
- pressurising local and national institutions and agencies: schools, youth clubs and organisations such as the Scouts and Guides, National Youth Agency, Youth Clubs UK, the Woodcraft Folk etc. to listen to their voices and act with them;
- lobbying and joining political and campaigning groups and parties to ensure that the views of young people are heard.

Something to get the brain cells ticking!

Before we ever contemplated writing this book, we were involved with many friends and colleagues in the UK and elsewhere who have been active on the environmental front. The UK has been slow to pick up the 'green' banner of action to stop wasting energy, cut pollution or establish radical, but achievable targets towards a sustainable environment. In Germany, for instance, over ten per cent of the population votes for the German Green Party and the other parties have agreed policies on renewable energy sources such as solar power. In Denmark, there is the Energy 2000 Plan, which plans to reduce carbon dioxide emissions by 20 per cent by 2005, and very actively encourage energy efficiency both for residential homes and industry.

The following article is something you might want to copy and give out to young people to start them thinking about the global issue of sustainability. It is written by George Firsoff and first appeared in slightly different forms in *Greenleaf* magazine which he edits.

A Deep Green Viewpoint

We want recycling of resources, wild land to be preserved and restored as a sacred heritage, we want cleaner motor vehicles, punishment of polluters, more ecologically sound food products and steps in these directions, however small, are welcome.

Nevertheless, it is easy to forget the Deep Green perspective within which this tinkering with the environment takes place. That perspective is that this civilisation is not sustainable. The Club of Rome were a group of scientists who investigated this by means of computer models, and published their report entitled, 'Limits to Growth' (1972). They identified five problems:
1. Accelerating industrialisation.
2. Rapid population growth.
3. Widespread malnutrition.
4. Depletion of non-renewable resources.
5. A deteriorating environment.

If we did nothing about these problems we would run out of resources.
If we doubled our resources we would choke on pollution.
If we curbed pollution we would run out of land to grow food on.
Even with every technological fix the scientists could devise, the system would collapse within the next one hundred years, with land erosion, mass starvation and poisoning of the population. The figures and details fed into the computers can be questioned, but the ultimate conclusion is that the Earth is a finite system. We cannot continue to grow without meeting disaster; all that clever technology can do is to delay the day. These are undeniable, common sense, conclusions.

The difficulty is that a political movement that says: "Consume less, agree to have smaller families, give up manufactured goods and live in low impact dwellings, meeting your own needs in local communities, while WE (that is a big We) work to maintain enough central government to ensure sensible national and global management of resources," is not only unattractive to most people but logically flawed, because we know peasant societies are no match for multinational exploiters. Green parties and green movements have philosophical and political problems to wrestle with.

Meanwhile, perhaps at least a generation of young people can believe in another way to live, while we tinker with the problems we meet on a daily basis, to improve our environment in the short term. It is a good thing that somebody cares. Belief that the Earth is a living Goddess and she owns everything we own, even our bodies are on loan, is a perspective that has great potential.

The next thousand years...........

It's not just that there are so many people, but they all want beefburgers, they all want motor cars, they all want newspapers; this places intolerable burdens on the environment. A hundred years ago the motor car was a novelty, the first pedestrian was killed by one. Fifty years ago there weren't that many. In the last twenty years we have been aware of the environmental crisis but have done little but tinker with the problems. All is perilous and unknown and it makes it hard for us to choose our path. More is required! The building of a new civilisation on the still struggling body of the old!

A very positive scenario would be that surprisingly soon there would be a big change in consciousness. A natural disaster might do it, just as Chernobyl really changed people's attitudes to nuclear power. Something really awesome might wake people up: they'd stabilise the human population, conserve energy, respect trees and wilderness, punish people who abuse the planet, go heavily into solar power, hydrogen power and massive tree planting, permaculture etc.

A slightly less rosy view is that some of the consciousness I have described takes off, at least among younger people (who will live longer into the deepening crisis) and things are slightly stabilised. The ruin is at least slowed down; there's still a period of stand-off between the old ways and the new, with the outcome still uncertain. That sounds very realistic, historically.

The last scenario is that it will go on getting worse. The whales will be killed, the seas will be poisoned, the Amazon trees will be cut down, England and Wales will be strip-mined, more people will drive cars, eat beef, and kill each other in deteriorating social conditions. Until Nature bites back with skin cancer epidemics, the pole melts drowning London and other major cities, we starve, choke to death on chemical disasters. Suddenly there is an Ice Age, something else we cannot imagine, a doomsday scenario caused by our terminal stupidity. We become extinct.

From the spiritual viewpoint, as magical beings, at least in the first instance, we can choose, we must choose, which of these ways we want, and act in accordance. Not wait for *them* to do it. As men and women of power we are *them,* and if we don't do our very best we may take the blame.

Greenleaf magazine is published quarterly costing 90 pence per issue and £3.70 per year from George Firsoff, 96 Church Road, Redfield, Bristol 5.

OUTDOOR AND ADVENTURE EXPERIENCES

Geoff Cooper, who is director of two outdoor education centres in the Lakeland area of Cumbria, contacted us with quite a stack of material on outdoor, environmental and adventure education. Like most of us these days, Geoff wears a number of hats, and is a fervent advocate of the value of environmental education of various sorts. His centres and the networks he belongs to, such as TOUCH, the European Environmental network, and the Adventure and Environmental Awareness Group have long grappled with many of the thorny questions such as:

access **v** damage and pollution

environmental use **v** ecosystem survival

competing sporting and recreational use (e.g. walkers, horses and mountain bikes)

legal regulation **v** voluntary self-regulation

use of wild areas or creation of specialist facilities on the urban fringes

Like Topsy, this list of conflicts can be made to grow very, very long indeed. We thought that some of these topics could well be used for staff training or senior member training in youth organisations.

One of the roles of environmental educators like Geoff seems to be to provide some guidelines on ways in which young people can be introduced to the natural environment and then make use of it in ways which do not destroy its beauty and grace. The Adventure and Environmental Awareness Group set its own aim as,
"...to encourage awareness, understanding and concern for the natural environment amongst those involved with education and recreation."

Their motto links the words: awareness; adventure; conservation and understanding, and it is in this fine balancing act that environmentalists have to engage with outdoor education and adventure leaders. Further to this there are national, international and global questions which the sporting and recreational use of the natural environment poses. In the following section we reprint Geoff's ten point guidelines for the 'greening' of outdoor centres (reprinted with thanks to Geoff and the Journal of Adventure Education). Perhaps this could be used as a discussion paper in staff and older member training, or as a part of a Local Agenda 21 initiative?

The Greening of Outdoor Centres

How should the modern outdoor/environmental centre differ from the traditional outdoor pursuits or field studies centre? To answer this, I've suggested a series of guidelines, reprinted below.

It is clear that changes must affect all aspects of the life of the centre. Saving aluminium cans or planting hedgerows does not make a centre 'green'. There is a need to establish a philosophy, where the aims relate to the process of environmental education. Who are the learners? What are they learning? Where does it take place? All these aspects should be compatible. A centre is far more than a set of buildings where a programme of activities is based. The ethos should permeate attitudes and behaviour of staff and students, organisational procedures, the curriculum (and the 'hidden' curriculum) as well as the physical environment (buildings, grounds etc.) of the centre.

1. The aim should be holistic education. Personal, social and environmental awareness and skills are all part of the same process. This ethos should permeate the work of the centre.
2. Centres should move away from narrow programmes based on academic fieldwork or physical outdoor activities. They should broaden their base to include other approaches, for example, through art, drama or problem solving, which encourage environmental learning.
3. Centres should question the importance they place on activities. Are they an end in themselves or used as a vehicle for learning? Are the learning outcomes of each activity clearly stated? Are there opportunities to 'plan, do and review'?
4. Centres should develop programmes in consultation with students to give a sense of ownership and foster self-reliance. The 'atmosphere' and organisation of the centre should be conducive to this process.
5. Teaching and learning styles should be varied and flexible depending on activities and situations. They should be designed to encourage all students to achieve their potential.
6. Centres should address all aspects of environmental education from awareness, understanding and development of skills to the discussion of attitudes and values and the ways in which action can be taken. They should tackle the major ecological concepts which govern all life on the planet. Through environmental issues they should also introduce economic and political systems and how they influence the environment. The aim should be to encourage citizens who are aware and environmentally competent.
7. Centres should have an 'open' policy fostering links with the local community and other organisations and agencies working towards similar aims. They should look at ways of sharing expertise with other centres and encourage in-service development of their own staff.

8. Centres should try to improve their own environmental actions, for instance in terms of energy saving, recycling and use of materials. They should examine their activities and use of sites and ensure that these are compatible with their overall aims. There should be attempts to improve environments through practical conservation.
9. Through their own example, centres should discuss with leaders and participants on courses, ways to make improvements in their own actions and encourage them to adopt more sustainable lifestyles.
10. Centres should try to relate local issues to global patterns. The message should be positive, forward-looking and attempt to broaden the horizons and foster international understanding.

Geoff Cooper can be contacted at Low Bank Outdoor Education Centre, Coniston, Cumbria LA21 8AA. Tel 015394 41314.

SAFETY CONSIDERATIONS
Introduction
Quite often, our work with young people on environmental issues will take groups of us into the outdoor environment, or young people themselves may elect to undertake conservation work, for example. This is a common feature of the Grizzly and Gruff Kids Challenge described in another section. In situations like these, safety becomes a paramount concern and leaders need to address safety issues as a core part of the planning process.

If part of your programme involves taking children to outdoor centres, you should make sure that the centre is licensed under the *Adventure Activities Licensing Regulations (1996)*. This is a legal requirement for centres accepting payment for activities, and flows from the *Activity Centres (Young Persons' Safety) Act (1995)*, which was enacted in response to a number of tragedies involving children at outdoor activity centres.

The regulations apply to, *"...anyone who provides, in return for payment, adventure activities to young people under 18".* The licensing is carried out by the Environmental Health Department of the local authority where the centre is based. So, if you have any doubt about a particular centre being licensed, contact the appropriate Environmental Health Department.

It is worth considering a discussion of safety issues as part of any ongoing programme of work involving young people. A good starting point can be the regulations which apply to particular institutions, such as schools, community centres, cinemas and theatres.

As an aid to those considering outdoor work, we include a checklist adapted from Alan Smith's book *Creative Outdoor Work with Young People*. This checklist can be used for local activities, as well as for residential camping trips or visits to outdoor activity centres.

Preparation and planning
Aims and Objectives of the Venture
One of the first tasks when planning any outdoor venture should be to establish clear educational aims – such as providing opportunities for young people to work together in a responsible and constructive way.

Leadership Qualities
Good leadership is of course very important in all aspects of outdoor work. One of the first questions we always ask ourselves before proceeding with an activity is, *'Would I be happy for my own children to take part in it?'* The 'in loco parentis' responsibilities of leaders when working with young people need careful consideration.

The Leader must:
- Have relevant experience of the activities to be pursued.
- Have undertaken suitable training and achieved recognised qualifications when these are relevant.
- Be alert and aware of the safety aspects of the activity.
- Maintain good discipline and check that the Country Code is being followed.
- Pre-plan remedial actions for foreseeable emergencies and be able to display sound judgement in difficult circumstances.
- Attain an appropriate level of physical and mental response.

Teamwork
In any planning it is of great benefit if the workload is shared between all adult members, and a clear strategy for responsibilities and duties agreed as early as possible. This becomes essential when planning residential ventures. Of course, teamwork should also include the young people involved, and many benefits can be gained by their full involvement during the planning and preparation stages.

Research and Reconnaissance
Using residential and outdoor centres and camp sites will require thorough research during the months preceding the expedition. Ordnance Survey maps, guide books, local interest books and publications from National Park Visitors' Centres and Tourist Information Centres can all provide valuable information and enhance the overall success of the visit. On many occasions a reconnaissance visit to the area can prove valuable. Study the general layout, the possibilities for training exercises, and the potential dangers and hazards. A thorough look around the camp site or the centre in advance will aid the smooth running of operations, and will enable staff to identify safe limits before the venture begins. It is also important to make use of local expertise and knowledge. This may be the staff of the centre you are going to use or other people who live and work in the area you are scheduled to visit. Many outdoor and adventure centres will not allow groups to use their facilities unless they have had earlier briefing sessions with the group.

Safety Preparations

There are a number of key questions which are of particular importance and have been included here to give special emphasis at the planning stage.

- Will staff be working within their own experience?
- Have all the risks been fully assessed?
- Are the planned activities appropriate for all the members of the group?
- Are all the leaders sufficiently experienced, trained or qualified?
- Have all staff completed appropriate first aid training?
- Will all staff be fully prepared and briefed?
- Will all vehicles be checked for their roadworthy condition?
- Do all staff know the emergency procedures and the location of emergency services?

Informing Others and Obtaining Approval

Good communications are essential in the planning stages of any off-site work. The written consent of parents/guardians is essential, and they should be informed as early as possible about the kind of activities that are contemplated. The youth organisation or school will have overall responsibility and will need to know full details of the plans at an early date, as will the local authority responsible for outdoor work. Other colleagues may need to be consulted where plans cut across their routines. Outside agencies including landowners and specific activity providers may need to be approached for permission or approval.

Briefings

For residential ventures, several briefing sessions will be necessary in the weeks leading up to the departure date. The final briefing session should be taken very seriously and emphasise the purpose of the visit, safety procedures, potential hazards, expectations and the standards of behaviour. In particular, strict rules concerning smoking, drinking, and sleeping arrangements should be clearly understood. This would be an appropriate time to remind participants about rewards and sanctions. Clothing and equipment will need to be checked before the party gets under way.

Discipline

It is with some regret that we feel the need to add some words of caution on this subject. Despite the planning and organisation that goes into outdoor activities, and regardless of much effort put in to make the exercise enjoyable, some young people will still be inclined towards activities that they might think of as mischief, but which staff might consider harmful or dangerous to themselves, to other members of the party or to the countryside generally. It is very important that the leaders know the young people in their charge, and occasionally exclusion may prove a safer option.

Environmental Concerns

As a point of some importance, the Country Code should be used as a resource. All outdoor groups need to be particularly conscious of the impact of their activities on the environment and local communities. Staff have a responsibility to educate the young people they work with to be considerate and sensitive towards environmental concerns. With careful thought, activities can be planned with minimal impact, and over-use of sites can be avoided.

It is often assumed that simply because an activity is taking place in the outdoors it will raise environmental awareness. Sadly, all too frequently this is not the case. And sometimes this is because the instructor, whether they are an orienteer, canoeist or sailor is so preoccupied with their particular sport that they miss the opportunity to take in the wonders of the environment, or fully share them with the members of their group. For many people their first appreciation of the range and beauty of the environment arrives on the back of less formal activities like walking or mountain bike riding, rather than through more obvious, planned environmental activities.

Alternative Plans

It is advisable to have some alternative ideas in mind in case the original plans need to be altered. The usual reason for having to abandon activities is bad weather. Many unexpected problems tend to spoil the original plans, and these could be disastrous for the venture unless alternative activities have been planned. For example, permission may unexpectedly be withdrawn for using a training area, the minibus may break down, a member of the group may suddenly become ill, or certain activities may become unavailable.

Insurance

Insurance cover is strongly recommended for most outdoor work. Leaders will need to check with their authority or organisation about the extent of insurance provision for their activities. Additional cover may be necessary for specific situations excluded in the policy. Parents/Guardians will need to be informed about these arrangements.

First Aid

Staff involved in outdoor work will need to be familiar with first aid techniques, including resuscitation. A minimum training level can be achieved by completing a one day Emergency Aid course run by the Red Cross or the St. John's Ambulance Brigade. Consideration should be given to higher qualifications in first aid for staff who are intending to spend a lot of time on off-site ventures. This is especially important when groups are split up to allow separate activities. First aid kits should be appropriate to the nature of the venture, and careful thought should be given to the best places to keep them, in case they are required in an emergency.

Equipment

The safety of participants depends largely on the generous provision of appropriate protective clothing and equipment to suit the nature of the activities and the outdoor conditions. Detailed lists of equipment are not included, as this information is contained in many of the well known outdoor handbooks, manuals and reference books. Leaders will need to decide on the suitability and safety of equipment. This includes inspecting items that are frequently in use and likely to become worn, and replacing them as necessary. Strong, comfortable footwear, waterproof clothing and enough layers of clothing to keep warm can all be of vital importance. Equipment checks are strongly recommended at the start of activities to ensure that all participants are equipped in an appropriate way. Much valuable outdoor work can be done in the local environment without the need for expensive equipment and clothing.

Accident and emergency procedures

The following recommended procedures have been extracted directly from the most up to date guidelines available, the Department for Education's *Safety in Outdoor Activity Centres.* Only the first section of the emergency procedures is given below. Leaders will need to study this document in full, especially for guidance on more serious incidents.

The recommended procedures are:
- Establish the nature and extent of the emergency.
- Make sure all other members of the party are accounted for and safe.
- If there are any injuries, immediately establish their extent, so far as possible, and administer appropriate first aid.
- Establish the name(s) of the injured and call whichever emergency services that are required.
- Advise other staff members of the incident and that the emergency procedures are in operation.
- Ensure that an adult from the party accompanies casualties to the hospital.
- Ensure that the remainder of the party are adequately supervised throughout and arrange for their early return to base.
- Arrange for one adult to remain at the incident site to liaise with the emergency services until the incident is over and all the children are accounted for.
- Control access to telephones.

ACTIVITIES FOR OUTDOORS
Background

This is one area of environmental work in which there are already some splendid resources available for teachers, youth workers and playworkers. Among some of the ones we have used with successful results are:
- *Joseph Bharat Cornell, Sharing Nature with Children, Exley Publications (US version, 1979).*
- *Joseph Bharat Cornell, Listening to Nature, Exley Publications, 1987.*
- *Joseph Bharat Cornell, Sharing the Joy of Nature, Dawn Publications, 1989.*
- *Gordon MacLellan, Talking to the Earth, Capall Bann (undated).*

- RSPB, Environmental Games Guide, RSPB Youth Unit (undated).
- RSPB, The Wildlife Action Awards, RSPB Youth Unit (undated).
- Steve Van Matre, Acclimatization, Earthwalk and other books, Institute of Earth Education (various).
- RSPB, First Nature (for 5-7 year olds) and Second Nature (7-12 year olds), RSPB Education Department (undated).
- Isobel Norris, Chase Schools Pack, Chase Nature Reserve, Dagenham (undated).
- Usborne Nature Trail Books: Ponds and Streams, Birdwatching, Wild Flowers, Insect Watching.

The list could become even longer. For this book, where nature and natural history activities are only one part of broader environmental concerns, we have chosen some examples of activities which have a high element of fun, but also convey useful and important messages about wildlife and habitats to the participants.

To kick off, we are indebted to Tony Whitehead, the Royal Society for the Protection of Birds (RSPB) Youth and Volunteer Officer for the South West. The first activity, Build a Creature, hasn't, as far as we know, been written up in this form. The second short set of activities come from the time when Tony worked at the RSPB Sandwell Valley Nature Reserve. The RSPB Young Ornithologists' Club (YOC) is the junior wing of the RSPB. Tony describes it as, "...the biggest environmental youth club in the world!" Membership info. and resources are available from RSPB , The Lodge, Sandy, Bedfordshire SG19 2DL.

After that we have included an example of the beautiful work/info. sheets designed and written by Isobel Norris, which are used with youth groups at the Chase Nature Reserve, which is situated between Dagenham and Hornchurch. It is managed by the London Wildlife Trust. The work described in the worksheets is a great way of introducing young people to the work of many environmental groups, among which is the national WATCH Education Service, which can be contacted at Wildlife Watch, The Green, Witham Park, Waterside South, Lincoln LN5 7JR.

Build a creature
The following is almost word-for-word how Tony explained the activity to us.

This is a lovely, imaginative activity which is ideal for 9-12 year olds, but may also be used with older young people. It introduces the idea of adaptation in plants and animals: the ways in which all living things have to be flexible to survive. It can also lead into discussion on how humans can make things either easier or harder for the other species on the planet........

The activity involves recycling old bits of scrap into fantastic animals. Tony usually starts the activity with the short discussion on how creatures are designed to live in particular types of environment: where they live, how they survive, what they eat, who hunts who. The challenge to the members of the youth group is then to make their own specially adapted animals using old bits of scrap such as card, paper, paper clips, lolly sticks, string, wool, cotton reels, in fact anything which comes to hand. As well as these materials, it is useful to have sticky tape, scissors and possibly other glue available for the construction of the animals.

This is where the twist in the tale (tail?) comes! Tony introduces far from usual places for the animals to live in. They include such diverse 'habitats' as:

- your coat pocket;
- a library shelf;
- in your fridge;
- under the sofa;
- in your sock;
- in your parent's car.

And that, as Tony says, is that! Everyone goes off thinking about what their creatures will eat? Where will they hide? Can they fly, walk, run, swim? Are they hunters or hunted?

Tony reports that using this activity has led to the creation of some wonderfully sophisticated creatures, such as the bookshelf being which eats dust and is camouflaged as a book, and which glides from shelf to shelf with its pages open; an all white fridge monster with infra red eyes for when the fridge door closes; and what Tony describes as a coat pocket 'detritivore' disguised as an old wrapper, feeding on forgotten sticky sweets. (Don't worry if you don't recognise this long word – we couldn't find it in our dictionary, either! Tony later explained that he thinks he made it up, as a composite of a few different words!)

All good fun and with a serious learning element.

Labels

The facilitator prepares in advance a number (say five) labels for each young participant. Prepare the labels with loops of string attached to each so that they can be hung from things. On each label is written a word, such as:

Cold, wet, fluffy, dry, smooth, large, rough.

The words should obviously be appropriate for the environment which is going to be used. The organiser hands out five labels to each person and helps them read them out if they are having any difficulty. Everyone is then invited to put their labels on things which seem suitable. In the Sandwell description:

" 'Wet? Where could we put this?'

'On the grass over here,' shouts Charlotte pointing at a patch of grass, heavy with dew.

'Think about where you put them and remember the places,' calls the organiser.

The children spread out. Adam finds a small puddle for his 'wet' label and helps Nicola discover a lovely big stone for her 'smooth' label. After a while, all the labels are placed and the organiser, Chris, goes round each in turn.
'That's excellent, you've all done a good job.'"

It's a simple activity, which introduces words and concepts to young people as well as creating a search and discovery type exercise. Tony added that he sometimes invites young people to make up poems about the labels and the things on which they have been hung, i.e. *"The cold, wet grass covered the wet path.....etc.etc.."* We'd suggest that the organiser should collect up all the labels to avoid leaving litter from the activity!

Kim's game

We used a version of this game in one of our games books. This version uses natural, found objects and again needs a little preparation by the organiser. To start the activity off, the leader produces six objects which are not too hard to find in the location where the group are standing. These are placed, one by one on the ground and then covered over with a handkerchief or a piece of cloth. The participants are invited to have studied all of them carefully before they are covered and then to go off individually or in pairs and collect as many of the six objects as they can in an agreed amount of time, say, ten minutes.

In the Sandwell example:
"Try to remember what the things are. A red leaf, a stick, a stone, a green leaf, an acorn and a blade of grass. After the children return from their search, Chris says, 'Who's got all six?'
A few hands are raised.
'Let's go through them.' Chris reaches under his hanky and pulls out the red leaf. 'Who's got a red leaf?'

Chris runs through all the natural objects. Some children have found four, some five, and one or two managed to find all six.
'Now, the important thing, of course, is to put them all back in exactly where you found them, the same way up and the same way round. Off you go!'
The children wander off, looking and trying to remember where the objects came from, placing the objects with care under bushes and by the trees."

Coloured eyes

This is a nice little activity which only requires the preparation of one piece of card with a hole in it for each person taking part. Around each hole is a band of colour. The organiser might introduce the activity in the same way as at Sandwell:

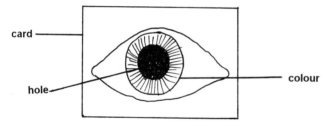

"The group reaches the stream.
'Look at all those colours!'
'What colours?' say the children in unison.
'All those colours over there on that tree; all these colours here on this bank, and
look at the sparkling water, wow!'
The children gaze around."

At this point the organiser produces the 'Colour Eyes', one for each person in the group.

> *" 'This is a colour eye. It helps us find colours. What you do is hold the card up*
> *to your eye, then look through it and see if you can match the colour on the ring*
> *around the hole with a colour in nature. Once you think you've got a match,*
> *zoom in and hold the colour eye right next to the thing you'd found.' "*

The use of the 'eyes' focus the attention of the young people on the amazing variety of colours which can be found in natural locations.

A word about worksheets

The next activities evolved through the work of the RSPB Educational Reserve at Sandwell Valley, near Birmingham. They are excellent examples of worksheets designed to get children and young people looking at the world around them, whilst having some fun. Virtually all nature reserves whether administered by the RSPB, Wildfowl and Wetlands Trust, The Wildlife Trusts or a local authority service will have worksheets or some similar resource for introducing young people to their facility.

This basically means, *"You don't have to be David Bellamy to take a group to a wildlife reserve".* Make contact with the reserve first and ask what educational services they offer. Although reserves can be more tuned in to school visits, educational staff are becoming more aware of the wonders of informal work with groups of children and young people from voluntary and local authority youth organisations.

As explained in the intro. to this section, the next handwritten pages come from the *Chase Schools Pack* published by the London Wildlife Trust, to whom we are very grateful for permission to reproduce examples.

Perhaps you or your group may be close enough to visit the Chase, or maybe you can help to produce similar information and activity sheets for a local environmental resource in your own area of the country.

Wetlands 1

① Birds of the wetland

The lakes and marshes of the Chase are great places for watching birds, both resident and migrant.

Approach quietly, keeping behind cover. Be patient and you will be rewarded. Birds will ignore stationary objects, however incongruous!

Stay behind the fence around the slack.

Who comes to bathe and drink?

Look for animal tracks as well as those of birds.

Watch for insects coming to drink.

Great Crested Grebe courtship display.

Quarrelsome coots.

Moorhens swim with jerky movements.

② Watching birds feed

Swallow catches flying insects

Kingfisher watches and dives for fish.

Heron waits for fish and frogs.

Shoveler dabbles in circles!

Great crested grebe eats fish.

Moorhen

Mallard eats plants.

Waders eg Redshank

Tufted duck eats vegetation and minibeasts.

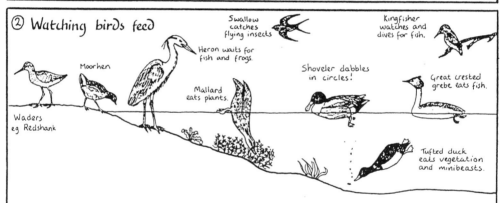

	on land	surface dabbling	head under water	up-ending	diving
Mallard					
Canada Goose					
Coot					
Swan					
Great Crested Grebe					
Redshank					

Record where different birds feed, and how they do it.

How does their feeding behaviour relate to the food they eat?

For how long do birds dive?

Look at the different neck lengths of swans, canada geese and mallards. All these birds eat water weeds. How might the birds' different neck lengths help to reduce feeding competition between them?

③ Beaks...

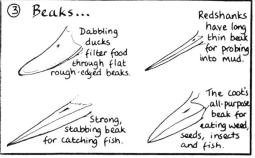

Dabbling ducks filter food through flat rough-edged beaks.

Redshanks have long thin beak for probing into mud.

Strong, stabbing beak for catching fish.

The coot's all-purpose beak for eating weed, seeds, insects and fish.

④ ... and feet!

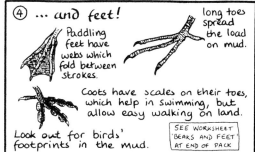

Paddling feet have webs which fold between strokes.

long toes spread the load on mud.

Coots have scales on their toes, which help in swimming, but allow easy walking on land.

Look out for birds' footprints in the mud.

SEE WORKSHEET 'BEAKS AND FEET' AT END OF PACK

⑤ Dandy drakes and dull ducks!

Male ducks (drakes) are often much brighter in colour than the drab females, who incubate the eggs.

Most ducks are ground nesting. How does the female's colouring help to protect her on the nest?

Why do males need their bright plumage?

⑥ Chicks

The chicks of ducks, geese, grebes and swans are 'precocial'! This means they are born with down and can swim and feed themselves within hours of hatching. They are also programmed to follow the first moving object they see when they hatch (imprinting). How are these features useful?

Watch parents with their chicks:-

Mallard ducks give a special quack to tell chicks to dive when danger threatens.

Tired grebe chicks hitch a ride on Mum or Dad, even holding on when the parent dives!

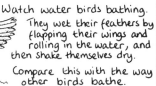

How are the chicks coloured?

How far do they go from their parents?

Birds which often nest off the ground, such as herons, have chicks which are born blind, naked and helpless. Why don't they need to be independent?

⑦ Keeping feathers clean

Watch water birds bathing.

They wet their feathers by flapping their wings and rolling in the water, and then shake themselves dry.

Compare this with the way other birds bathe.

⑧ Preening

Birds rub their heads on an oil gland just above the base of the tail. They rub the oil over the rest of their feathers to waterproof and condition them.

Watch how they spread the oil.

⑨ Each feather is then drawn through the bill. This repairs gaps in the vane and oils the feathers.

You can try this with ducks' feathers found at the Chase.

Put a tiny bit of cooking oil on your thumb and forefinger, and make them into a beak shape. Pull the feather through your 'beak' to preen it and 'zip up' any gaps.

Does water run off the feather? Compare your preened feather with a dirty one. Which repels water best?

⑩ What keeps feathers together?

Look under a lens

... but it's much clearer under a microscope.

shaft

barbs

⑪ Flight

How do birds use their wings for different manoeuvres?

taking off   landing   diving   gliding

Look over grassland for kestrels hovering. Listen too, for the clapping flight of wood pigeons and the whistle of swans and Canada geese.

⑫ Aerofoils

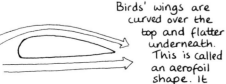

Birds' wings are curved over the top and flatter underneath. This is called an aerofoil shape. It gives much more lift than a flat wing. The air going over the top has further to go, and gets more 'spread out' than the air underneath. The result is higher air pressure underneath, which pushes the wing upwards.

⑬ Make cardboard gliders:

fold

with flat wings

sticky tape

with aerofoils

Launch gently into the air. Which flies furthest?
Compare long and short winged gliders.

⑭ Distance or manoevrability?

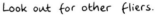

Swift

Kingfisher

long thin wings - good for fast gliding but poor for take-off and manoeuvrability. The swift may fly for 3 years before it lands! Swifts only land to breed, even sleeping on the wing.
Watch their flight.
How much of the time do their wings beat?

Short stubby wings - good for rapid take-off and sharp turns, but not for long distance. The kingfisher can brake in mid-flight to dive!

Find some other wing shapes.

⑮ Who else flies?

Look out for other fliers.

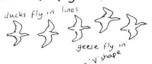

Hawker dragonflies are very strong fliers. They can hover, and even fly backwards.

Damselflies are much weaker fliers.

Look out for water beetles and boatmen too!

Why can't we fly? It has been calculated that no bird over 18 kg can fly, because it could not have enough muscle to power flight. Flying takes a lot of energy; birds have minimised weight, with hollow bones, and very large flight muscles.

⑯ How many birds?

To estimate how many birds are in a flock, count a block of 10 birds. Then decide what fraction that is of the whole flock. Multiply to obtain the total size of the flock.

⑰ Staying together

Watch for flights of ducks and geese.

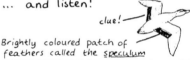

ducks fly in lines

How do they stay in formation?

geese fly in a 'v' shape

Look ... and listen!

clue!

Brightly coloured patch of feathers called the speculum

⑱ Migration

Some birds migrate on a daily basis, between feeding and roosting sites. Watch starlings flocking into the warmer town centre as a winter evening sets in. There is also seasonal migration over short distances, such as the movement from woodland to gardens in winter, where extra food is provided by humans.

For some birds, migration involves journeys of many thousands of miles. Swallows only breed from June to August, but at this time it is winter in South Africa where they spend much of the year. They fly about 6000 miles north to breed in Europe, where the northern summer provides enough food for rearing young. Swallows begin arriving here in April, leaving in September for the South African summer.

Fieldfares spend the summer in Scandinavia, flying to Britain for our less severe winter.

Keep records of bird sightings in the Chase Diary. When do birds arrive and when do they leave?
Which birds are here all year, and which are seasonal visitors?

Build up a picture of bird movements. Can you tell which birds breed here, and which are just stopping off on their way to another destination?

Use books to find out where birds go from the Chase:

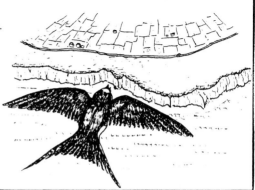

	Summer	Winter
Swallow	The Chase	South Africa
Yellow wagtail	The Chase	West Africa
Fieldfare	Scandinavia	The Chase

Can the class find the places on a map and draw in the birds' summer and winter migration routes?

Birds are not the only animals visiting us. Find out about butterflies such as red admirals and painted ladies.

⑲ A migration adventure

Migration is a very hazardous operation. Birds die from exhaustion, are picked off by predators, and shot for "fun" by 'sportsmen'.

Stories can be written about the journeys a swallow makes each year. Which countries does the bird fly over? Describe the different landscapes and people; from rainforest to desert, farmland to city...

A journey could be made into a play with the whole class taking part.

THE DUKE OF EDINBURGH'S AWARD AND THE ENVIRONMENT

Introduction

The Duke of Edinburgh's Award is for all young people between the ages of 14 and 25. Whilst it is one of the best known providers of opportunities for personal achievements, adventure, community and social involvement and a widening of interests for young people it is not in itself a youth organisation. Responsibility for the operation of the scheme is delegated under licence to Operating Authorities to be able to grant awards.

It is this dynamic structure of the Award Scheme that makes it an attractive method of engaging young people in environmental action. There are three Awards:

- Bronze, for those over 14;
- Silver for those over 15, and
- Gold, for those over 16.

To qualify for an Award a young person must satisfy the requirements for the four sections: Service; Expeditions; Skills and Physical Recreation. For the Gold Award a young person must also undertake a residential project. Although this arrangement appears very structured, young people have the opportunity to design the Award to suit their particular needs.

Because of the high profile of the Award, a number of environmental organisations create opportunities for young people specifically tailored to the Award.

The RSPB offers special membership rates to Award participants. RSPB has produced a pamphlet called *Flying for Gold* which details opportunities for young people to take environmental action and get the Award. Through the RSPB young people can fulfil the requirements for the Skills, Service and Residential Sections of the Award.

The National Trust is currently offering a Free Entry Pass to all Award participants.

The Youth Hostels Association, whose facilities offer an excellent method of gaining low-cost access to the countryside for all sorts of Award activities, offers free group membership and half-price individual membership to Award participants.

In addition, other organisations like the Wildlife Trusts, the Wildfowl and Wetlands Trust, the Groundwork Foundation, Friends of the Earth, The John Muir Trust, Peak National Park Centre, the Field Studies Council, British Trust for Conservation Volunteers and the RSPCA are receptive to requests to provide action packed environmental opportunities for young people following the Award.

Examples of the kind of environmental activities that young people have engaged in through the Award Scheme are:

- Campaigning for improved cycle routes.
- Helping with the construction, repair of footpaths, stiles, fences and stone walls.
- Helping with urban conservation projects such as improving areas of wasteland.
- Assisting with raising awareness about recycling and waste-collection projects.
- Undertaking surveys of wildlife and plants in conjunction with a conservation group or trust, e.g. Badger Watch, Bats, Barn Owls.
- Taking part in fund-raising activities or events.
- Improving natural habitats and encouraging the increase of specific types of flora and fauna

There are very few pieces of environmental action that cannot be undertaken within the framework of the Duke of Edinburgh's Award; the only limit is the imagination of the young participants and those working with them.

For more information about the Award in general or its environmental opportunities in particular, contact:

The Duke of Edinburgh's Award
Gulliver House
Madeira Walk, Windsor
Berkshire SL4 1EU

Tel: 01753 810753
Fax: 01753 810666
Email: AwardHQ@dea.sonnet.co.uk

Or check out their web-site on HTTP//www.sonnet.co.uk.dea

WOODCRAFT

When we were compiling information for this book, one of our concerns was to make sure that 'environment' included a range of things, especially those which are close to us at home, school or work – rather than just the 'great outdoors'. We stand by this view but are keenly aware that there is something very special about outdoor living and community participation. This 'something' is connected to our essential humanness and can create some very powerful, positive and creative experiences for young people. Above all, a humble appreciation of 'outdoors' is necessary if we are really to appreciate the awesome beauty and wholeness of nature and the wanton destruction our modern day market economies wreak on it.

The 'specialness' of outdoor living can be hard to define but certainly includes the communal challenge against the elements and the feeling of freedom which can only be had in the wide open spaces of the countryside. Living outdoors in groups is also one of the best ways of building group identity and cohesion, as many youth workers will tell you. It is only in this kind of setting that we return to primitive methods of existence like the use of open fires for cooking and warmth. Cooking fires and camp fires are arguably the very epitome of outdoor living. There is something magical about watching the endless play of the flames and sparks in the evening, and the warm glow reflected from the faces of the people circling the fire for warmth and companionship.

Much of this is covered by the broad term 'woodcraft' which includes the philosophy behind living outdoors, as well as what you do with bits of wood. For those who espouse this way of life, the philosophy (and the sense of purpose and camaraderie) is always more important than pitching your tent correctly or being able to light a fire in a force 8 gale!

The Woodcraft Folk, Order of Woodcraft Chivalry and Forest School Camps are the main organisations promoting the 'Woodcraft Way' of first-hand experience and the chivalrous spirit of helping others. The movement was started in the early 1900s in America by Ernest Thompson Seton, who was heavily influenced by the lifestyle, beliefs and skills of native American Indians. Interestingly (perhaps!) Alan has an old, but very interesting 1920s American book entitled *A Book of Symbols for Camp Fire Girls*. In it the authors say,

> "All progress has been made by one generation building upon the work of the generations of the past, and thus the founders of the Camp Fire Girls, searching for a past that was worthy of superstructure, turned to the symbolism of the Indian people, as the most expressive and highly developed yet simple in its elements."

The Camp Fire Girls used native Indian symbols as a useful induction for their members and each girl designed their own personal symbol from elemental signs and symbols from a variety of different tribes. If you can get hold of a book it might be good fun and interesting for a modern youth group.

THE SNOW MOON
January

THE WILD GOOSE MOON
April

THE THUNDER MOON
July

THE LEAF FALLING MOON
October

THE HUNGER MOON
February

THE SONG OR PLANT-ING MOON
May

THE GREEN CORN OR RED MOON
August

THE ICE-FORMING MOON
November

THE CROW MOON
March

THE ROSE MOON
June

THE HUNTING MOON
September

THE LONG NIGHT MOON
December

From the *Camp Fire Girls Book*

Howie has worked at a number of Forest School Camps. They organise several 'standing camps' for young people during the spring, summer and autumn – as well as mobile camps using bicycles or canoes. A standing camp may have as many as 80 or 90 young people and 20 to 30 volunteer staff. Believe it or not, it is tremendous fun to spend a fortnight in a remote field in north Wales making one's own food, entertainment etc.!

At a Forest School Camp

During a standing camp, everyone comes together at least once a day at 'Rally' where the programme is discussed and relevant issues ironed out – also, it can be used as an opportunity for individuals to make a contribution by way of a joke, poem or comment. Tom Soper (a story-teller by trade) was on Howie's first camp and would talk at Rally about the way our ancestors lived. He has, we think, put his finger on the 'something' we mentioned earlier and we include his article from the *Forest School Camps* magazine. And after Tom's contribution is a piece from Ben Law of the Order of Woodcraft Chivalry, on building a sweat lodge to purify body and spirit.

FOLK MEMORY

Sometimes being on a Forest School Camp can be so satisfying. I find myself, body and soul, moving into a state of great contentment and a strange feeling of 'rightness', so much so that I begin to wonder what I do in my daily life that keeps me from feeling this way more often.

Maybe it's the day-long physical exercise. Maybe it's being out in the elements, close to nature. Maybe it's living so intimately with other people – eating, playing, working, sleeping – and the same people day after day. Maybe it's creating, in a way, your own mini-society; having to make our own entertainment, our own culture of songs, festivities, stories, running jokes. Maybe it's knowing (and seeing it proved) that everything you do affects someone else, that your voice counts and your contribution shapes your world. Maybe it's all of these things put together.

So why do these things feel so right? Well, the answer may lie in the past. We need to go back less than ten generations to find our forebears living in a pre-industrial world, and whether they lived in the city or the countryside (as in the case of the vast majority) they were living a life that involved greater physical exertion, less protection from the vagaries of nature, and a greater sense of belonging to a specific community of people.

Less than a hundred generations takes us back to the times of Christ (line them up and they'd perhaps reach to the corner shop). Two hundred generations back and we come to a time when, in this country (and virtually everywhere else in the world except the Near East and parts of Southern Europe), there was no knowledge of agriculture at all, settled village life had not yet been adopted. People, our ancestors, lived in tribal groups migrating with the seasons. And here you have a way of life that to us moderns has an almost unimaginable vulnerability to the natural elements; where 'physical exercise' as we call it was a grim necessity of survival; where whether eating, working or sleeping the individual was constantly in the company of people they knew intimately, often from birth; where the only sources of 'culture' – music, stories, dances – were the people themselves; where, by virtue of the group's small size, the individual's voice was heard and could have an impact on the community of which he or she was a part.

Our ancestors lived like this not for tens or hundreds, or even thousands of generations, but tens of thousands of generations. It's hard to be exact, of course, but some sources estimate that 20,000 generations had the use of fire, and 100,000 generations used stone tools. Further back than this and we are in the realm of the Apeman.

So this way of living is fairly firmly established in our ancestry and, I am sure, deep in our unconscious. As a species we are very adaptable but I find it hard to imagine that the long repeated sound of that way of life isn't still echoing deep inside us. Are ten generations, or even two hundred generations, long enough for that sound to die out?

It would be wrong to picture this past as a lost paradise and the modern world as a fall from grace. People in industrialised countries are better housed, clothed and fed than their forebears ever dreamt of. But each successive wave of new technologies has brought about, and continues to bring about, great changes in the way we live. The amount of physical exertion required of us has greatly diminished, and the traditional communities in which we once lived have, for good or ill, largely been eroded and displaced. There's more distance between people, and between people and nature. As for culture, that's now done for us by the mass media, and we are involved in such huge societies that the chances of our individual voices being heard often seem remote.

A Forest School Camp is a long, long way from the hard life our hunter-gatherer ancestors lived, but it contains enough similar elements for something inside us to wake up and say, "Yes I remember this!" And for a week or two we are blessed with the opportunity to live a life far more in tune with that which our ancestors lived, and one which satisfies so many of the deep human needs that our modern civilisation fails to meet.

Tom Soper
Forest School Camps magazine

SWEAT LODGE

A sweat lodge is a Native American purification ceremony and in its simplest form involves taking an outside sauna; in a more traditional sweat many prayers will be sent, give-aways intended and traditional chants sung. To me the beauty of the sweat lodge is in the deep connection to the elements and the bonding and sense of harmony and openness which becomes established by all those who sweat together.

A typical bender

A sweat lodge is made by first constructing a 'bender', hazel or willow poles cut green and bent to form a domed structure. At camp we cut green willow and stripped some of the bark which made strong ties to secure the poles. The preparation for a sweat is a long process but this is part of its beauty as all the different parts start to come together as the sun begins to set. We started construction just after five in the evening. First we built a large pyre, with limestone rocks resting on a platform in the pyre. It is traditional that the youngest should light the fire to bring the spirit of innocence into the heart of the fire: Charlotte lit the pyre and, with the help of a fire-lighting song, there was soon a huge blaze. We then constructed the lodge 'shell' from willow and then covered the structure in blankets, carpets and tarpaulins. In the centre a pit was dug for the rocks and the soil was used to create a spirit line from the fire to the lodge.

At about 9.30 the first glowing rocks were taken into the sweat. Entering into the womb-like lodge in darkness with just the red glow of the hot rocks and the heat coming off touches chords deep within me every time. At around 10.00 the main sweat took place and the lodge was filled with members of all ages; more glowing red rocks appeared through the doorway and we welcomed each one in as the heat grew and sweat poured off our bodies into the earth below. Once we had shared how we were feeling and were in need of cooling off we would leave the lodge and plunge into the icy cold water of the plunge pool we had constructed earlier by damming the stream. When the last of us left the lodge and sat naked around the fire, it was already the next day; shooting stars were in abundance and beautiful friendships had been deepened.

Ben Law
From 'Pine Cone' O.W.C. quarterly journal

FURTHER INFORMATION

Forest School Camps

Forest School Camps organise around 35 camps each year, typically weekend and one week camps during spring and autumn and two week 'standing' camps in the summer. Most camps are in the English and Welsh countryside. It is an entirely voluntary organisation and is always in need of volunteers of all ages to help staff the camps.

Programme Requests
and New Member Enquiries:
Filton House
42 Payne Avenue
Aldrington
Hove
East Sussex BN3 5HD

New Staff Enquiries
Lisa Hallgarten
75 St. Thomas's Road
London N4

Special Enrolments – social workers, teachers, care workers, foster parents and others wishing to enrol children should contact:
Joan Wilmot
19b McGregor Road
London W11 1DE

The Woodcraft Folk

The Woodcraft Folk run a nationwide organisation of youth groups for young people which focus on outdoor and environmental issues.

England & Wales.
13 Ritherdon Road
London SW17 8QE

Scotland.
95 Morrison Street
Glasgow G5 8LP

Order of Woodcraft Chivalry

This is a small family based organisation with about 140 member families. It is an educational and social fellowship, for all ages and sexes, which is non-political and non-denominational.

Julian Brown
73 Willow Way
Luton
Bedfordshire
LU3 2SA

CONSERVATION, WORKING HOLIDAYS AND BASECAMP ACCOMMODATION:

The National Trust Conservation projects

Each year the National Trust welcomes over 4,500 volunteers to their conservation projects programme. From a youth work point of view, these are only suitable for older young people, the minimum age of involvement being 17 for young people from Britain, and 18 for those from overseas. The Trust is also interested in recruiting new volunteer project leaders, who receive training and preparation for the task before being let loose with any groups!

In any year, the Trust volunteers tackle about 450 projects, for instance:
- constructing a heathland boardwalk;
- building a dry-stone wall;
- surveying woodland wildlife habitats;
- repairing a coastal path;
- repuddling (what a lovely word!) a dew pond;
- woodland maintenance;
- construction projects, for instance maintenance to bridges and Trust estate properties.

Volunteers stay in a variety of accommodation, from Trust basecamps with showers and bunk beds, through to holiday cottages and even village halls. At the time of writing, early in 1997, volunteers contributed about £50 per week, or about £20 for a weekend for their board and lodging while working on the project. All participants bring old working clothes, strong footwear, waterproofs and sleeping bag. Each group works under the co-ordination of two volunteer project leaders, who have received training from the Trust. Self-catering facilities are used by the group for meals.

A relatively new development are the Venture Projects, which involve spending between nine and fourteen days living, working and socialising with volunteers from other countries. The Trust runs these projects along with Concordia Trust.

The National Trust told us that anyone can volunteer as long as they are reasonably fit and are happy to accept the simple, yet friendly way of countryside life. Each year the Trust publishes a detailed brochure which gives details of the individual projects and all the info. on insurance, travel etc. Send two first class stamps and an envelope to: **National Trust Working Holidays,** PO Box 84, Cirencester, Glos GL7 1ZP. Tel. 01285 657935.

Basecamps and bothies

The National Trust has 35 purpose-built or converted buildings (the basecamps) which it uses for groups working on the conservation projects. There are also five bothies, which offer more basic accommodation, often situated in isolated locations. In addition to being used for the conservation working holidays, they are also available for a whole range of youth and educational groups, sports groups, recreational groups and corporate groups. If you are looking for a base for an environmental field trip, these might be just what you and your group are looking for!

Peel Bothy: a romantic but very basic stone bothy near Bardon Mill, only 200 metres from Hadrian's Wall and adjacent to the Pennine Way

To obtain a copy of the **Basecamp Guide** which gives full details, costs and contact details for all of the basecamps and bothies, write with a large SAE to the Volunteers Office, 33 Sheep Street, Cirencester, Glos GL7 1QW. Tel. 01285 651818.

British Trust for Conservation Volunteers

BTCV are the UK's largest practical conservation organisation. Like the National Trust they organise conservation-based working holidays, both in the UK and abroad. They have also organised conservation work involving 85,000 volunteers, including:

- renovation of footpaths;
- practical and management work on wetland, heathland and grassland sites;
- training courses;
- helping school and community groups renovate and improve their grounds;
- extensive tree planting programmes;
- hedge repairs;
- running Agenda 21 projects, and participated in other initiatives such as Rural Action and the work of the Tree Council;
- developing a trading arm, BTCV Enterprises, which supplies products and services relating to conservation, ranging from trees to clothing and publications.

Their *Natural Breaks* offer a very extensive range of working holidays which cost between £32 and £80 per week to cover food and accommodation in the UK. They also have links with organisations in 21 other countries and where working holidays have been organised. As well as a general leaflet about their work, they also produce specific leaflets about aspects of their work such as: local volunteering; Natural Breaks; International conservation working holidays; training opportunities, and managing land.

To receive more information send your request with two second class stamps to: **BTCV**, 36 St Mary's Street, Wallingford, Oxfordshire OX10 0BR.

GRIZZLY CHALLENGE AND THE GRUFF KIDS
Background
Jessie Todd, Chief Executive of Youth Clubs Scotland, says of this exciting and innovative range of young people's environmental projects,

> *"Once upon a time there were young people all over Scotland being recognised as no hopers, vandals and muggers of the environment. Now, because of the Grizzly Challenge (for 14-18 year olds) and the Gruff Kids' Programme (for 10-13 year olds) there is a well supported range of opportunities for young people to try and change their worlds for better in locations throughout Scotland."*

So, what makes these programmes different from local youth and community environmental initiatives in other places?

That's always harder to put into words. Partly it's a matter of quality and quantity. In 1996, in its sixth year of operation, the two project programmes were open to any Scottish young people through their youth clubs or youth organisations. Over 120 teams have already participated. From turning a field into a playground for disabled children through to rebuilding a riverside walkway, the projects have all improved the local environment, often in very socially and economically disadvantaged communities. The project outcomes have varied enormously, but each project has been characterised by:

- having the incentive of a substantial prize from BP Exploration, which for the overall category winners is a trip abroad;
- involving teams of five members working together for nine weeks at a time;
- requiring planning, imagination, innovation and lots of hard work;
- providing part time and full time support (meaning guidance and advice, not orders!) through volunteers to assist the teams;
- involvement of increasing numbers of members of local communities ranging from councillors, environmentalists, teachers, business people through to the whole community of residents;
- fun, new ideas, involvement and commitment of young people.

Jessie says,

> *"The Grizzly Challenge and Gruff Kids' Programme is a success because it allows space for personal and community growth, time for recognition and change, and attractive learning that can be transferred positively."*

So much for the hyperbole; the following pages of the book offer some actual real life, practical examples of the projects and how they have helped encourage young people to change their own environments for the better...

Some of the Challenges

To take part the challenge teams must comprise between three and five members and are divided into two age groups:

      Grizzly teams are aged 14 to 18.

      Gruff teams are aged 10 to 13.

Members of Dickshill Youth Club taking part in adventure residential at Dounan's Camp

Newburgh

The project undertaken by *Newburgh Youth Club*, in the north of Scotland, is a good example of a complex project which brought substantial benefit to the local community by way of improved facilities and a tourist attraction. The group planned to build on the work of the previous year's Grizzly team – they had tidied up a wood near the beach and provided picnic areas. Now the group hoped to construct a fairly lengthy walkway from the wood to the beach incorporating an observation platform and bird hide, as the area is well known for its birdlife.

As the land they wanted to work on was in the process of being handed over from a local estate to the village, they were involved in tricky negotiations between the estate, SNH (Scottish Natural Heritage) and the local council. As is often the case with such negotiations, there were several disappointments and times when it looked as if the project would not get off the ground. The group had actually begun to construct the walkway when they were told that the proposed bird hide would need planning permission. Undaunted, the group descended on the local planning department and emerged fully five hours later with a completed (and submitted) planning application. This kind of tenacity and refusal to accept defeat characterises the indomitable spirit of the most successful Grizzly teams.

By the end of their ten week planning and construction period the team had:

- Completed the walkway and boardwalk from the wood to the beach. This work included shifting, spreading and flattening six lorry loads of 'blinding' to construct a traditional pathway.
- Constructed an observation platform and commissioned a £3,000 information sign to be placed beside the platform.
- Successfully applied for funding to SNH, the council and Scottish Power.
- Created a picnic area complete with tables and benches.
- Planted 3,000 native trees.
- Created a local fund (with £2,000) to provide for the ongoing maintenance of the walkway.
- Raised substantial amounts of cash through an open day and booklet sales.

This was the obvious result of their work but not the sum total of it. Along the way they also found time to research, write and publish an excellent history of the local area. This was produced to a very high standard, which was probably just as well, as sales of the booklet provided quite a lot of the cash needed to fund the project! The team also began the preparation of two other booklets – on local birdlife and on the area's maritime history, and this work continues.

This project combined complex planning and preparation with very high levels of strenuous effort, and is perhaps the kind of project which only young people – with their boundless enthusiasm and high energy levels – could possibly have completed within the timescale.

Two notable events from the team's scrapbook were: one member working by torchlight at midnight to finish off work on a section of the boardwalk; and when all seemed lost a squad of 15 turning up, complete with shovels, led by two members of the previous year's Grizzly team!

Craigmillar

A similarly monumental task was undertaken by the *Craigmillar Out of School Project*. This time it was a younger age group Gruff Kids team and their efforts are therefore all the more impressive. Their project involved repair work to the fabric of the local Arts Centre building and improvements to the garden area outside the centre. Unusual tasks included the removal, repair and reinstatement of a 'finial', which is the decorative bunch of foliage etc. which sits on top of spires and steeples. The team also had to seek advice from the council on removing Giant Hogweed from the site. This is very dangerous, poisonous stuff which needs to be handled carefully and is very difficult to eradicate unless you deal with it correctly.

This team also managed to:

- Remove trees and tidy the garden area – this included turfing, slabbing and tree planting.
- Repair a cellar and annexe roof.
- Create a patio and barbecue area.
- Repair and paint the boundary fence.
- Install disabled toilet facilities and floodlighting.

All in all, an impressive list of achievements involving considerable physical effort. It is typical of this team's enthusiasm that often it was only darkness which stopped them working.

Carpenter's Arms

The Carpenter's Arms Grizzly team undertook the internal renovation of their local hall. Initially, they had planned to arrange for the outside of the building to be painted. They had just found a painter who would have done the job free of charge, as long as they provided the paint, when they discovered that the building had a Grade II listing and they would therefore need to apply for planning permission. Apparently it would have taken a minimum of 12 weeks for the decision to be made and the team had no option but to abandon the idea of painting the outside of the building.

Undaunted they decided to add the painting of the kitchen and toilets to their proposed list. By the end of the project they had:

- Dismantled the stage curtains for cleaning and made a new pulley system.
- Weeded and cleared glass from the outside areas.
- Arranged for a joiner to completely replace the stage flooring, which was riddled with woodworm.
- Painted the foyer, kitchen and toilets.
- Laid lino in the toilets.
- Spent ages on the phone calling theatres up and down the country, and eventually found a theatre supplier in Dundee who were willing to donate four theatre lights to the hall.
- Painted a badminton court on the hall floor.

The efforts of this team really illustrates what can be achieved by determined 'ferreting about'. Although the team managed to raise some cash from two banks, virtually all the materials were donated by local firms, from whom the team had tremendous support. The stage curtains, for example, were cleaned free of charge, a job which would have normally cost £400.

Information on the Grizzly and Gruff Kids Challenge can be obtained from:

Youth Clubs Scotland
Balfour House
19 Bonnington Grove
EDINBURGH EH6 4BL
Tel: 0131 554 2561

TRAINING FOR LIFE: Environmental Challenges
Introduction
An increasing number of agencies are turning to environmental activities as a means of delivering social and personal development programmes of youth work. These include social and life skills courses, conservation projects and programmes to assist the young unemployed. Below we offer two examples of such work.

Groundwork
Groundwork in particular has run a variety of successful schemes. One such project is their Young Leaders' programme. Sponsored by the Bank of Scotland, Young Leaders aims to help the young unemployed break the vicious cycle of joblessness. Young people take part in various personal development training courses (there were 20 projects throughout the UK in August 1996) where they act as leaders of other young people working on a wide range of environmental regeneration projects.

Research sponsored by Barclays Bank (*SiteSavers Report,* 1996) confirmed that the process of involving local people – especially young local people – in reclamation projects, is as important as the reclamation itself.

Another innovative Groundwork scheme supported by the Rural Development Commission is 'The More to Life' project. Through this scheme at least 60 young people in Durham and Cumbria aged 14-20 will be offered the opportunity to take part in a programme of community action, further education and new experiences intended to give them a better understanding of the factors affecting their lives and their communities and providing benefits to both.

Drive For Youth in Snowdonia, Wales
Chaired by TV news presenter, Martyn Lewis, Drive for Youth (DFY) is sited in the Snowdonia national park. It is a national youth training organisation which prioritises work with some of the most disadvantaged young people in the UK. Martyn says,
> "Drive For Youth's mission is to develop the potential skills and attitudes of disadvantage, unemployed young people, aged 18-26 years, enabling them to gain a job and a positive role in society."

Their Welsh base in a group of buildings known as Celmi is an ideal site for offering involvement in local environmental projects as part of the overall 22 week programme. After this background section describing some of the work of DFY, there is a case-study of one such environmental community project with the Corris Railway Society. The complete programme has a number of elements, as can be readily seen from the chart below.

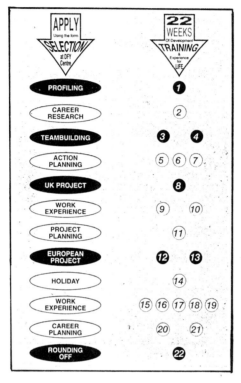

The background of the participants has many common elements. All have been unemployed for at least six months, and based on research findings:

- 11% have tried glue or solvents;
- 70% have tried marijuana;
- 48% have taken acid and ecstasy;
- 25% have taken amphetamines, cocaine, crack or heroin;
- 18% have previous convictions;
- 44% have been homeless for some time;
- 48% have spent periods in special hostels;
- 15% have been in residential care;
- 74% have had serious home difficulties;
- 66% have been out of work for over a year;
- 40% have never worked.

Recruitment on to the scheme is by a mixture of self-referral and referral from a whole range of agencies associated with the socially and economically disadvantaged throughout the UK. These include job centres, youth clubs, probation offices and agencies specifically working with young people with problems due to offending behaviour, drug use and homelessness. DFY sends recruitment officers to areas such as Glasgow, Leeds, Birmingham and Bristol to actively encourage applications from eligible young people who are seen as likely to benefit from the scheme which offers a challenging range of experiences at Celmi, on placements and back in the participant's home area.

The Celmi Centre in Snowdonia

Selection takes place through a two day residential 'taster' at Celmi. During these two days they take part in an outdoor activity, a team-based problem solving exercise, and an interview with experienced members of staff. There are plenty of opportunities for them to mix informally with both staff and other participants. The key to selection is a recognition from a person that they need to build up their skills and self-sufficiency, and that this is likely to require a change in behaviour and attitude.

Not everyone gets onto the courses, but they often still benefit from the experience and some re-apply when the time is more appropriate. The 22 week courses require full commitment from participants and those taking part can obtain a number of benefits including:
- a City and Guilds certificate;
- an improved level of self-reliance and confidence;
- new skills;
- more understanding of how groups and individuals work together;
- about a 60% chance of moving into employment at the end of the programme.

Funding comes from a wide range of big and small companies including Coopers and Lybrand, KPMG, and Marks and Spencers. There is also a considerable amount of additional support in terms of staff secondment to the organisation which supports the work of the organisation to the tune of nearly half a million pounds per annum. The balance of funding (about 50 per cent) is received from the Training and Local Enterprise Councils in the areas from which the young people are recruited. DFY have also started to develop new programmes in collaboration with partners, such as Groundwork, who have concentrated on specific regeneration sites.

Previous participants have said,

"...being on DFY has given me more confidence in myself and I'm not so shy anymore. I would honestly recommend the course to anyone. I've started to look for jobs now whereas before I didn't have the confidence."

"Learning to display initiative and make decisions with confidence has led to me to find new direction. Following the work experience during the DFY programme, I am now on a childcare course, working within a school for children with special needs...I now realise that I have a lot to offer and am prepared to put 100 per cent effort into my new life." Kim.

"DFY gave me the opportunity to broaden my horizons, it built up my confidence and allowed me to meet people I probably wouldn't normally mix with. It also helped me to use skills to help others and this made me see I was capable of doing much more than I thought. I am now working as a mobile park ranger with Haringey Parks Department." Emile.

Staffing and the programme. The Team Advisors, who act as facilitators for DFY, are mostly professionally trained teachers and youth workers, plus a number of people who are seconded from management and training positions in industry and public service. During the residential components of the programme it gives the staff and trainees a chance to get to know one another as individuals, rather than conforming to stereotypes. This has been a major factor in the success of the scheme for many participants (and seconded staff members), who have taken their new understandings back to their own communities. Some quite strict rules are adhered to during the residential components. No drinks or drugs use is allowed, nor stealing or abusive behaviour, and those who ignore these rules are automatically sent home. One can imagine that this must appear rather draconian to many of the 18 to 26 year olds who have grown used to urban street culture!

For more information about Drive For Youth, you can contact them through Freepost CS 125A, Tywyn, Gwynedd LL36 9BR, or on freephone 0800 616258.

Extracts from 'A cold week in December at the Corris Railway' by DFY's Richard Greenhough

     Following the success of the August working week with a group of Drive For Youth trainees working on the Corris Railway, the chance of another week later in the year came up. This time, it was the first week of December on offer, from Monday 4th to Friday 8th. One thing could be said with reasonable confidence - there would be no cases of heatstroke this time!

     Once again, I managed to obtain clearance from my Guv'nor (what a nice man!) to go railwaying with the group, as before, subject to the rider that if anything urgent came up at the office, I would have to go in to sort it out. Fortunately, it proved possible to manage matters by means of a phone call first thing each morning, although it did leave me with a pile of paper to catch up with on my return. With the possibility of having to return to the Celmi base during the week in mind, I sought a suitable support from the Corris Railway Society, and fortunately Bronwyn was available for most of the week. This not only provided an experienced worker, but also a second engine driver, and more importantly still, one who can usually persuade No.5 to start in the mornings !

     DFY's staffers for this group were Pamela, short of stature and red of hair, and Steve, sometime Inspector with the Metropolitan Police on secondment to DFY for a year. Their charges were Darren from Nottingham, Paul from Manchester, Nathan from Nottingham, and Grant from London. As with the August group, they had been booked into the Cells in Corris and, as the weekend immediately beforehand was a working weekend, they were able to come along on the Sunday afternoon to see the sort of things they would be doing. Despite this, they all turned up at Maespoeth on the Monday morning, ready and keen to start work!

     The section of line set aside for the week was immediately north of an area known as the Triangle, continuing from where the previous group had left off. In the meantime, CRS members had cleared most of the topsoil from under the track and on the east (valley) side of the line, and a start had been made on the cess. The group was to continue the work, finishing a section between cross-drains by digging out the cess, jacking up the track and cleaning under the sleepers, removing baseplates where necessary, laying in the blue plastic land drain, covering the drain with ballast, and then ballasting across the track under the sleepers.

Having successfully persuaded No.5 into fume, we filled the two tippers with ballast, loaded the tools and the workers into the CAT carriage, and set off up the line to the worksite. Fortunately, the wet weather of that Saturday had given way to dry-ish and cold, a good incentive to get going with the work to keep warm ! The lads set to with a will, using the arisings to strengthen the embankment below the line - somewhat eroded over the years by sheep - and soon the first section of cess was ready for the drain to be brought up.

On some sections the original cross-drains reappear as topsoil clearance takes place; here, with the line having been dug up for the Dulas Valley Hotel's sewage pipe, there is nothing to indicate where they lay. We therefore ran the cess until a physical obstacle barred progress - either a shallow section of living rock, shaped from the mountain by the long-ago railway builders, or a large and permanent-seeming boulder! A cross-drain would then be dug to the north (uphill) side of the obstacle, and the drain run from its south side to the next cross-drain down.

It had been hoped that one of the Bentley colliery waggons, 216, would be available to move ballast during the week, but due to problems with the side doors, we used the tried and trusted tippers. However, 216 was nevertheless pressed into service. A new length of land-drain pipe was to be used, and opening out a roll of this stuff is like wrestling with an angry python! If opening it out is difficult, trying to persuade it to go back into a transportable format is well-nigh impossible. Waggon 216's first duty in Corris service was therefore to act as a land-drain transporting vehicle. It proved possible, just, to persuade the pipe to fit into the well of the waggon and to tie it down inside so that it could be transported back to Maespoeth at the end of the week..

Monday went well, but Tuesday dawned colder, and during the day snow flurries started, becoming heavier as the day went on. Nevertheless, our doughty gang continued their efforts, and steady progress resulted, defying everything the weather could throw at us! This section of trackbed suffers from minor slippages of loose material from the steep hillside above, between the old Upper Corris Tramway trackbed and the main line. Previous partial excavation of the cess hereabouts had been buried by such slippages. So, to prevent this happening to our newly-ballasted cess and drain, we decided to build a low dry-stone wall immediately above the cess, with a flat area behind, to catch the slipping material before it messed up the new drainage. Pamela proclaimed herself an expert at dry-stone walling, and while some of us took the train back to Maespoeth for more ballast, she proved that this was no idle boast, so that when we returned, a fine rustic wall had begun to take shape along the west side of the track.

Wednesday arrived much as Tuesday had - cold and snowy ! Each morning, the group brought the DFY minibus down to Maespoeth, and commenced the day's work by filling the ballast waggons, while Bron and I persuaded No.5 to fire up. In return for their efforts, each of the group were allowed on the loco footplate for a journey up or down the line, always accompanied by either myself or Bron, and this greatly added to their enjoyment of the work.

Sadly, on Thursday, we lost Darren, who had to go home for personal reasons, but the rest of the group were prepared for another day's hard work, on what turned out to be the coldest day of the week. However, No.5 was not of the same mind, and after firing up once and running for a few seconds, it conked out and refused to show any further interest in running. We carried on loading ballast, and one after another tried to persuade the loco to burst into life; we ended up with seven weary people and one silent loco. Although everyone was warned of the dangers to their ribs if the starting handle slipped, Pamela managed to whack herself in the chest, but being female, her natural cushioning seemed to protect her from more than a mild bruise; for a mere male, a whack from the starting handle can mean being unable to sleep on the left side for up to six weeks !

We therefore pushed the loaded ballast waggons, with the tools on top, up to the worksite, and carried on regardless. No loco, of course, meant no CAT carriage either, so when lunchtime arrived, we all headed back to Maespoeth with the empty tippers, to load some more ballast, and see whether No.5 had stopped sulking. Eventually, with a shower of sparks and some thick black smoke, it burst reluctantly into life, and for the rest of the day ran as though there had never been a problem.

Friday was (relatively) warm, and the loco decided that one awkward day was enough, and got up fume without difficulty. With a need to clean out the Cells and return to DFY that night, work was scheduled to end at midday, but another good morning's work was done beforehand. Progress during the week had been excellent, with a good length of cess laid, a fine length of rustic dry-stone wall installed, and a further section of sleepers lifted off the mud and laid on ballast. The trainees had performed well, and they and the 'staffers' had enjoyed themselves, while Bron and I had enjoyed working alongside them.

After tools had been collected up and loaded ready to return to Maespoeth, various photos were taken, and the gang made a last trip down the line. On reaching the shed, a small presentation was made to your Editor; in view of my noted sartorial elegance when working on the railway, a multi-coloured woollen hat had been acquired to set off the rest of my outfit, and the wearing of this was naturally the cue for more photos !

If proof was needed, this week demonstrated that working outdoors in the winter can be successful, and that cold and snow is infinitely preferable to driving rain! Thanks are due to the four lads for their efforts, and to Pamela and Steve for their guidance and hard work alongside them. Thanks too to Bronwyn, who made it much easier for me by sharing supervisory duties and enabling the loco to be down the line collecting ballast with a couple of the lads while the rest continued at the worksite. A few more weeks like this and we will be finished to Corris and thinking about extending towards Machynlleth!

AGENDA 21 YOUTH PARTICIPATION

Background

After the 1992 agreement at the Earth Summit in Rio de Janeiro between the 179 countries who attended, Agenda 21 became the environmental action plan for the 21st Century. The UK accepted the action plan, and part of it, Chapter 25, stated clearly that young people had an active part to play in the process of sustainable development. To be precise it says,

"Governments....should take measures to establish procedures allowing for consultation and possible participation of youth in decision-making processes with regard to the environment, involving youth at the local, national and regional levels."

Agenda 21 is an international agreement, but two thirds of its proposals can only be achieved at the local level. Supporting young people in their actions under the Agenda 21 umbrella is one way to achieve this. Many initiatives have been taking place linked to local authorities taking on and developing the idea of Local Agenda 21 and there has been a commitment to involving young people in the process in most of these. In this section we offer a number of examples of local and national initiatives which have taken place.

CEE/LGMB roundtable: young people and Local Agenda 21

A roundtable event was held in March 1996, co-ordinated by CEE and the Local Government Management Board, with the aim of producing guidelines for local authority staff and youth workers to help them ensure the involvement of young people in the Local Agenda 21 process. The initiative is itself an excellent example of the successful participation of young people in the Local Agenda 21 process.

CEE/LGMB Roundtable: Young People and Local Agenda 21. (Keith Emmitt photo)

The aim was for at least 50:50 representation of young people and 'older' people and this was more than achieved – on the day, 34 people took part, 18 of whom were young people under 25. The participants represented a wide range of perspectives and expertise, from the voluntary and statutory youth service, local authorities, NGOs and environmental organisations. Many of the young people were involved in environmental initiatives in their schools, colleges, youth groups and communities; some were already working with their local authorities on Local Agenda 21 issues.

Delegates explored the environmental concerns most important to young people and identified barriers to young people's involvement in Local Agenda 21 which need to be addressed in order to ensure lasting and meaningful participation. They also considered a range of projects involving young people, and were able to analyse the characteristics of these successful projects which demonstrated the most meaningful involvement of young people. Following this, they drew up a list of recommendations and suggested strategies for involving and consulting young people in Local Agenda 21 initiatives. These recommendations appear in the guideline document, together with a range of case study examples.

Local Agenda 21 and young people, no. 12 in the LGMB's Local Agenda 21 guidance series, is available from CEE (please send 50p p&p).

The Next Generation Council
In the London Borough of Richmond, a local organisation, EcoAction, has taken up the challenge and worked with a group of young people, the Next Generation Council, to develop a Young People's Vision for the Future for the local area around Richmond. The intention has been to:
- ensure that the adult-led Agenda 21 Sustainability Forum hears (and hopefully listens to) the views of local young people;
- make the concept of 'sustainability' actually mean something to the community, through action.

Jane Elmslie from EcoAction puts it quite neatly,
"Sustainability is about changing people's attitudes as well as improving things like the public transport system. A major difficulty lies in overcoming cynicism – as a confirmed cynic, I know!....Beginning to consider your own environmental impact, and joining together with others who are thinking about theirs, can open your mind to larger issues and give you a voice......Sustainable development means meeting the needs of today without destroying the planet's capacity to meet the needs of future generations....How do you improve the quality of life today without jeopardising that of future generations?"

What have the Next Generation Council been doing?
The Next Generation Council members are in the age range 7-18 years old. The aim has been to get as many young people as possible involved in looking at environmental issues which are local, regional, national and international. They have been involved in the following ways:
- A local Next Generation Conference acted as the focal point for developing a greater understanding of environmental issues, and identifying issues which

could be tackled locally by young people through action and lobbying.

- They have presented their own vision of a future Richmond to the Sustainability Forum. In this vision, "the noise of machinery would be replaced by the sounds of nature."

- Two of their members, Hannah Streeter and Chloe Bridge represented the Richmond group at the International Environmental Children's Conference, entitled 'Leave it to us'. Some of the demands of the young people were:
    -We challenge shops in all countries of the world to follow the example of Malawi and to stop using plastic carrier bags by 1988; instead customers must bring their own.
    -We challenge governments to use money from tourism to take care of wildlife areas and endangered species.

Hannah Streeter and Chloe Bridge

- The Times on 26.11.95 printed the following account of that conference:

Gummer shouted down by children

Hundreds of children silenced John Gummer, the Environment Secretary, yesterday. Four minutes into his speech at the International Children's Conference, Eastbourne, young delegates shouted: "You are behaving like an adult." To the 800 children at the environment conference the phrase is an insult, meaning too much talk and too little content. Mr Gummer quickly sat down.

He also felt the children's anger, however, during a debate on French nuclear testing. Children from New Zealand called on everyone at the Devonshire Park Conference Centre to stand up if they disagreed with the actions of France. Mr Gummer remained firmly seated, prompting boos from the audience.

- Hannah's particular concerns are the availability of cycle paths and campaigning on litter and recycling; Chloe's primary concerns are the wildlife in the cities, especially the deer in Richmond Park, many of whom have died as a result of eating litter, and who may also suffer as a result of car pollution.
- Members have been actively involved in the Peace Child International initiative: 'Rescue Mission-Planet Earth'. Through this they have produced local indicators of sustainability. Put into plain English this means that they are looking at positive and negative aspects of the environment. These are things like industrial development and waste; levels of waste recycling; air quality; sports and recreational amenities; water quality; biodiversity (the number and variety of plants and animals in any area), human rights; employment/unemployment, and transport and communications. (see Rescue Mission information later in this section).
- They took part in a riverside litter pick during the Tidy Britain's national campaign week.
- A video and the written views of young people were prepared for inclusion in Richmond's Agenda 21 Legacy Time Capsule.
- They conducted a questionnaire amongst over 100 young people about issues which concerned them. A sample page from the questionnaire is reprinted below with the results.

WHAT DO YOUNG PEOPLE THINK THEY CAN DO TO PROTECT THE PLANET?

*pick up/don't drop litter	32%
*recycle	24%
*walk or cycle more	13%
*reduce energy	10%
*don't waste paper	10%
*support greengroups	8%
*stop using CFC'S	4%
*plant trees	3%

other comments: don't have lifts for short journeys

WHAT DO YOUNG PEOPLE THINK THEIR PARENTS CAN DO TO PROTECT THE PLANET?

*walk, not drive	33%
*recycle	20%
*reduce energy use	9%
*use unleaded petrol	8%
*avoid CFC'S	8%
*don't litter	7%
*stop smoking	6%
*buy green products	4%
*join a green group	4%

other comments: sell one of their cars, stop people from sunbathing

WHAT COULD THE GOVERNMENT DO TO PROTECT THE PLANET?

*stricter pollution laws	32%
*encourage recycling	15%
*reduce car use	14%
*invest in green projects	9%
*protect wildlife	9%
*more street sweepers	9%
*encourage solar power	5%

other comments:increase the price of petrol, resign, no wars, invest in environmental education.

WHICH ADULTS WOULD YOUNG PEOPLE LIKE TO QUESTION ABOUT THE ENVIRONMENT?

*John Major	25%	other suggestions:
*David Bellamy	8%	
*The Queen	8%	Paddy Ashdown
*Mum & Dad	8%	John Gummer
*The Government	7%	The Gladiators
*Richmond Council	6%	Rolf Harris
*Jeremy Hanley	6%	Factory owners
*Environment Minister	6%	Grandad
*The Mayor	5%	Michael Howard

What future?

The Next Generation Council is very much a project still in existence. They are lobbying to try and make some of their 'visions' for the future become realities. The following are some of their ideas. *Why not develop your own wants list for your own local vision?*

The Richmond vision includes:
- there would be fewer cars and the town centre would be pedestrianised;
- public transport would be cheaper and more efficient in order to encourage people to use it;
- the air would be clean and alternative energy sources would be used as much as possible (solar and wind power, for instance)
- everyone would receive better environmental education so that people cared for their environment and understood its importance.
- the river would become a focal point for the local area – it would be less polluted and there would be a riverbus service.

The National Young People's Environment Network (NYPEN)

In April 1996 five national voluntary youth organisations made a successful application to the Department for Education and Employment for funding to develop a National Young People's Environment Network over a three-year period. The five organisations are: Youth Clubs UK, The Royal Society for the Protection of Birds, The Wildlife Trusts, The National Federation of Young Farmers Clubs and the Council for Environmental Education.

Between September 1996 and March 1997 the NYPEN partner organisations ran a pilot project in the City of Bath. This involved 15-20 young people aged 13-19, planning and carrying out an environmental awareness-raising activity. The young people were drawn from the NYPEN partner organisations and given the task of raising the awareness of a further 150 of their peers. At the time of writing the programme is to extend to operate six regional fora and will operate over a two year period. Each forum will be provided with financial support for travel costs, programme costs and facilitation. Advisory support from the NYPEN partner organisations will also be available. In addition, the fora will be encouraged to maintain contact with each other and will gather annually at a national event to share their experiences.

NYPEN was developed as a result of a number of environmental and youth organisations agreeing the following statements:
- There is evidence that young people aged 13-19 have environmental concerns but few opportunities for them to develop their concerns into action.
- Environmental organisations often offer opportunities for environmental action by young people, but tend to concentrate their activities on a younger audience.
- National youth organisations have undertaken environmental projects but these are restricted to their own organisations.
- The UK government has an obligation under the international Agenda 21 agreement to consult with young people at local, regional and national level on environment and development issues.
- The effective way to establish a national environmental youth movement is to work through existing structures and develop an inter-agency initiative at a local/regional level.
- Such a structure would enable young men and women to effect change within their own youth organisations, their own communities, and their own lives.

The NYPEN programme aims to promote partnership and co-operation between National Voluntary Youth Organisations and other agencies at local, regional and national level through the development of a national young people's environment network. It will also support and develop the participation of young people in environmental policy formulation, management and decision making at local, regional and national level. In addition it will create a structure which enables young people to be consulted as part of the local and national Agenda 21 processes. For more information about NYPEN developments, contact the CEE.

Rescue Mission: indicators for action
Background
Many users of this book will have come into contact with the *Rescue Mission: Planet Earth* materials. Their Indicators project has turned into one of the biggest participative, environmental youth projects ever seen. Whilst mostly used by school groups, the *Indicators for Action Pack* has also been used by some youth groups and organisations and as part of Local Agenda 21 initiatives.

Rescue Mission Planet Earth was set up the United Nations after the Rio Earth Summit in 1992. The primary aim has been to involve young people in an organisation which actually has a structure whereby it is run by young people in equal partnership with adults. The Indicators Project has been the core enterprise involving young people in 120 countries taking the pulse of their own countries. The pack itself provides a leader's guide, 16 indicator sheets and 10 copies of the UN Passport to the Future. It is described organisers as being,
> "...a magnificent tool to teach 11-16 year olds the concept of Sustainable Development."

The Indicators Project is continuing into 1997 and may well continue on an annual basis well into the future. In addition to the Indicators Pack, Rescue Mission is actively organising youth exchanges for 17-25 year olds to get involved in both the Indicators Projects and whole gamut of sustainable enterprises and eco-action.

For more information, and prices for their publications and the Indicators Pack, contact:
Rescue Mission: Planet Earth, The White House, Buntingford, Herts SG9 9AH. Tel. 0176 327 4459.

The Manchester Indicators Project: Acting locally – thinking globally!

Chris Smith is the very active Young People's Co-ordinator for Local Agenda 21 in Manchester. Along with Wayne Talbot and a whole host of young people in Manchester she helped to turn the Indicators Pack into something which could be used by individuals, schools and youth groups. In fact, this is one of the only areas in the UK that we know about, where a specific youth workers' version of the Indicators Project has been created.

To give you a flavour of the Indicators Project and how Manchester translated it into a form suitable for use by youth workers, we have reprinted a section of their version, but have left out the word Manchester, so that you can fill in the name of your own area. Even if you don't actually manage to return the outcomes to Rescue Mission HQ, it may well be a useful exercise for your community in relation to Planning for Real or other development forums. Incidentally, Planning for Real is a technique devised by the Neighbourhood Initiatives Foundation (NIF). Information packs are available from the NIF, Suite 23-25, Horsehay, Telford TF4 3PY. Tel. 01952 503628. The most widely used of the packs is based upon the principle of supporting communities to identify problems and issues, generate ideas, set priorities and produce a three-dimensional model. This model can then be modified to take account of people's ideas for changing or developing their neighbourhood.

Returning to the Manchester Indicators Project, they defined the aims and areas of skill development to include:

- a new series of activities that allow young people to monitor the health of their local community;
- youth/adult partnerships to improve local conditions and solve local problems;
- an understanding and experience of how decision making processes work;
- connections between the local and global issues that young people and adults encounter;
- an understanding of what sustainability means;
- communication skills including discussion, reporting and structured debate; collecting, recording and interpreting data; understanding the conflicts of social, economic and natural issues designing solutions.

The Manchester Indicators Project defined the task as:

How would you design the _____ of the future so that it is safe, secure, pollution free. The activities on this sheet will help you decide. All you need to do is design three computer screens:

✓ A description of the best and worst bits of
   _____ today.
✓ An outline of the solutions to today's problems.
✓ A vision of _____ in 2096 when your solutions have been working for a short while.

The following material is from the Manchester Indicators Project.

STEP 1. Making the Headlines.

OBJECT: To find the best and worst things about your life and living in _____

☺ Sit quietly for a few minutes, think about what you like about where you live,
what are the problems about living in _____ ? Think of three good things
and three bad things

☺ Look at the grid below. Write the benefits and problems down in the appropriate
columns.

GOOD NEWS	BAD NEWS
1	1
2	2
3	3

Use this list to help encourage discussion. It summarises some of the issues in ~ Agenda 21:

☺ Employment and work
☺ Education and training
☺ Energy and resources use
☺ Open space and conservation
☺ Health and Safer cities
☺ Transport
☺ Pollution
☺ Entertainment.

Step 2. Hanging the Issues out to Dry

OBJECTIVE: To share your ideas and see if you can build a picture of the problems mentioned most often.

☺ Get into a circle with your Good News - Bad News Grids in front of you.
☺ Go round the circle writing down on one big piece of paper or a board what everyone says are the bad bits. If they are mentioned more than once put a tick next to the problem.
☺ Now repeat for the good news.

An alternative is to string a washing line across the room. Give each person six pegs or clips. At one end put positive suggestions. At the other put negative suggestions. If something is repeated clip them together. The biggest bundles are the most popular best bits, or the biggest problems.

Congratulations,you can now draw a computer screen of the best and worst bits of _____today using everyone's ideas.

Step 3 The Great Green Grid.

OBJECTIVE; To identify the effects of and the solutions to the cities problems. This activity will provide ideas for your second computer screen.

☺ Get into small groups with the most popular problems. You may choose these from the last activity or use your groups lists.
☺ Look at the grid below and redraw it on a large piece of paper.
☺ Write the problem in the problem column.
☺ Write down the effect the problem has on you, the part of the city you live in, the whole city.
☺ In the final column try to think of a solution to the problem and write that down. Try to keep it simple and easy.

Problem	Effect on me	Effects on the place I live in	Effects on the city	Simple solutions

You can now use the solution ideas to draw a second computer screen, outlining the solutions to the problems in _____ .

Screen title:
- ☐   199   Problems of living in_____
- ☐   199   Solutions to the problems
- ☐   2096 The perfect _____ Tick correct title

problem/issue	solutions/comments

Name:
Address:

Age

Return forms to

Key words on next screen:

Use these words to link your screens

Screen title:

☐ Problems of living in _____

☐ Solutions to the problems

☐ 2096 The perfect _____

Tick correct title

Name...

Address...
....
.... ☐

In addition to the Indicators Project, Chris and her colleagues in Manchester have been developing a number of other resources for schools and youth groups to use in environmental education. One major resource is the *Junk Jam 4 Pack* which consists of a leader's handbook; audio cassette; cartoons; instrument building instructions; star profile sheets; star picture sheets and a song sheet. The whole pack is aimed encouraging young people to actively think about rubbish and the four 'R words': *Reduce, Re-use, Repair and Recycle.*

They have also produced a photo pack entitled, *Manchester – Creating a Future.* This includes 24 colour photos and a handbook full of ideas on how to explore sustainability issues. Although based on Manchester and aimed at primary schools, the pack is still a good resource for youth workers, especially those in urban areas. At the time of writing, a complementary pack for 11+ youth groups is being compiled.

For info. on any of the **Manchester initiatives** contact **Chris Smith** at the Technical Services Department, Manchester City Council, PO Box 488, Town Hall, Manchester M60 2JT.

Agenda 21 interactive environmental workshops
Background
Filton College played host to the Eco 95 conference which involved David Bellamy and was attended by over two hundred participants. Subsequently, it became the

David Bellamy with the organisers and youth ambassadors at Eco 95

catalyst for the establishment of a wide range of environmental initiatives. Central to these is the Northavon Local Agenda 21 Youth Initiative, which, under local government reorganisation, has become the South Gloucestershire Agenda 21 Youth Forum. Lesley Kinsley organised the original conference and is involved in a number of ways in keeping the impetus going through in addition to her support work with the Youth Forum:

- partnership working with young people and members of the business sector; education sector, local authorities and the voluntary sector;
- cycle to school/college week during Green Transport Week;
- BUG schemes – this neat little acronym stands for Bicycle User Groups;
- project work with schools, colleges and youth groups on recycling, environmental improvement, tree planting, landscaping, supporting the establishment of environmental 'arms' in schools' councils and student councils etc.;
- raising awareness through environmental curriculum development – Lesley is working within the college and in partnership with businesses, the voluntary sector and the local authority to broaden the environmental curriculum and emphasise its importance as a core area; (teachers/lecturers have a crucial role to play in raising awareness and developing environmental aspects of their courses and materials);
- developmental and outreach work involving Youth Ambassadors from the Agenda 21 Youth Forum, including work with young people from Germany, Finland, Luton and Hereford; and, for the future,
- involvement in a 'Festival of Youth' to be co-ordinated by the University of Bristol.

The majority of Lesley's work has been with groups of young people from schools and colleges, including feeder primary schools. Agenda 21 is central to most of the work. Lesley told us that the work is very school based, *"...because these are ready made communities within which it is fairly easy to successfully set up projects."* She, like us, hopes that the local Youth Forum will widen its constituency to include many more young people who are members of youth organisations and others who are not.

Running interactive workshops
At the Eco 95 conference, Lesley organised a set of interactive workshops which were designed to help participants to think individually, collectively, and in partnership with other external agencies, about how they could best achieve environmental change. The process during 75 minutes, involved:
1. Brainstorming a list of ideas of what people would wish to change to achieve a greener future.
2. Prioritising a small number (between four and six) of the actions needed to achieve change.
3. Designing a plan for how to carry out one plan of action.

We thought that Lesley's material and process could be very helpful in a practical way for other people who are involved in organising local Agenda 21 events, or indeed any other environmental gathering using participatory workshops. Reprinted on the next pages are the actual resource handouts and OHP masters which Lesley used.

INTERACTIVE WORKSHOPS

Reconvene in marquee at 11.45am for a 5 minute **dramatic reading.** When this has finished you notice posters around the edge of the marquee displaying MONTHS of the year. You will then be given several minutes to gather around the person who is holding the poster displaying your BIRTHDAY month. You will then be led to your workshop room to carry out the following exercises. Months with a large number of birthdays will be divided into two.

Exercise ONE (10 minutes)

Divide into subgroups of about four people. Try to have mixed sector groups where possible.

Each group has a large piece of paper and a felt tip pen.

Using OHP **WHAT?** as a stimulus BRAINSTORM what you would like to change for the better under any **one** of these headings at **any** level - as an individual, family, organisation - it doesn't matter.

One 'scribe' writes **everything** down - no discussion or argument. Write as much down as possible.

Exercise TWO (10 minutes)

Pick out from your list the 6 best actions you could best carry out in partnerships between:

schools/colleges/universities

businesses

voluntary organisations

local authorities

You must agree as a group.

Write each **one** of the six on each of 6 'post its' and stick over your brainstorm.

Exercise THREE (10 minutes)

On another large piece of paper.

Pick **ONE** of your actions.

Decide **how** you would **carry this out** in partnership.

Use the **HOW** OHP as a stimulus. The 'scribe' writes short ACTION POINTS on how to make this happen.

- How do you start?

- What do you need to do? **LIST**

- Who will do it? **LIST** - this may involve partnerships

- Do you need money?

  Where do you get this?

- Do you need other resources?

  What are they?

  Where do you get these?

- Do you need permission?

  How and where do you get this?

ASTERISK all those points which involve partnership.

Your 2 large sheets will be displayed in

We will start DAY 2 with a short summary of the outcomes.

A more detailed summary will be published and posted to you after the conference.

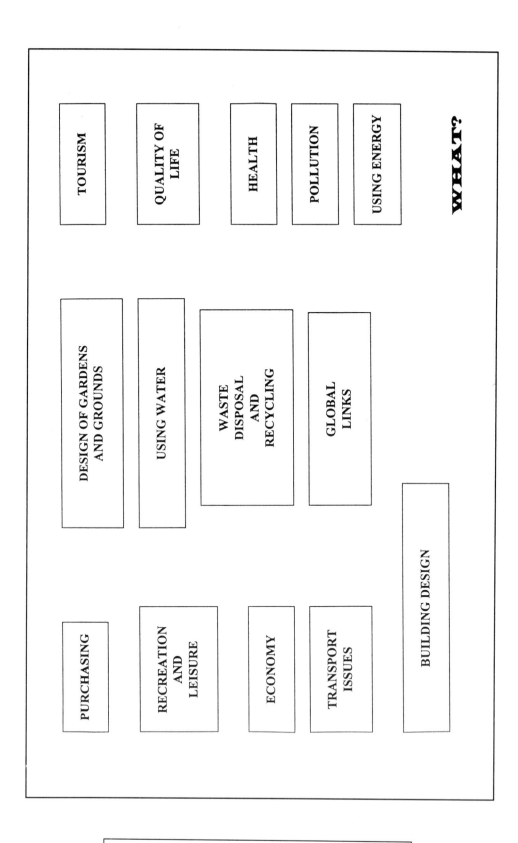

WHAT?

TOURISM

QUALITY OF
LIFE

HEALTH

POLLUTION

USING ENERGY

DESIGN OF GARDENS
AND GROUNDS

USING WATER

WASTE
DISPOSAL
AND
RECYCLING

GLOBAL
LINKS

BUILDING DESIGN

PURCHASING

RECREATION
AND
LEISURE

ECONOMY

TRANSPORT
ISSUES

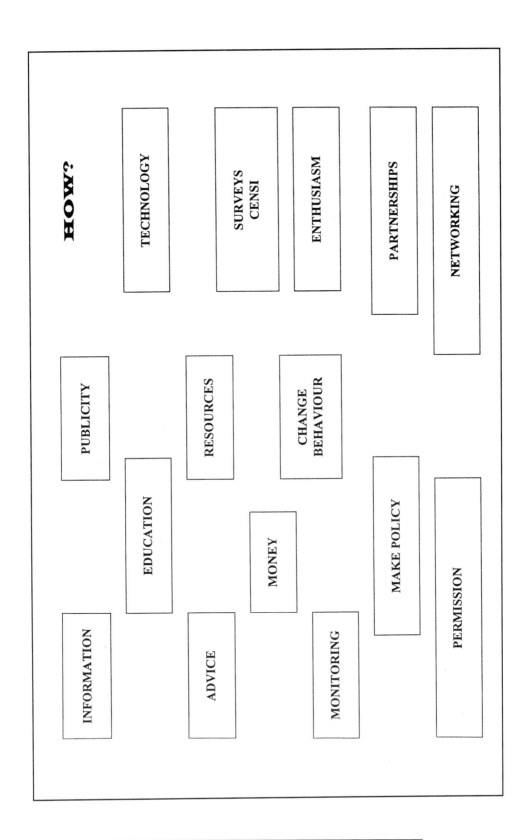

HOW?

TECHNOLOGY

SURVEYS CENSI

ENTHUSIASM

PARTNERSHIPS

NETWORKING

PUBLICITY

RESOURCES

CHANGE BEHAVIOUR

EDUCATION

MONEY

MAKE POLICY

INFORMATION

ADVICE

MONITORING

PERMISSION

Filton
College
Bristol

If you would like to get in touch with Lesley Kinsley, she is the Environmental Development Officer, Filton College North, Filton Avenue, Bristol BS12 7AT.

ENVIRONMENTAL YOUTH ACTIVITIES
The EARTHworks pack

The first and second editions of the *EARTHworks* pack were developed by Jill Edbrooke, Lisbeth Grundy and Alan Rogers for the Council for Environmental Education Youth Work Unit in 1990 and 1992 respectively. Keith Phelpstead provided the illustrations. In many ways it was the forerunner of this publication. That pack is now out of print and in preparing this new book, Alan and Howie contacted past users of *EARTHworks,* and as a result of that survey decided together with CEE staff which bits to reintroduce into this book.

These activities introduce three levels of environmental work with young people:

1. Young people's attitudes.
2. Is your club/organisation environmentally friendly?
3. The wider environment.

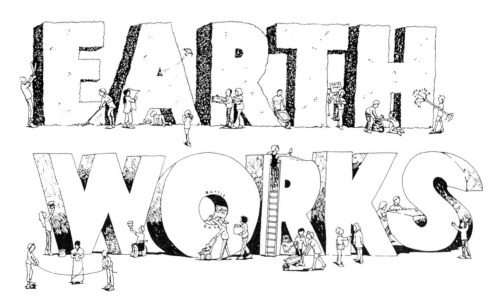

The material on the next nine pages all comes from that pack. We decided to keep this material in its original format. Thanks to the authors! We hope that you and the young people you work with find it useful.

Using Video, Camera or Tape Recordings to get Young People's Views

Technology has an appeal for many young people. It is also a useful way of stimulating self expression. In these exercises the equipment is used as a means to an end, although the people using it will need to be familiar with how each bit works. For most of the exercises a camera, video recorder or tape recorder could be used, but for clarity examples are given for each.

Self image

AIMS:

To examine the environments in which young people feel at ease. This activity is based on IMAGE – an ever-present concern of young people!

WHAT TO DO:

Start by taking self portraits. You can do this in various ways.

- Put a blank back drop (a sheet or very large piece of paper) against a wall and get individuals to pose for the camera. If they want they can add props to the back drop such as giant speech bubbles, a ghetto blaster, a giant pair of trainers (cut out of paper) OR
- Let them take photos of themselves in part of the club or the local area that they use a lot and like being in, alone or with their friends.

When the photos have been developed they can add comments to go with their own photo. You might want to suggest sub-titles e.g.

my name is ______________________

my best back drop is ______________________

because I am ______________________

PRACTICAL TIPS

Do you need a room that you can use where you won't be interrupted?

Watch out for trigger happy photographers!

OTHER IDEAS USING CAMERAS:

Photo Album

• Simply record and label different views and put them into a book.

Advertising

• You can look at how using parts of a picture can affect the image and help to sell something.

Newspaper

• Produce a photo and/or article about the area for the local newspaper – perhaps something like the articles on the back pages of Sunday magazines ...
'A day in the life of .....' or
'My favourite room'.

DISCUSSION POINTS:

While the portraits are being taken try to draw out some of the features of our self image and what we seem to others.

• Does what we wear represent a particular group of people, a lifestyle, a state of mind, conformity or individuality?
• How do others see us?....is this a true reflection?
• What type of surroundings go with our image?
• Can we create these surroundings?
• Will our tastes last?

VARIATIONS:

As an alternative or follow up to the activity, suggest having an image swapping session. If you can, bring in a load of jumble sale clothes and see what outfits and images the group can create out of it. Put posters of other images up around the club to spark off ideas.

Discussion points here could include:

• Why does a garment suggest a certain image?
• What sort of back drop would they give this image?
• Why don't they want this image themselves?
• Are the things it represents really that bad/unobtainable?

PREPARATION:

Camera and film. Props (including large sheets of scrap paper e.g. wallpaper). Paints and pens. -

These sessions will also raise all sorts of issues about stereotyping. Be prepared to discuss these and challenge them.

You may find that the environmental issues become secondary, or they may come out in different ways
e.g. one group got into the idea of recycling clothes and after going to some more jumble sales put on a fashion show.

Eyelites & eyesores

AIMS:
To help young people to think critically about their local environment and express their views.

WHAT TO DO:
If the town/village is involved in a competition like the Best Kept Village, bring in some press cuttings about it. Ask if anyone thinks it is a good idea. Which parts will the judges like? Can anyone think of areas that the judges might miss, but which are important for young people?

Suggest that the club could run a competition like this, but taking the views of young people into account, by making a video and ask for volunteers to produce it.

Spend an evening looking around the community (if you are in a large town, you may need to use the local community rather than the whole town). Make a list of what the group thinks are the eyelites and eyesores from their point of view. Select three or four examples of each and plan what the group wants to say about them. Think about how they can make best use of the camera. For example, emphasise the beauty of an area by filming it on a sunny day, or film a dirty shopping arcade at dusk with the camera at knee level...

If there are more than half a dozen people in the group, you may want to divide them up for the filming, or suggest they take responsibility for different tasks such as scripting, filming and editing.

When the video is completed have an evening performance and round the event off with a vote for the Best 'Eyelite' and Biggest 'Eyesore'. (Would the group like to invite anyone to this – a local councillor or M.P. for example?)

Make sure the group knows how the video works.

The members of the group may want to be on the video as well – if so, make sure that the scene includes the eyelite/eyesore tool

DISCUSSION POINTS:
When the group is reviewing the video, some of these questions might be useful:
• Did everyone choose the same spots to record?
• Which sights would other members of the community choose?
• Were the eyesores permanent (ugly buildings for example), or temporary (litter etc)?
• Could anything be done about the eyesores?
• Were any of the eyelites or eyesores there because of young people?

VARIATIONS:
When the club has voted for the Biggest Eyesore, you might want to follow this up and visit representatives of the Eyesore to see if the club can get involved in improving it.

Try this exercise over different times of the year – which parts are particularly good/bad in different seasons?

If you do not have access to a video, a camera can be used, or simple sketches.

PREPARATION:
Video camera and T.V. in working order.

This is my world

AIMS:
To identify which parts of their environment are important to young people.

WHAT TO DO:
Ask if anyone would like to make a video about their 'patch'. Emphasise that the contents of the video will be decided by them and it is up to them where they take the camera (within reason and walking distance)!!

Before setting off, work out roughly where your route will take you and shoot an introductory scene in the club. Members of the group will be acting as reporters, so give each of them a chance to be filmed at the beginning. This trial run is important as it gives you a chance to check the equipment and techniques (you will need to decide who does the filming at this stage).

Sort out the ground rules for behaviour during practical discussions about the organisation of the filming and how individuals perform in front of the camera.

DISCUSSION POINTS:
While you are 'on location' you could start discussions on various aspects:
- Where do the group spend most of their time?
- Which parts are their favourites and why?
- If they have 'secret places', do they want to reveal these?
- Where don't they like going?.... what is it about these places that they find off-putting?

VARIATIONS:
Look at the local environment as a personal history.
- Where did they play when they were little?
- What areas do they use now?
- What areas do they think they may use in the future?

PREPARATION:
Portable video and film.

OTHER IDEAS USING VIDEOS:

Documentary
- Individuals or small groups do research on different aspects of the story.

Fiction
- Role play or drama with the discussion coming through development of the plot.

News Flash
- Similar to the idea suggested for tape recorders but with a young person as reporter.

Rapping
- If members are interested in music or rapping, video could be a vehicle for their ideas.
-

Party political broadcast
- On behalf of a local branch of the YPWS (Young People Want a Say Party).

PRACTICAL TIPS

Because of the equipment being used you will have to work with a small group.

Make sure that other leaders know that you will be out of the club for the session.

Watch out for the unexpected – one group decided to film the 'Haunted House'. An irate neighbour saw the group as vandals rather than young people playing. He almost flattened the youth worker who he felt should be responsible for their behaviour.

Check all the equipment thoroughly before you start – especially batteries.

Information and ideas

'How Green is your Club' challenge

The Club Challenge could provide a good way of getting started on environmental action. Remember though, that it could well lead to suggestions or demands that the club is run differently... are you prepared to work with the consequences of using it? You could use it with the staff team as well as using it with young people. Used with the other materials, it provides a comprehensive look at how global environmental issues affect the youth club.

HOW GREEN IS YOUR CLUB?

Score a point for every question that you can say YES to.
For some of the questions it may not be your responsibility, for example buying light bulbs.
If this is the case, you will need to ask the person who is responsible.

This is quite a difficult quiz – if you don't know why something will help the environment,
see if you can find out... then try this quiz again in a couple of months.

1. Do you recycle...
   (a) paper that you use in the office, club activities etc? ☐Yes ☐No
   (b) waste paper? ☐Yes ☐No

2. Do you recycle aluminium drinks cans? ☐Yes ☐No

3. Has the club stopped using spray cans that contain CFC's....
   (a) in cleaning materials and the office? ☐Yes ☐No
   (b) in art work? ☐Yes ☐No

4. Have you checked that there are no solvents in the felt pens and tippex? ☐Yes ☐No

5. Has the cleaner been asked to...
   (a) avoid using bleaches? ☐Yes ☐No
       (Score a bonus point if you can suggest alternatives)
   (b) only use cleaning materials that are fully biodegradeable? ☐Yes ☐No
   (c) avoid using cleaning materials that contain phosphates? ☐Yes ☐No

6. Are there any low energy light bulbs in the club? ☐Yes ☐No

7. Do you know if the fire extinguishers contain CFC's ☐Yes ☐No
   (Bonus point if they don't)

8. Do you buy recycled...
   (a) paper for art work and the office? (If there is one) ☐Yes ☐No
   (b) toilet paper ☐Yes ☐No

9. When you break equipment is it...
   (a) repaired if possible? ☐Yes ☐No
   (b) used for another activity? ☐Yes ☐No
   (c) thrown away? (Lose a point) ☐Yes ☐No

10. Are people discouraged from smoking in the club? ☐Yes ☐No

11. If there are tampons in the girls toilets have you stopped using ☐Yes ☐No
    ones that are chlorine bleached?
    (Can you think of other paper in the club that is bleached with
    chlorine?)

12. Do you use rechargeable batteries? ☐Yes ☐No
    (Score a bonus point if you don't use batteries at all)

13. The last time that you used block board/chip board/plywood, ☐Yes ☐No
    did you check whether it was made of wood from sustainably
    managed forests?
    (Score three bonus points if you can explain what 'sustainable
    management' means)

14. Do you use stains, varnishes and paints that are based on plant ☐Yes ☐No
    products?

15. Do you know if animals were used to   ne soap that you use ☐Yes ☐No
    in the club?
    (Extra point if it wasn't)

HOW GREEN IS YOUR CLUB?

16. Have you done anything to improve the environment outside the club for wildlife?   Yes No

17. Have you had the fridge serviced in the last three years or descaled the kettle/urn in the last six months? (One point for each)   Yes No

18. Have you thought about the products that you sell over the coffee bar...

   (a) what sort of 'E' numbers and additives they contain?   Yes No

   (b) what effect there is on the environment where the products were grown?   Yes No
   (Two bonus points if you know where the ingredients are grown)

19. Is there a water filter in the kitchen?   Yes No

20. Some environmentally friendly products are more expensive than the alternatives you usually use. Have you ever thought about raising money (in an environmentally friendly way of course!) to pay for some of these?   Yes No

WHAT DOES YOUR SCORE MEAN?

Less than 10
MAY DAY MAY DAY – there is something wrong with the way your club is being run! Even if you aren't concerned about environmental issues, you could be saving money and improving your health. Take the matter to those responsible and challenge them to make some DRASTIC changes!

10 – 24
Your club is thinking about some of the ways it can improve the environment of the club and some of the things it can do about environmental issues. There is potential for improvement – why did you get this score?

• Because you didn't know about some of the ways you can take action?

• Because some things you can do are more expensive?
  (If you aren't in charge of how money is spent, do you agree with the decisions that are being made?)

• Because the effect of your decisions seems so tiny in comparison to the problems?

Take heart!
Your actions DO matter.... The more you know, the more you can do....
Encourage those who control the purse strings at least to think about how they are spending the money.

25 – 30
Congratulations, your club seems to be working as a team. You are obviously well-informed and concerned about environmental issues. Keep it up! Why not try to help other people in the community to be as positive as you are...?

Over 30
AMAZING! Write to the papers and ˙ everyone know – you are probably 'greener' than the greenest organisa¹ and don't really need to be using this quiz unless you are on an ego tri¡

Photomontage

AIMS:

To let young people express what they like about different environments in a creative way. To use photomontage as a way of focusing on what kind of environment young people like to use for leisure activities.

WHAT TO DO:

Explain that anyone interested can use the magazines you have brought to make a picture of their ideal place. They can cut out whatever they want – it doesn't have to be a whole object.

When a picture is complete stick it onto a wall temporarily so that it doesn't get chopped up again and encourage people to do another one with a different theme. There is no right or wrong for this activity and it can take as long as the individual wants (some will find it a lot easier than others). If they picture themselves indoors, encourage an outdoor version – what about places that they feel uncomfortable in or an outer space version....?

Depending on how the session develops you may want to link the activity to a discussion of places that a group could visit.

Before the session finishes make a display of the finished works and see if you can get titles for them.

VARIATIONS:

You might begin by working on a representation of where you live before moving on to the 'ideal environment'.

PREPARATION:

Collect a selection of magazines, newspapers, brochures and other material together before the activity. Think about the group you will be working with when you are collecting the magazines – when one group of Asian boys were doing this activity there were no images of people that they could identify with. However, they made very good use of old snapshots of themselves...

You will also need:

Glue/pritt stick; blu-tack; large surface for working on; bin liners to clear bits into; backing paper; scissors.

Let individuals come and go if they want to – some of them may take a while to get interested in what can be seen as 'arty' stuff.

Watch out for the magazines' contents – a Littlewoods catalogue 'underwear' section proved an attraction for one group of young men.

If you have any spare photos of the young people or can photocopy some to chop up and stick on to the pictures, they are a great help in stimulating interest. You will need to lay down ground rules about individuals respecting each others work and only using pictures of themselves.

Places I'd like to visit

AIMS:
To help young people to think about the kind of environment they like/dislike using for different purposes. To increase the involvement of young people in planning trips and residentials.

WHAT TO DO:
Put up large pictures of different environments around the room. Ask people to list in order of preference where they would like to go, for example:

'Spend a weekend' or 'Go for a trip'.

The question will depend on what the pictures are of and what you want them to discuss.

Put all the votes together and see which picture is most popular. Ask why they made the choices and relate this to the plans you are making for the trip/residential. Can they reach a group consensus?

DISCUSSION POINTS:
If, for example, you are planning a residential you might have put up pictures of different types of houses – a remote cottage, a Victorian town house, a block of flats or a luxury mansion.

• Why did they pick one type of house and not another?
• Was it because they have never stayed in, say, a remote country cottage?
• Did the prospect appeal to them because of this – or did it frighten them?
• Did they pick a house because they had stayed in a similar one when they were younger and it had good memories?
• Did they pick it because of the 'kind' of person they imagine would live there?

VARIATION:
Use collections of pictures with different themes e.g. activities, places to meet friends, romantic places, exciting places etc.

Ask each person to place one of the pictures on a line marked 'best ——— worst'. Let the group negotiate about where the pictures should go until they have ranked them in some way.

PREPARATION:
Make a collection of different pictures around the theme you want to discuss and number them. Either prepare individual sheets for scoring or put up a master sheet with First choice........ Last choice (five or six pictures is a reasonable number).

PRACTICAL TIPS

Travel agents usually have spare posters, especially at the end of a season.

Larger libraries with education resource sections may have teaching packs with posters/photos of different environments.

You may find working with different small groups during the course of a session is easier than trying to have discussions in a large group.

Postcards can be good, if they aren't too expensive.

LOCAL/GLOBAL GRID

This exercise proved very popular in the original *EARTHworks* publication. It is based on the 'think *global* - act *local*' philosophy. In other words, the actions we can take to counter global environmental problems are often to be found at an individual or local level. This is an important point for people to take on board because it leads to the realisation that no matter how big the issue or problem there is usually something that 'little old me' can do about it!

The local/global grid is used to encourage young people to relate their everyday experiences and environment to global environmental issues. It also helps to highlight gaps in the knowledge that young people have about a particular issue.

Two types of blank grid are provided – an *effect* grid, and an *action* grid. These can be photocopied for people to work on individually or in twos or threes. For small group work it is probably best to copy the sheets onto flipchart paper which can be fixed to a stand or a wall so that the whole group can see and work on them.

Stage one
Brainstorm a number of environmental issues with the group and invite them to select a few to work on. Group leaders should always be prepared to suggest issues if they are slow in being identified by the group. Alternatively, the leader can provide a range of objects which represent a particular issue or theme, e.g. product packaging, plastic/glass containers, piece of coal etc..

Stage two
Select an issue and put it in the *effect* grid. Now ask people to write down the global, national/local and individual effect of that issue in the appropriate square. Remember that one of the aims of the exercise is to identify gaps in knowledge, so don't insist that each square is filled in.

Example
Issue – paper packaging.
Global – loss of trees; global warming; species loss; pollution.
Local – waste disposal; litter; employment; recycling.
National – as above.
Individual – advertising and what we buy; litter and health.

Stage three
Put the same issue in the *action* grid and work out what actions can be taken to alter or reduce the identified effects.

Stage four
Lead a discussion on what the group has discovered about the issue. Some relevant questions may be:
- Were some of the squares easier to fill in than others?
- Where can we get more information from?
- Are all individuals affected in the same way?
- What kind of action – direct or indirect – can an individual take?
- How can we influence local or national politicians?
- Can the group do anything to raise awareness about this issue, e.g. by publicising it or fund-raising?
- What stops us taking action about this kind of issue?

Stage five
Repeat the process for one or two other issues identified by the group.

Variations
- Collect background information on likely issues so that the group can do 'on the spot' research. If gaps in knowledge still exist, discuss how to find more information.
- The grid can be used to examine the individual (i.e. personal) relevance of social issues such as poverty in the developing/developed world, racism, sexism or disability. Although at first glance these issues may appear to have little relevance to the environment, a detailed examination using the grid will usually throw up a number of environmental factors.

WHAT *EFFECT* DO ENVIRONMENTAL ISSUES HAVE ON US?

EFFECT	Issue	Issue	Issue
Individual			
Local			
National			
Global			

WHAT *ACTION* CAN WE TAKE ABOUT AN ISSUE?

EFFECT	Issue	Issue	Issue
Individual			
Local			
National			
Global			

DISCONNECTIONS CARDS

This way of using the 'Issues Cards' (shown on the next page) proved to be popular with users of *EARTHworks* – and kept folk on their toes, as it encourages 'several steps removed' links to environmental issues.

Disconnections can be played in a small or large group. First, prepare a set of cards; you can photocopy the Issues Cards and add to them if you like – or generate ideas from the group using a brainstorm. Place the set of cards face down in the centre of the group and invite someone to take a card and read it out. The fun element comes from the fact that now they have to state a word that is totally unconnected with the issue on the card.

Play continues round the group with each person having to state a word completely unconnected with the previous one. Players can be challenged, and if a word does have some connection with the issue, they lose a life (from a set number available, e.g. 3 or 5). Following a successful challenge – or one or two rounds – the next person (in turn from the original one) should take a card. Don't allow successful challengers to be the ones who take the next cards (except perhaps in a very large group) as this can cut some young people out and provide others with the opportunity of dominating play.

Other uses for the Issues Cards
Ask individuals, partners or groups to arrange the cards in a value line –

from most to least important – and stimulate discussion on the various arrangements:

- Use the 'Who am I?' technique (see the *New Youth Games Book* page 40) or, as it is in this case 'What issue am I?' First, pin an issue card on someone's back – they have to guess the issue by asking questions of individuals or the group. Only YES/NO answers are allowed.
- Try the 'Charades' technique, e.g. with one person miming each syllable and the rest trying to guess what the whole issue is.
- Hide letters to make up one of the issues around the room or building, and give clues as necessary. Once all the letters are found, can the group rearrange them into the issue?

ISSUES CARDS

Acid Rain	Roads and Transport
Global Warming	Animal Rights
Ozone layer	Waste
Recycling	Natural Habitats
Nature Conservation	Agriculture
Alternative Technology	Human Rights
Nuclear Power	Sustainable Development

EARTH SPIRIT ACTIVITIES
Talking to the Earth

This is the title of a rather special little book and set of A4 work sheets originated by Gordon MacLellan (Capall Bann Publishing). Currently development worker with the Sacred Earth Trust, Gordon's work as an environmental educator is becoming increasingly well known. He describes his book as, *"...a collection of activities to let the artist out in everyone.......it is a mixed collection of 'art' and 'spirit' activities."* We feel that many of his activities represent the very essence of the spirit of environmental youth work. Gordon himself says it is,

> *"...about change; about encouraging people to understand their world and where they belong in it; to appreciate the wonder and diversity of it, and to be prepared to make their own informed decisions about what they feel should happen to it."*

It seems as a good a definition as we've seen!

Gordon has field tested his activities mostly with young people aged 8-12 years. They are also, we think, ideal for a slightly older age group and the youth club or social education setting. A lot of Gordon's work centres on the way in which the cultures of many indigenous people around the world show a far greater awareness than we do of the interconnectedness of all things in the environment – the elements: earth, water, sky, fire, animals and plants, marine life and humans.

In the following pages we offer Gordon's activities for producing Mapsticks and a Charm or Token. We are very grateful to Gordon and Capall Bann Publishing for permission to include our version of this material. Capall Bann are based at Freshfields, Chieveley, Berks RG20 8TF.

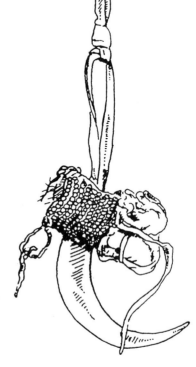

Bear Medicine: Blackfoot, North America

Gordon offers a few words about cultures.

"In our world, we tend to record events as written words: diaries, letters, accounts in exercise books; increasingly we even hang onto precise recordings such as photographs or video. We seem to be moving away from remembering significant moments for their meaning and the impressions they leave, and towards hanging a picture of the event itself.

In other cultures, that pin-point accuracy is often less important than the change a situation heralds and the long term consequences for an individual's life. A naming ceremony may, for example, identify and place a person within their community and connects them to a whole lineage of spiritual and cultural associations and obligations. The enduring feature of such an event is not the moment itself (we might keep a baptism photograph) but the connection that is made, a link that may last the rest of a person's life.

Recording such situations in a non-literate culture can take place in many ways – as songs or stories, dances, drawings or tokens. (In these activities) we shall draw upon the idea that takes an incident, large or small and turns it into a 'thing' – a 'medicine object', or just medicine, in Native American parlance. Here, colour, shape, materials and texture can all encompass meaning – all contribute to the message contained within a shaped and structured artefact."

Such objects can be found and constructed in our normal UK environment. If an adult worker introduces the activity in an appropriate way, the significance of the individual totem can be very powerful and very personal. Gordon reckons they can also act as memory triggers in the future, recalling the story of the making. In a lesser way, hair-braiding and friendship bracelets, which we described in our *New Youth Arts and Crafts Book,* can have a similar significance for the maker and the wearer. The two activities which Gordon explains can be simple structures as in the charm or token, or more complex and linked to a specific story, quest or journey as with mapsticks. Perhaps they even convey something of the spirit of the people involved and the place and time where they evolved!

The Charm or Token

Materials: minimal – twine, string, scissors and or a penknife are useful for the adult facilitator to have available. Other materials are searched for and discovered by the participants. The activity can involve a group working singly, or in pairs, with the young people making the charms either for themselves or to give as a gift to their partner. Gordon suggests that anything up to half an hour should be allowed for the activity, and that, *"It is probably best to let people spread out and find their own places to stop and reflect and enjoy a bit of peace and quiet."*

The method: locate a special place on a walk; a place where there are a reasonably abundant supply of available found materials, leaves, sticks, stones, leaves, feathers etc. Invite the group to enjoy the feeling and spirit of the place. They can then try and find materials which can be bound together to make a token or charm which will remind them or a friend of the visit to the specific location. The finished token can then be kept or gifted, or even left behind as a 'thank you' to the place itself!

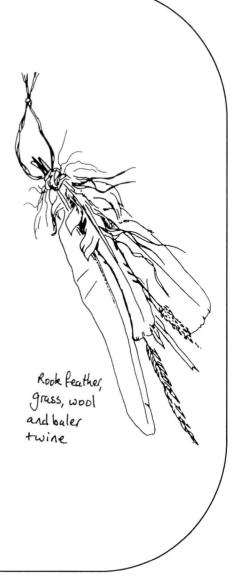

Rook feather, grass, wool and baler twine

Mapsticks

This is a more substantial activity and requires between one a half and two hours to undertake. It also needs a little more preparation. Gordon shares a common love with us for the famous children's book *The Phantom Tollbooth,* by Norton Juster. In that book it is proclaimed that,

> *"The most important reason for going from one place to another is to see what's in between."*

It is the very essence of this activity.

The organiser needs a small pair of scissors for each group member and lots of small lengths of different coloured wool to hand out to the participants. It is a good idea if each individual has a bag with handles in which to collect the findings. Usually it is safest to start off by defining clearly the boundaries in which the group should go 'exploring'. The task should be explained:

Search for a suitable stick on which to attach mementoes of their journey.
Each pair or group should go about their personal quests enjoying the place, looking for what Gordon calls, *"...the juicy bits, the exciting bits, the places they'd like to take someone else to."*

When we have done this type of activity we usually suggest that the participants search in pairs, hopefully without getting on each other's nerves! Gordon recommends small groups each containing an adult member. Get them to meet up again at regular intervals, say every, 20 minutes or so after searching around the meeting point in different directions. After perhaps two of these expeditions, the facilitator should suggest that every one settles down at the meeting place to make their own mapstick of their personal journeys.

Afterwards, Gordon gets the group members to sit down together and explain their own journeys with reference to their mapsticks. This should help everyone to get to know and understand the whole site really well. As additional activities, Gordon suggests that individuals give mapstick guided tours around their exploration. The mapstick is a very personal record of a place and its meaning to an individual.

In Native American culture, Crazy Horse was a famous mystic and was likely to have taken part in the Ghost Dance, which was outlawed by the White authorities. The Ghost Dance was the ultimate evocation of the power of the land and its spirits. You might like to use the following passage from one of the great mystics, or offer some pieces of prose or even poetry or song which conjure up the magic of the particular place, or re-tell its tales and legends.

> *"When the last red man shall have become a myth among the white man, when your children's children think themselves alone in the field, upon the highway or in the silence of pathless woods, they will not be alone. In all the earth there is no place dedicated to solitude. At night when the streets of your cities are silent, and you think them deserted, they will throng with the returning hosts that once filled them and still love this beautiful land. The white man will never be alone."*
> **Chief Seattle.**

An example of a mapstick adventure from *Talking to the Earth* is presented next.

A MAPSTICK

The journey

My journey began by a pond of cool, clear water with rushes growing around it (*blue wool with plaited rushes making a pond shape*)

Leaving the pond, I followed a path across a field. I liked this section and even though the distance was quite short, I spent a long time here (*green wool with grass stalks and leaves woven into it*)

Moving on, I walked over bare earth in a wood of alder and birch trees. There were holes among the tree-roots where I found a rabbit bone (*brown and black wool, alder cones, birch leaves*)

3. **Keep talking** (if only to yourself). Everything that goes onto the stick is part of the story of your journey. Talking helps you tie object, colour and incident together.

At the end of my walk, I came out onto a field with out a path and there I stopped (*green wool with grass woven into it*)

This walk was in the early morning - the sky was clear and blue, birds were singing and the sun was rising (*pale blue wool, feathers and an orange and yellow "sun" weaving*)

5. **Special items** could be added out-of-sequence to show their importance: a single wellington boot turned up on one occasion.

Making the mapstick

1. When wrapping, **keep the wool tight,** feeding one colour into the next so no unexplained bits of twig are exposed.

2. **Don't start at the very bottom or work right to the very tip.** A bare base gives space to thrust the finished mapstick into the ground for a useful display style, and if you work right to the end, does that mean you have finished your journey and you have nowhere else to go? At all? Do journeys ever end?

4. Be adventurous. **Think about colour** - wool may reflect changing colours in the environment, the skies, how you feel. Create shapes out of things you have found: ponds woven from their rushes, a boardwalk of cracked birch twigs, a five-bar gate.

LYME REGIS ALPHABET PROJECT

Background

An original Alphabet for Britain was produced by a number of professional artists for Common Ground, the national arts and environment organisation, which is based in Covent Garden. Simon Rodwell wrote the words for the Common Ground alphabet which were adopted as the Common Ground Rules for the organisation. The whole work was then reproduced as a full page advert in a number of daily newspapers and sold as a poster. Alan was very impressed with the concept and asked for permission to blank out the national images and use the remaining skeleton version as the basis for an environmental arts project in his own local area. The overall name was changed from *'Celebrating Local Distinctiveness'* to the *'Lyme Regis Alphabet'*.

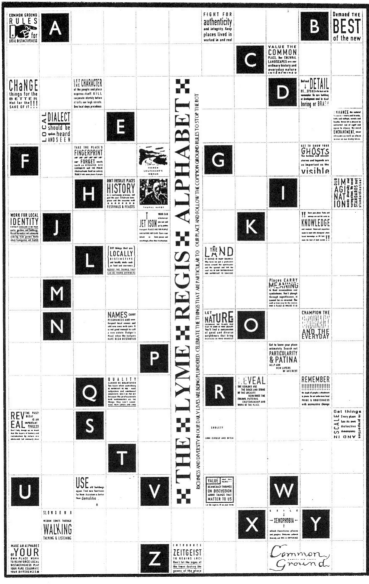

With Common Ground's encouragement and permission, this project is now shared with users of this book as an ideal way in which to engage young people to produce a piece of art which:

- is locally based;
- can involve a number of members of the community, especially young people;
- encourages people to look at the local environment and its cultural and natural diversity – the place where we live or work;
- is suitable for exhibition and going on show to the public as an end product of the work.

One of the final squares of the original Common Ground creation invited users to

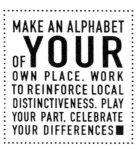

This is how Alan did it...

Having the permission to undertake the local project version of the Alphabet, Alan created the blank and then wrote to the local papers, schools, youth club and put up posters about the project inviting participation. The local Philpot Museum was contacted and it was agreed that the finished piece could go on show over the following Christmas and New Year holiday. The timescale had to be a fairly long one since there are so many squares to be filled

Participants were given two levels of instruction:
1. Try to find images of the area which reflect its present, past and individuality.
2. Produce drawings no bigger than 2½" x 2½", preferably in black and white.

During the period between July and December, after initial 'brainstorm' sessions to identify potential subjects for the squares using the different letters of the alphabet, over 360 drawings were produced with over seventy people involved, many of them year nine pupils from the local Woodroffe School. Alan enlisted the assistance of community artist, Andy Wood, and together they selected and photo-reduced the final images for inclusion and created the exhibition which comprised of the framed, finished alphabet and nine large panels containing all the original submissions.

The feedback from the exhibition was very positive. The young people and other members of the community who had been involved in the project were surprised by what a striking and uniquely local tapestry of the area was produced at the end of the exercise. Dot Page, the Woodroffe teacher who helped co-ordinate a lot of the drawings, was impressed that a number of young people who were not normally attracted to artwork had produced unusual and attractive images for the display. And councillors, museum staff and members of the public who visited the

exhibition commented about the scope of the project and the blend of images used to represent the town of Lyme and its local environment. Four young people, Gemma Pritchard, Lucy Campbell, Gemma Wood and Lucy Jack became so involved in the project that their school allowed them to research and draw the images as part of their term time work, and they eventually produced over one hundred drawings between them!

Some of the alphabet images:

The Common Ground poster, *Celebrating Local Distinctiveness* across Britain is available from Common Ground, 44 Earlham Street, Covent Garden, London WC2H 9LA, price £4.50.

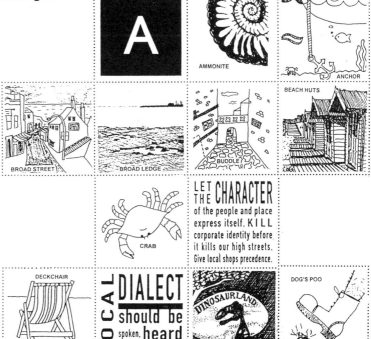

ANIMATE THE EARTH

*"Animation: to breathe
life into the Earth......"*
Millie Young

Millimations projects

Millie Young, based in Brighton, has been making quite a lot of ripples in the worlds of art, education, youth work and the environment in the south of England. Her *Millimations Workshops* are environmentally focused, and have been involving, intriguing and entrancing hundreds of young people in youth clubs, schools and community groups. Animation as a method and a means of work has at least two meanings. Animation is a style of work, all about empowering and facilitating people to take control of their own futures and destinies. Animation is also a method of bringing cartoons, objects and drawings, leaping into life through the medium of camera and film. Still other Millimations projects have involved building fantastic creatures out of scrap; using powerful environmental themes. We'd describe Millie as both an animator and an *animateur,* the French word for a person who helps make things happen! Her work is funded from a rich variety of sources including the Prince's Youth Business Trust, the Museum of the Moving Image and the Arts Council.

One Millimations Workshop

At the CEE national conference, *Engaging young people in environmental action* in Reading, 1996, Alan ran a workshop about the collation of this book. At the beginning of the session he showed a compilation video of animations produced by young people in Millimations workshops – they provoked a lot of interest, showing as they did a mixture of humour, environmental images, music and simple story lines about our fragile relationship with the natural world.

Millimations workshops include: *Illusion Workshop (zoetropes, praxinoscopes and flickbooks); Environmental and other Animation Workshops using PAR broadcast quality animation equipment (usually using cut-out animation work in 2-D, but 3-D images can be incorporated if planned for in advance. A VHS copy of the finished work is then supplied to the group); Longer term Animation Courses suitable for sixth formers and older young people and community groups; Litter the Monster, Scrap Monster Sculpture; Mural Workshops. Millimations also collates work for a compilation of* **Animate the Earth films** *to be shown at Animation Festivals, such as the Cardiff International Animation Festival and the Young Persons' Co-op Festival.*

Some of the ideas in action...

Millie describes her work,

> "Environmental Animation workshops can be put together using any or all of the many varied themes thrown up by environmental issues. Part of what Millimations purpose is to use accessible communications mediums as the vehicles for exploration and expression for individual and group concerns. In particular young people's. With the advent of the forthcoming Millennium celebrations my aim is to spread the possibilities to as wide an audience as possible."

Millie's approach is practical, low cost and transferable. She calls the core project of making a short animation, *Animate the Earth.* A drop-in workshop requires at least two hours to function effectively, and ideally a day is the minimum to produce a coherent end product. Operating through workshops of between 10 and 20, short animation films are made by individuals and small groups of two to five people work though a process which involves:

- an opening brainstorm session with the whole group to identify ideas, themes and processes;
- division into small groups;
- small group task to create a simple story board/storyline; each group then tells their story to the whole group;
- further advice from the facilitator on techniques, available materials, and things like keeping ideas and stories simple, use of music etc.;
- preparation and making of the materials for the film (between one hour and two or three days);
- tidying up, additional artwork and actual film making.

Millie adds,

> "The natural progression of the groups' ideas and abilities usually creates staggered filming time. This allows each group to film and mount artwork at the end in turn. This does not always work, and so a second activity for those waiting to film needs to be available. I often have a number of videos to show - EcoToons and Green Animation , both produced by the Worldwide Fund for

Nature are good. Alternatively, some people can be devising a soundtrack of produce a poster to advertise the film. Usually they are interested in the progress of other groups' film work and don't want to make something else! I aim to finish in time to clear up and then all sit together and watch the films. At this stage they are likely to be silent movies; at a later stage I help them to put sound and vision together."

Equipment and materials

Most groups end up using a video camera with tripod, monitor and lights using whatever stop frame facility is included. This is the most immediate system. Super 8 and other film mediums are good, but lose the immediacy of quick replay. Millie uses the PAR computer System with a rostrum camera and an EOS animation video controller. She suggests that local colleges may have the equipment and expertise to support local youth groups and schools, or it is worth getting in contact with the ASIFA national animation network organisations, listed at the end of this section. Sometimes if the particular project is of interest, youth groups may be able to negotiate special deals.

For animation materials, she suggests:
- paper and magazines for cutting out, which are easy to use and allow for the people who are not confident with drawing;
- pixillation - the animation of people/objects in real life, e.g. people, sand, litter, mud, boxes, toys, machines, bottles, cans, wood, twigs, in fact, anything! Good fun, and easy to achieve great effects;
- puppets and models are great for long term projects. Can be difficult to balance and great care is needed to move the joints to create movement.

Resource contacts

Millimations c/o Conscious Cinema, PO Box 2679, Brighton, East Sussex. Tel. 01273 605128. Fax. 01273 621390.
ASIFA Workshops Jessica Langford, Winton Hill Animation, 2 Winton Hill Cottages, Pencaitland, East Lothian, Scotland EH34 5AY.
ASIFA UK Pat Raine Webb, ASIFA International, 61 Railwayside, Barnes, London SW13 0PQ.

A WALK ON THE WILD SIDE

Background

Nature Trails, Woodland Walks and Sculpture Trails have all been developed with varying degrees of success and environmental sensitivity throughout the UK. The common ideas behind the development of these specialist walks include:
- encouraging more people (or young people specifically) to learn about their local area and to develop an understanding of the diversity of the local environment;
- to promote art and sculpture work which is appropriate to the place and landscape of a particular area;
- to specifically engage young people in conservation and wildlife projects (see also the sections on, Training for Life (Drive For Youth) the National Trust and the British Trust for Conservation Volunteers).

In preparing the material for this book, both of us found our own awareness changing of what is possible and what has already been undertaken. The high profile Sculpture Trail in the Forest of Dean had always impressed our adult sensibilities, but it seemed a bit esoteric for many young people. What we were looking for were examples of walks and trails which could more actively engage young people as participants. We found what were looking for from a number of sources. Perhaps most important was the Common Ground organisation, who it seemed to us had already identified lots of good reasons for people to engage with their own landscape, and had developed a whole host of processes and good ideas to make it happen. The following extracts from their pack *Celebrating Local Distinctiveness* hopefully shares their overwhelming sense of enthusiasm and optimism. (Common Ground, Seven Dials Warehouse, 44 Earlham Street, London WC2H 9LA.) They can also underlie some good, hands-on, practical environmental youth activities.

From *Celebrating Local Distinctiveness (Common Ground)*

"Of course the thing we take most for granted is that places stay put. Their geography may be fixed but places are a mixed bag of nature, history, legends and lives, and they are changing all the time."

"(All around us is a) cultural landscape: our history and nature's so intertwined that we have conspired to make it more diverse than nature would have achieved without us. And because of this it means a great deal to us."

"**Meaning and Significance.** Something lies at the heart of the place. Imagine....in the centre of the square stands an ancient oak. It is more than a botanical specimen, a home for hundreds of creatures, a wardrobe in waiting. It is the centre of the place, venerable, enduring......It stands as a reminder that here people gathered and made decisions, here news from the outside was first heard, here goods were exchanged........When the cars crowd in, the tree is cut back and then down, we are left with 'noplace', soulless, useless, somewhere to hurry through."

"**Identity.** Places like people do not need to be rich, famous or beautiful to have dignity. A place which is losing its identity because of pit closures, crowds of tourists, or huge new developments, is in danger of losing its integrity."

Common Ground also stress the need for what they call **authenticity**, meaning preserving real crafts and traditions rather than recreating a plastic, fabricated shadow version, **detail,** all the smells, sounds and small episodes which surround us and make our environment distinctive, and, finally, **patina,** the accumulated layers of meaning that time has enriched our buildings, woodlands and streams with. Places are wealthier because of the ways in which they connect the past with the present.

"Together they can create places which we want to be in, which we want to share."

Walking and Talking

An exciting and innovative example of the sort of project which can involve young people comes from the work of the Common Players, a rather unusual theatre company based in Exeter. They are strolling players born out of time, but recreating a form of local People's Theatre, which takes the show to people and makes the people an integral part of the show! They mostly perform in places where you wouldn't expect a touring theatre company, on village greens and in some cases, literally in the middle of footpath walks. In their community walk pieces with young people in Devon they do not usually perform themselves, instead they enthuse, galvanise and pass on skills so that the locals have the confidence to perform. The approach consists of:

- first, getting to know the different members of the local community;
- encouraging community members to share their tales, legends and stories about their local area;
- empowerment work with youth clubs, school groups, youth theatres and other community groups to create a framework for the Walk event. This is both the geography of the walk and the subject matter which can be related to it. The performance can then bring the locality to life and move from place to place where stories can be re-enacted;
- then the route is determined and 'locals' join the actors from the company to determine a script or series of scripts, songs or whatever. These are then rehearsed, fine tuned; props and special effects are created, all ready for,
- the Big Day, when, with the local performers are sited around the route of the walk and the audience joins in...............

The Dulverton Old Crow's Ramble
photo by Piers Rawson, courtesy of Take Art

The Common Players have used this process in a number of locations. In Dulverton, over 200 people joined the walk entitled *The Old Crow's Ramble.* The effects of the 'performance' on that audience were variously, confusion, amusement and engagement. The dramatic image of a resident afloat on her bed in the middle of the River Barle after a local flood was particularly striking, as were the many humanoid crows!. The Ramble event was ultimately a success because so much of the activity was based on the Common Ground principle of celebrating a place and its meaning for the people themselves.

Anthony Richards, Director of the Common Players remembers the event, saying,
> *"In Dulverton, the Common Players did not perform as such, rather they dressed as crows (yellow peaked baseball caps and black coats), and marshalled walkers around the route.*
>
> *Along the way, events and objects were located around the route.*
> 1. *Wayside songs and raps, composed to fit the location.*
> 2. *Visual artworks, for instance, mud sculptures and tree hangings.*
> 3. *A short mummer's play about a local legend.*
> 4. *A monologue about the flood in Dulverton. This was spoken from a bed in the middle of the river, with carrots supposedly washed up and dangling from the surrounding trees!*
> 5. *An improvised re-enactment of iron age activities in a hilltop settlement.*
> 6. *Secret messages for walkers in hidden places.*
> 7. *A giant buzzard puppet (worn by the headmaster) was chased by crows (carried by his pupils)."*

The way in which the event was 'sold' to the local people is self evident in the handbill:

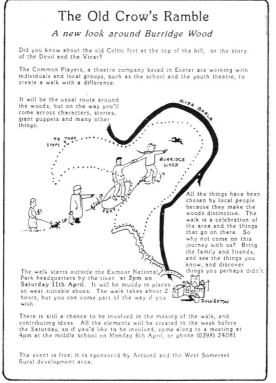

The Old Crow's Ramble

A new look around Burridge Wood

Did you know about the old Celtic fort at the top of the hill, or the story of the Devil and the Vicar?

The Common Players, a theatre company based in Exeter are working with individuals and local groups, such as the school and the youth theatre, to create a walk with a difference.

It will be the usual route around the woods, but on the way you'll come across characters, stories, giant puppets and many other things.

All the things have been chosen by local people because they make the woods distinctive. The walk is a celebration of the area and the things that go on there. So why not come on this journey with us? Bring the family and friends, and see the things you know, and discover things you perhaps didn't.

The walk starts outside the Exmoor National Park headquarters by the river at 2pm on Saturday 11th April. It will be muddy in places so wear suitable shoes. The walk takes about 2 hours, but you can come part of the way if you wish.

There is still a chance to be involved in the making of the walk, and contributing ideas. All the elements will be created in the week before the Saturday, so if you'd like to be involved, come along to a meeting at 4pm at the middle school on Monday 6th April, or phone (0398) 24081

The event is free; it is sponsored by Artsced and the West Somerset Rural development area.

Lessons to be learned

Talking to Anthony Richards about the organisation of the walks, he stressed that it is not really as daunting as it may sound. If handled with humour, enthusiasm and some tact, local people, including a lot of young members of a community, can use such an event to learn or relearn a love and appreciation for the place where they live. The performance aspects of the event and the need to construct the activity at people's own pace means that the version of the Common Players' timetable which we have created needs careful consideration. It also requires a group of people at the helm who have skills to handle quite complex event management, and communicate effectively with all the different individuals and groups involved.

Possible Timetable

1. Begin negotiation with key groups such as the Youth and Community Office, District Council, Rotary, Arts Council for help on access and funding. Basically the reconnaissance period.
2. At least ten weeks before the event, begin meetings and discussions with groups of young people and other community groups who could be directly involved.
3. Identify a potential route and check it out involving local people. Simultaneously, develop the raw material for the event by finding out from locals about legends, local history, customs and ceremonies etc.
4. Continue to publicise the Walk event by word of mouth and handbills/posters.
5. The Common Players become 'resident' in the community in the week before an event. In practice, this means that they are available for workshops, rehearsals, helping the young people and community members to build props and move the event to fruition.
6. The event itself with a potential fallback date if the weather is bad.

(The Common Players can be contacted at the Exeter and Devon Arts Centre, Bradninch Place, Gandy Street, Exeter EX4 3LS. Kneehigh Theatre in Cornwall have also worked with Common Ground to develop theatrical walks for local people. There may be theatre groups in your own area who would be keen to work in this way).

THE SEATON MOSAIC PROJECT

Background

Seaton is a small seaside resort with about 5,000 residents nestling in the flat floodplain of the River Axe. Amongst the young people of the East Devon town, many feel that the town and its predominantly older population do not either appreciate or value the younger members of the community. Seaton itself has been identified as being in need of a bit of a 'kick up the backside' which has resulted in the creation of the Seaton Regeneration Forum. This group is actively looking at new ways of involving the local population in a wide range of potential schemes, from a new Nature (and possibly Arts) Trail through to a BMX and Mountain Bike Park.

However, prior to this adult-led activity, the young people down at Seaton Youth Centre had decided to make their own contribution to changing the face of the town.

Seaton Youth Centre

Most youth facilities in the UK, even in the voluntary sector, are in some way attached to, or financially supported by the Education or Leisure departments of their local or county council. Not so Seaton Youth Centre. Like a Phoenix rising from the ashes of the previous local authority youth club, this fiercely independent centre was established nine years ago by a group of adults concerned that the local young people were being undervalued and scapegoated by their own community. What happened then, was that Chris Byrne Jones, his wife Dee, his friend, Bob Grimshaw and his wife had more than one bottle of wine, took a very deep breath, and together became the founding four Trustees of the centre, which now costs £25,000 a year just to keep going! Much of this money is raised by making lettings to local community groups in the daytime, such as dance classes and an indoor car boot sale. Compared with many youth facilities there are relatively few rules governing involvement. At present, members range from 9-22 years old, and 23 entirely voluntary, and deeply committed staff, keep the club open six nights a week all year round. Chris says,

> "We're not youth leaders, we try to be led by the young people....The centre is more like a night club for young people.....we get about 60 per night in the summer, 120 in the winter mid-week, dropping in and out, using the coffee bar, satellite TV, lounge, juke box, sports and other facilities. Then, up to 300 at weekends for karaoke and discos.......we also have special nights where we offer circus skills, pantomime, bar-fly, laser clay pigeon shooting etc."

The aims of the Mosaic Project

Developed out of their 1994 Summer Playscheme project in collaboration with Exeter and Devon Arts Centre, the Mosaic Project was initially the brainchild of the Arts worker, Andy Boal, and a group of six young people aged between 14 and 18. The focus project was always meant to be something which was, *"Mucky and hands on".* Rather than being a mosaic for the youth centre, the group were adamant that the mosaic should be,

> "...for the whole town, since people think that young people never do anything for others."

This led to much discussion on what should be depicted in the mosaic and where the best possible site was. The group eventually identified 15 potential site options. The subject for the mosaic might have been youth or global issues, tourism, sport, or peace, but the group eventually plumped for, 'Seaton through the ages and into the future,' and therefore a site on the front of a long wall with eight natural panel areas was deemed the most appropriate. It was thought to be especially suitable because it was close to the youth centre (about 100 metres away); well lit, and highly visible from the road and pavements.

The development process

Initially, the involvement of the arts designer working in discussion and in preparatory mosaic work with the six young people took about three months. This was funded as a 'Spearhead' project from East Devon Alive and the Exeter and Devon Arts Centre. Chris says that project took far too long, especially the stage where planning permission was sought.

> *"What should have taken six weeks took six months."*

This, coupled with the effect of the key arts worker, Andy Boal, having had a long illness, meant that the process of turning designs into constructions was delayed.

The original Marshlands' Day Centre walls

However, even at this stage, the group researched potential subjects for the panels, using the local museum and other sources to find out about key aspects of the town's development. They also experimented designing panels, using adhesives and pieces of broken tiles and china. An unusual level of suspicion towards the mosaic existed in the town because the last piece of community art in the town, an 18 foot high sculpture on the seafront entitled, 'Erosion of the Emotions' had engendered such horror, criticism and vandalism, it eventually led, after a petition of 4,728 signatures, to its removal! By carefully consulting with the planning authorities through the town and district councils, about the nature, location and content of the eight mosaic panels, and with support from Exeter and Devon Arts Centre, and Julie Clark from East Devon Amenities department, the eventual planning permission was granted.

Not all of the original drawings for the panels were used, partly because of insufficient historical information. Among the possible panel subjects were: a Roman settlement; landings by the Vikings; local smugglers; the local stone quarry at Beer; the arrival of the railway in town; the Victorians in Seaton; the new Tramway terminal, and the proposed new Youth Centre.

Site plans for the mosaics

Nicola Holbrook (then aged 16) was the main designer of the artwork for the panels. She scaled up her drawings onto eight by four foot boards and the slow process of marking up areas for tiles and the actual gluing and grouting began. The construction process on the eight panels involved about 25 young people. Thanks to the generosity of local individuals and businesses, a lot of the tiles and other china for making the mosaics become a reality, and were donated to the youth centre after an appeal through the local media.

Construction details

- Each wooden panel was marked up in chalk, scaled up from Nicola's original designs.
- The finicky process of gluing the individual tiles in place was done by centre members, and especially, Karen Farndon who seemed to get great pleasure out of this laborious task.
- Once the tiles were affixed, more adhesive was added between the tiles and then they were grouted.

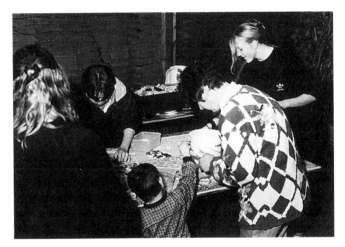

Under construction

- The back of the panels were treated with wood preservative and then the front and the back of the boards were given final coats of protective varnish.
- The walls on which the eight panels were to be mounted were re-painted white, which put an extra cost of £150 onto the project.
- Finally, the panels were mounted in place using stainless steel rag bolts and adhesive.

Outcomes from the project

The Mosaic Project cost nearly £1,000 to complete, a lot of money for an independently run and funded youth centre. But, within three months of its completion in March 1996, half of the costs were covered by public donation. Furthermore, the project has started to benefit the young people, the youth centre and indeed the local community.

- Individuals and community groups have communicated their wholehearted praise for the nature and execution of the Seaton murals.

- Young people and the youth centre have become highly visible for making a very positive contribution to the town environment.
- The mosaics are already becoming a tourist attraction, especially since they are within easy reach of the seafront and are opposite the popular Tramway terminal.

The Seaton Mosaics – pride of the town

- Individuals involved in the project are keen to be involved in further mural work and feel that they have learned useful skills.
- The youth centre is hoping to obtain funding, perhaps from Shell, to produce more murals in the town, having identified a number of other suitable sites. Indeed, Seaton may even be able to develop its murals as a tourist theme.
- The profile of youth and community arts has been given a boost and the youth centre are hoping to obtain funds to develop other arts based activities, particularly around music.
- The Seaton Regeneration Forum is hoping to involve more young people from the town in other projects such as the nature trail, which will improve the overall environment for both community members and visitors to East Devon.
- Nicola Holbrook, having left school and started work with no wish for further education, is now returning to college to do an art and design course – the Mosaic Project changed one person's life!

SIMULATION ACTIVITIES

Next comes an example of a simulation game that illustrates how an ecosystem works. Simulation games and drama activities are very useful tools for introducing complex environmental issues. In particular, development agencies like Oxfam and Christian Aid have developed a number of useful activities. Also the National Youth Agency's *One World Pack* offers a worthwhile simulation. Our own publications, *The New Youth Games Book* and *World Youth Games,* also offer a range of easily adaptable simulations, sequences, activities and games which are designed for use with youth groups.

Although these kind of activities could be seen as trivialising important issues, they offer a range of very interesting and interactive approaches. In our experience as youth workers we have found that young people quickly overcome the manufactured nature of the scenario and become passionately engaged in the process.

The Ecology Game
Background
This quite complicated simulation activity was kindly supplied to us by Andrew Backhouse of the Quakers (Religious Society of Friends). The aim is to involve quite a large number of young people (ideally about 15-30) in an exercise which shows to them in a graphic way how an ecosystem works. In other words, all species on the planet exist through interaction, and therefore any action will have a reaction. In particular, it offers young people an opportunity to look at the effect which humans have on other species in the ecosystem of the planet. Four adults or older young people are required to supervise the activity. The first two take on specific roles:

- **The March of Time** person acts as the general referee, exacts 'tolls' (penalties) from players and overseas the 'chases'.
- **The Earth** person keeps hold of the central stock of paper cups and beans for awarding to *Planties.*
- The other two facilitators operate in the *Planties* and *Nibblers* groups, keeping an eye on progress and clarifying rules.

Equipment required:
Lots of paper cups
Lots of beans

Time:
You need to allow between about one and one a quarter hours to explain the rules, set up the groups and take part in the activity for long enough to understand the 'meaning'. A short **debriefing session** at the end is useful for participants to consider,
a) what they thought was happening, and
b) how it felt to be part of the interdependent ecosystem.

Age range:
Because the basic concept and group rules are a bit complicated, we feel that it is best played with a 12 plus age range.

Setting up:
Four groups of young people are required to represent four species. The numbers in each can be varied but try to keep the percentage proportions roughly the same: *Planties* 60 per cent; *Nibblers* 10 per cent; *Crunchers* 15 per cent; *Hummies* 15 per cent. It can help if each of the species either has a coloured badge or sash to identify it, or makes a characteristic noise to identify its species! This can also add fun to the game.

Play:
The object of the game is for each group of players (Planties, Nibblers etc.) to reproduce as often as possible and sustain **THE MAXIMUM NUMBER** of members of their species group, within the constraints of their group rules. As all the groups are interdependent, this will involve decisions as to the best distribution of resources. Each group has its own code of rules. (see below)

Basically, each individual within a species of organism (whether Plantie, Nibbler, Cruncher or Hummie) is represented by a cup and the beans within it. Below a certain number of beans, the organism dies. (Their cup and remaining beans are returned to the Earth). Once an individual organism has collected a certain number of beans, the organism can reproduce; i.e. get a new cup and transfer the beans needed from the first cup.

Other rules:
Every five minutes, the *March of Time* calls, 'Chase', which is when Nibblers are allowed to chase and capture beans off Planties; Crunchers can 'attack' (strictly within the rules of the game!) Nibblers, and, once Hummies have entered the games arena, they can attack any other species.

After a chase, lasting, perhaps three or four minutes, 'a period of time' has passed and the *March of Time* exacts a toll from each organism which is paid to the *Earth.*

Some organisms will probably die at this point and players involved should leave the simulation.

The Hummies are introduced once the system is working – about two *time periods into the game.*

Planties
1) Start with 5 beans each.
2) Die if they have less than 5 beans each.
3) Give a toll to the *March of Time* of 1 bean for each passage of time.
4) Collect extra beans (a bit like worker ants) from the *Earth,* one bean at a time, by going round in a never ending queue.
5) Reproduce at 10 beans (i.e. start a new cup with 5 beans in it) if you want. Remember that you are trying to make as many Planties as possible. This can bring new participants into the game.
6) You <u>cannot</u> resist Nibblers.

Nibblers
1) Start with 10 beans each.
2) Die if they have less than 6 beans each.
3) Give a toll to the *March of Time* of 2 beans for each passage of time.
4) Reproduce at 22 beans (i.e. start a new cup with 10 beans in it) if you want.
    Remember you are trying to make as many Nibblers as possible.
5) Get more beans by taking cups of Planties, who cannot resist. For each cup you
    have to pay 2 beans to the *March of Time.*
6) If you are chased by a Cruncher you can pay beans to the *March of Time*, to try
    to escape. If you are reduced to less than 6 beans the Nibbler dies.

Crunchers
1) Start with 20 beans each.
2) Die if they have less than 10 beans each.
3) Give a toll to *March of Time* of 3 beans for each passage of time.
4) Reproduce at 44 beans (i.e. start a new cup with 20 beans in it) if you want.
    Remember, you are trying to make as many Crunchers as possible.
5) Get more beans by taking cups from Nibblers. Go with a Nibbler to the *March of
    Time*. If the Nibbler wishes to escape it pays beans to the *March of Time*.
    Crunchers have to match the Nibbler bean for bean. If the Nibbler dies, the
    Cruncher takes the remaining beans. Crunchers can stop chasing at any time.

Hummies
1) Start with 20 beans each.
2) Die if they have less than 15 beans each.
3) Give a toll to the *March of Time* of 4 beans for each passage of time.
4) Reproduce at 45 beans (i.e. start a new cup with 20 beans in it) if you want.
    Remember, you are trying to make as many Hummies as possible.
5) Get more beans by taking them from Planties, Nibblers and Crunchers.
6) After about three passages of time, Hummies can change any rule they wish,
    apart from the levels of beans at which organisms die and the tolls the *March
    of Time.*

Comment
We have to admit that we found this simulation a bit complicated, though the group
we tried it with did have fun in amongst the chaos of spilled cups, and hundreds of
beans. It also seemed a bit of a waste of dried beans! Our suggestion is that you
have a look at the basic rules and try to modify them into a form which you feel
confident that you can explain and referee! Have a happy ecosystem!

LAND ACCESS
Introduction
The natural beauty of the landscape is a delicate creature. It is there to be enjoyed,
but it also needs our care and protection. Conflicting interests between landowners,
conservationists, planners and developers, businesses, walkers, cyclists, to name
but a few, put an increasing amount of pressure on the landscape. This is equally
true in both of the wild and remote places, and in the local open spaces in rural and
urban areas, their hedgerows, trees and wildlife.

Access denied

There is also a central question about ownership of and access to land. Different countries have varying rules for allowing or disallowing access to land. Elsewhere in this book we have offered material which can be used to introduce young people to concepts such as an ecosystem, biodiversity and sustainability. These are all vital concepts when young (or older) people plan to use the outdoor environment. We have also provided material to raise issues surrounding road building and transport policies; housing and homelessness; travellers and low impact dwellings; trees and wildlife; agriculture and farming, and opencast mining.

Much of this book is aimed at encouraging people to make creative use of the environment, to get involved in conservation work, and/or environmental campaigning. But achieving a balance which actually proves environmentally and ecologically friendly is extremely complex. It is full of paradoxes. For instance, additional recreational use can quite quickly lead to erosion in the most used areas. Yet, it has become increasingly difficult to persuade landowners, and the national custodians of our land (such as the Ministry of Defence and the Forestry Commission) to allow more areas to be opened for access to the public.

In reality, virtually all land in Britain includes some elements of human use. And it is the use by people of paths and trackways on foot and horses, which has led to the effective establishment of the English and Welsh footpath network of 140,000 miles, and a limited 'right to roam' on moors, mountains and other open land. On the next pages, we highlight some aspects of two national organisations who are working hard to provide more access and opportunities for active use of the countryside. The first is the Ramblers' Association who have now been at the forefront of environmental campaigning for over 60 years; the second piece outlines some of the plans of Sustrans, who are developing the National Cycle Network as part of the Millennium Project. Obviously, these are only two of the many organisations which may be able to offer special support for young people. Others includes:
The Youth Hostels Association (YHA), Trevelyan House, 8 St Stephen's Hill, St Albans, Herts AL1 2DY. Tel. 01727 855215.

The Wildlife Trusts, The Green, Witham Park, Waterside South, Lincoln LN5 7JR. Tel 01522 544400.
The Open Spaces Society, 25a Bell Street, Henley-upon-Thames, Oxon RG9 2BA. Tel. 01491 573535.
The Long Distance Walkers' Association, 21 Upcroft, Windsor, Berks SL4 3NH. Tel. 01753 866685.

The Ramblers' Association (RA): *Working for Walkers*

Those working with young people in youth centres have often used the Youth Hostels Association as an organisation offering accommodation for youth groups going on a walking or cycling holiday, but may be less familiar with the work of the Ramblers' Association. During their 60 plus years in existence, and now with over 118,000 members, the RA have been one of the key pressure groups engaged in:

- fighting to open up neglected footpaths;
- saving existing rights of way from so-called rationalisation;
- campaigning against monoculture conifer forestry, and proactive work to re-establish more broadleaved woodlands;
- keeping open rights of way across and around farmers' fields;
- seeking restrictions on dangerous animals such as bulls in fields containing public rights of way;
- campaigning for the adoption of the law of *allemansratt,* which exists in Sweden and which allows people to walk freely anywhere in the countryside as long as they do no damage and respect privacy;
- public enquiries and parliamentary lobbying on road building and land access issues.

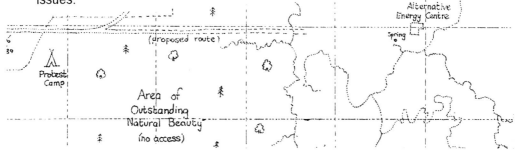

Each year the RA publishes a yearbook which includes over 3,000 accommodation addresses, including bunkhouses, hostels, camping barns and accommodation specifically geared to group needs. This 300 page book also includes a useful legal rights summary on access to the countryside , information on long distance paths, public transport and safety aspects. In addition, they organise specific events and campaigns designed to involve members and supporters in all aspects of their work.

Their network of over 400 local groups are keen to support youth organisations and the national office has an extensive selection of maps, guides and resources available for individuals and groups who want to be actively involved in the preservation of countryside access. Membership is open to adults, unwaged, students, retired, disabled, families and under 18s.

The Ramblers' Association can be contacted at 1-5 Wandsworth Road, London SW8 2XX. Tel 0171 582 6878.

We are also offering some quotes which might be useful for using for photocopying as a handout to get discussion going about **land, ownership and access.** (You might also like to look at the Landgrab section from Homeless International).

Whose Land is it, anyway?

Teach your children
what we have taught our children,
that the earth is our mother.
Whatever befalls the earth,
befalls the sons of the earth.
The earth does not belong to the white man,
the white man belongs to the earth.
This we know.
All things are connected.
How can you buy or sell the sky?
How can we sell these things to you
and how can you buy them?
(adapted from words by Ted Perry, inspired by Chief Seattle, 19th century chief of the Suquamish tribe in North America)

When you've spent half your political life dealing with humdrum issues like the environment, it's exciting to have a real crisis on your hands.
(Margaret Thatcher, 1981, at the time of the Falklands War)

Some people take a walk in the rain
Others just get wet...
(graffiti on motorway, courtesy of Matt Smith)

The Earth belongs to anyone who stops for a moment,
gazes and goes on their way
(Colette, French author, 1873-1954)

No owner or occupier of open country shall be entitled to exclude any person from walking or being on such land for the purposes of recreation or scientific study, or molest him or her in so walking.
(Sir James Bryce's Access to the Mountains (Scotland) Bill, 1884)

Many landowners, however, are so hostile to the paths that walkers in England and Wales have on average only a one in three chance of being able to complete a two mile walk on rights of way.
(Fay Godwin, photographer and author and past President of the Ramblers' Association.)

You cannot teach a child to care about the environment until he or she has learned to love it.
(Cliff Dean, Winchelsea primary school teacher)

Sustrans – National Cycle Network

Now in receipt of a four year grant of £42.5 million from the Lottery for the Millennium Routes (the first 2,500 miles) of the 6,500 mile National Cycle Network, Sustrans is an organisation obviously in tune with both government and popular thinking. The enterprise has lots of different aspects and many of them are very much in tune with Agenda 21 principles for local environmental initiatives. The overall aim is to establish the National Cycle Network which is aimed at providing safe and scenic routes for cyclists, walkers and wheelchair users.

However, within this there are obvious initiatives which would be ideal for involving youth organisations and individual young people. Fear of traffic and pollution are the main barriers to much cycle use and the new Network and all the local schemes to improve and develop new cycle routes should help to overcome these major hurdles. On the plus side, cycling can help encourage a healthy lifestyle, increase recreational opportunities, and combat the pollution of motor vehicles.

Among the ventures in which young people and their organisations can get involved are:
1. Holidays and short cycling adventures on the new trail routes such as the C2C route which crosses Britain between Whitehaven and Sunderland; the Camel Trail in Cornwall; the Tarka Trail in Devon; Lon Las Cymru (the Welsh National Cycle route), and Carlisle to Inverness. New mapped and signed routes which will be opened in 1997 include: Hull to Harwich and Padstow to Bristol and Bath.
2. Helping define the ways in which local routes can be developed and linked to the national network.
3. Joining Sustrans, subscribing to *Network News* (quarterly), or engaging in their Local Agenda 21 initiatives.
4. Active involvement in the *Safe Routes to Schools* project which aims to counter the fact that fewer and fewer children are allowed to cycle to school (and indeed youth clubs) because of safety on the roads.
5. Conservation and route building, for instance, along old canal tow paths and disused rail lines. Summer workcamps are planned, with children being accompanied by an adult.

Fun, safety and recreation on the cycleways

Sustrans are growing fast as a resource organisation and produce a range of useful and nicely designed materials. These include an information pack on the Agenda 21; Safe Routes to Schools; maps of the new cycle routes and information sheets on various aspects of the schemes including shared use; wildlife and people with disabilities. A publications catalogue is available from Sustrans.

Sustrans head office is at 35 King Street, Bristol BS1 4DZ. Tel 0117 929 0888.

TREE LIFE
What's special about trees?
There's something magical about trees. And, it is the young people of the world today who seem to be most aware of that spirit. This section of the book begins with some general comments, then offers some specific suggestions for activities which young people can engage in within their own communities. Towards the end of the book, we are pleased to include the continuing story of Jenny James, who is desperately trying to protect sections of the Colombian forest in South America (see International Action section). The disappearing rainforests, road building programmes and the continuing encroachment of agriculture, industry and settlements into forests and woodland are increasingly destroying the rich diversity of trees and the crucial role they play in the eco-structure of both local environments and the planet as a whole.

Trees are our lungs, humidifiers and air conditioning units. They soak up carbon dioxide, and purify the air by releasing huge quantities of water into the atmosphere. Forests and woodlands are also home to many of the world's plants, animals, birds and insects. Destroy the woodland and the biodiversity of the planet is seriously upset. Yet, in the name of progress, that is exactly what is happening throughout the world, even though there is more than enough technical 'know-how' available to ensure that trees are treated with respect and as a sustainable resource which must be replenished and cherished.

Myth and inspiration
Traditionally, most cultures have celebrated the existence of their trees. The spirit of trees has been evoked time and time again in fertility rites, marriage rites, and for their healing powers. Long before Christianity it was under the oak that couples were married. Jason with his Argonauts sailed aboard the 'Argo', which was built with oak trees from Dodona, the sacred oakgrove of Zeus. There is a wealth of tree related festivals, legends and events which have the tree as the central image. As Jacqueline Memory Paterson says in her fascinating new book, *Tree Wisdom* (Thorsons, 1996),

> "The oak was revered as a happy symbol, and people bedecked themselves with its leaves and boughs, which they were given permission to pick from certain woods. This celebration is thought to be a continuance from an older Druidic Oak Apple Day and is still being celebrated in certain parts of Wiltshire. Over time the Royal Oak Day celebrations became absorbed into the May Day celebrations at the beginning of the month, where the Oak Man or Jack in the Green (the May King), wreathed in oak and hawthorn leaves with only his face exposed, danced symbolically through the streets before claiming the May Queen."

Coincidentally, Alan used to live on a narrow boat at Upton upon Severn in Worcestershire, and Oak Apple Day is celebrated there on the late May Bank Holiday Saturday each year, as a reminder that Charles II hid up an oak tree before successfully reclaiming the throne from Oliver Cromwell in 1660. The event is a local, but lively affair, with lots of Morris-type dancing in the streets and sprigs of leaves and acorns adorning the local shops and houses. Jacqueline's *Tree Wisdom* book would be a useful resource if you wanted to organise a series of community workshops on the lore, customs and healing properties of trees and plants.

Nowadays, Alan is based down in Dorset, where one of the most popular local folk-rock duos are 'Show of Hands'. One of their most memorable songs is entitled 'The Oak', which was originally written as a celebratory performance song, inspired by the Beaminster Oak, in the centre of that village.

(Words from **The Oak** by Steve Knightley and Kim O' Loughlin)

For shelter and shade has the oak tree grown,
the ship, the cradle, the hearth, and home.
Arms so strong they hold the sky,
stood so long that the heart can't die.

The limbs, the veins, the head and the heart.
The earth, the roots, the leaves and the bark.

Trees deserve some of our reverence. John Fowles wrote in 1979, in *The Tree,*

"I suspect some religious element in my feelings towards woods. Their mysterious atmospheres, their silences...all of these must recall the holy man-made place. We know the very first holy places in Neolithic times, long before Stonehenge (which is only a petrified copse), were artificial wooden groves made of felled, transported and re-erected tree trunks..."

Historically, trees featured significantly in the Essene Teachings in the Dead Sea Scrolls, which in part was translated from the original Hebrew and Aramaic as:

"Go towards the high growing Trees,
And before one of them
Which is beautiful, high growing and mighty,
Say these words:
Hail be unto Thee!
O good living Tree,
Made by the Creator."

To see beauty and solidity in a tree
is to see these qualities in yourself.

TREES – The great recyclers for all seasons

Thanks to Dave Kelf, Seaton Tree Warden,
for providing the Essene piece and the drawing.

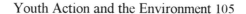

Some examples

There are a large number of organisations in Britain which own and/or actively protect the woodland areas. Among them are:
the Woodland Trust, Common Ground, the Forestry Commission, the Wildlife Trusts, the Countryside Commission, the National Trust, the Royal Society for Nature Conservation, Tree Spirit, the International Tree Foundation, British Trust for Conservation Volunteers, Coed Cymru, Scottish Community Woods Campaign and the Tree Council.

Many of these organisations are involved in projects designed to get people more actively involved with trees and tree issues. These include:

The Esso Treewatch project

The most recent project from Wildlife Watch (the junior branch of the Wildlife Trusts), and part of the Esso Living Tree campaign, this project includes a survey pack for young people, *Trees where you live*, to help them investigate trees and tree issues in their home, garden, street and neighbourhood. There is also a pack for leaders containing activity guidelines on creatively involving young people with trees.
Contact Phil Budd, Shropshire Wildlife Trust, Conservation Centre, 167 Frankwell, Shrewsbury SY3 8LG.

Trees enhance the walled town of Berwick on Tweed

The Community Forests Initiative (Countryside Commission)

The Countryside Commission has created 12 Community Forests around our major cities, in partnership with local authorities, the Forestry Commission and other organisations. These major projects, covering 1730 square miles, will create new landscapes on large areas of derelict land, provide recreation and help the local economy. As the name suggests, local people are encouraged to get involved in planning, developing and using these areas.

The Countryside Commission, John Dower House, Crescent Place, Cheltenham, Glos GL50 3RA

A little bit of history

In Britain there are about 60 tree species which are known as the native species. These trees were part of the original Wildwood, which dates back to about 8000 BC. The predominant types of trees differed in the various parts of the country. In Scotland, the most common trees were birch and pine; in the north-east of England and in much of Wales, oak and hazel were the main species; the south-west of England had the highest percentage of elm and a lot of hazel, and over the rest of the country it is believed that the lime was the most common single species. This is rather at odds with the common view that Britain was one great forest of oak trees. Neither did the Wildwood still exist by the time of the Domesday Book in 1086. Trees were managed. In practice this meant that many of the woodlands were harvested and trees were coppiced and pollarded to produce faster growth. Trees were long ago regarded as a resource and their wood was used for building homes, smelting and fuel. It was only in the eighteenth century that brick built houses became commonplace. The relationship between woodland and industry has always been one of demand and supply. The development of the iron industry and the British navy led to the destruction of many of the country's oldest trees and the growth of settlements and arable farming brought about the destruction of many former forests.

What can we do?

That destruction is still the responsibility of all of us. It isn't just the developers of Britain or the cattle ranchers of South America who cause the destruction of the forests. We demand cheap beef, which may be imported from Central America or the Amazonian basin, or hardwoods such as mahogany or teak for our furniture, yet fail to see this as a contributory factor to the destruction of forests.

Awareness of, and consciousness-raising about the role and intrinsic beauty of trees, can best start with the young people. We can no longer take for granted the continued existence of the trees on this planet. You might like to use the following sheet as a handout for your youth group (or for yourself and friends) to get the braincells moving on the subject of trees.

Some other Tree facts:

- Each year, 1.8 per cent of the remaining rainforests are being eliminated (Porritt, *Where on Earth are we going?*). Each year 12 million hectares of forests throughout the world are cleared for agriculture and fuel, and a further 4.5 hectares are cut in commercial logging. Some new forests are being planted, but there is definitely a net loss and a loss in biodiversity. (Howson, *Young Person's Guide to the Environment*).

- Rainforests are the most species-rich habitats on the planet. A single bush in a forest in Peru is likely to be home to as many ant species as exist in the whole of Britain. In a 125 acre patch of Malaysia there are more varieties of trees than exist in the whole of North America. In some regions of the world, many of the trees, and the plant life that surrounds them, have never been classified.

- The rainforest habitat has supplied the 'answer' to some of the world's greatest medical problems. For instance wild yams from Mexican forests were formulated into the contraceptive pill; the Madagascan periwinkle is used in a drug to fight leukaemia and Hodgkin's disease.

- Common Ground say, "*A fallen tree is not a dead tree...with only a quarter of its roots left in the ground, it may survive and become a fascinating old character. Even large trees will grow horizontally given half a chance. Only if a tree has fallen dangerously should removal be the sole option...otherwise wait and see. Insects, birds, animals and fungi need old trees and so do we.*"

- In Britain, the problem has been that new forests are planted for their fast growth potential, not beauty or biodiversity. Called a 'monoculture', these largely single species forests do not allow trees a pattern of natural growth and older trees are not tolerated. Britain's legacy, its old trees, need protecting from tree managers who see old trees as senile and overmature, rather than grand and spiritual.

- From Thomas Hinde's *Forests of Britain* (1985): "*As a result of [the first World War] the Forestry Commission was established and since then has created huge plantations, largely of conifer, all over the country. In one sense these have reforested the country...All the same, conifers have destroyed even more of the country's ancient woods than farmers who grubbed them up or the villages and towns which have sprawled over them. Below conifers, once they are well grown, no underwood survives and the complex biological systems of many centuries are finally destroyed.*"

Protecting local trees: Ideas for Action

The following is adapted from material included in, *In a Nutshell: A manifesto for trees and a guide to growing them and protecting them* (second edition 1990) by Neil Sinden for Common Ground. It's well worth adding to your library or resource collection. Common Ground is based at 44 Earlham Street, Covent Garden, London WC2H 9LA. Our thanks and admiration to them for their pioneering work in this area.

Trees are damaged or felled because no-one has taken the bother to keep an eye on them and their well-being. Young people can make a very positive contribution to this process. Here are some ideas:

- Make local maps of the trees in your area. The local planning authority should be able to supply a large scale map if you are based in a town. In rural areas, the Ordnance Survey 2.5 inches to the mile maps should be readily available. Locate trees, chart their types, ages, condition, problems etc., and use this information to monitor any natural or unnatural threats to their continued well-being. (Other ideas in this section can be integrated into a local tree map survey. Your local Tree Warden may already have done this exercise, or may appreciate help in a specific area).
- Encourage young people to identify trees in their area which have special value to them. For instance, conker trees; trees with rope swings; good climbing trees; trees with romantic connections!
- Get young people to take photos or make drawings of trees which are especially old or are unusual shapes. Every tree is unique and like people they deserve to be valued. Organise a 'Favourite Tree' project, and get individuals to say why they particularly like their tree.

- Find out who are the local naturalists and the tree warden in your area. Make contact with them and invite them to spend some time with your group of young people, perhaps taking the group for a walk through particular woodlands or showing photos and slides about the different types of trees and describing their characteristics.
- Try to find out about the history of your area through its trees. Were trees planted, or did they grow wild? Who has cared for them in the past? How has the land been used over time? Has any historically important event ever taken place in the vicinity of the trees?
- Could a community tree nursery, wood or orchard be started in your area? Does one already exist, perhaps started or cared for by a group such as the Woodland Trust? Could a local school premises be used to develop a new orchard of unusual apples or pears, and serve as an outside classroom space in

the summer months?

- Is there already a local commercial nursery for native tree species?
- Some trees are already protected under the law; others could be. Try to help protect the trees in your area by:

  – Finding out which trees in your area are currently protected by Tree Preservation Orders. Identify other trees which could be protected and then apply to the local council tree officer to ask for an order (a TPO) to be placed on the tree. TPOs can be granted if they are an important home for wildlife; if they are intrinsically beautiful; if they are a locally scarce type; if they shield an eyesore, or, if they contribute to the landscape.

  – Contacting the local tree officer if a tree is under threat of felling, lopping, topping or uprooting. They may be able to restrain the owner using an emergency TPO, or a TPO may already be in place.

  – The local Woodland Trust or Tree Warden may appreciate help with the maintenance of newly planted trees; the use of mulch mats, ties, guards etc.

  – Finding out whether the area is designated as a Conservation area, which should give added protection to the trees in your area. Common Ground's slogan is worth repeating: **Every tree counts**.

In addition, young people may want to know more about the road/tree protest movement. More information is given in the next, Alternative Lifestyles section, on how to contact organisations and groups involved in direct action.

Protest Vigil at the Fairmile Eviction January 1997 (Graeme Strike)

Tree dressing

This is the reinvention of a very old tradition. Trees are the oldest and largest living creatures on the Earth's surface (underground, the fungi win the competition with specimens up to half a mile across!). We are all familiar with decorating our Christmas trees, however, living trees used to be decorated as a celebration of their place in the community. The forms of decoration are infinitely variable. Tree dressing is once again being celebrated in Britain, largely thanks to Common Ground who have been supporting a national Tree Dressing Day during the first weekend in December. In Japan the ancient Shinto religion sanctified trees by tying strips of cloth or paper to the branches; the Buddhist religion has a similar ceremony. It is also very similar to well-dressing, which still occurs at some wells which are regarded as sacred or having special healing powers. For instance, at the Cloutie Well, near Dingwall in Scotland and at the Rag Well at Walton in Yorkshire, coloured rags are tied to fencing and trees above and besides the wells by people who have used the well water and felt cleansed or cured.

Since 1990, community and youth groups, schools, charities such as Barnardos, and local authorities have all been involved in tree dressing. It's an ideal activity for youth groups and can be combined very easily with performance arts such as drama, carnival, street theatre, music and sculpture and murals. Examples we have seen include coloured kites, red inflatable balls looking like giant cherries, huge letters suspended in branches, and giant papier mache insects.

Common Ground publish a well illustrated newsletter about previous events and also two colourful posters of examples of how to dress a tree. Ultimately the aim is to:

- draw community attention to the singular beauty and uniqueness of trees;
- bring communities together in group celebration;
- motivate people towards looking after trees.

Woodland Skills Training Project

Based in Glastonbury, the Friends and Families of Travellers (FFT) organisation are trying to organise a small scale, but national, training project for those older young people (18 plus) who are part of the traveller community, are homeless, or are poor and living in rural areas where work opportunities are scarce. These groups are frequently disadvantaged and disaffected, yet are often amongst those who are keenest to demonstrate sustainable styles of living with low impact on the environment. The aim of the Woodland Project is to provide a certificated course in basic woodland skills such as coppicing, pollarding, hurdle making, charcoal manufacture etc., which can help woodland environments to survive, by providing sustainable management of woods without endangering the biodiversity of those woods.

Currently there are an estimated 100,000 acres of unmanaged woodland in England and Wales which in the words of FFT,

> *"...are crying out to become managed and productive, as they were in the past. The project aims to set up a mobile training skills project using a Yurt tent as a base. Each course would last six weeks during the winter half of the year. 12 people would be trained on each course. Initial planning is for two sessions in Somerset, one in Gloucestershire, one in Sussex and two others depending upon geographical demand. A throughput of 72 students will be attained in the first year. The pilot project will run for an initial two year period."*

The Tudor Trust and the National Lottery have already promised about £41,000 towards the two year project, and at the time of compiling this book, the FFT were seeking match funding from the European Social Fund. FFT are based at 33 High Street, Glastonbury, Somerset BA6 9HT

ALTERNATIVE LIFESTYLES
So, what does 'alternative' mean?
From beatniks to flower children, hippies to ravers, CND to Greenham Common, travellers to eco-rads, feminists, black power and black rights workers, squatters, communards, gay rights activists, animal rights campaigners, road protesters, permaculturalists, herbalists and arboriculturalists – the list of countercultural groups who have tried to operate outside, or on the fringes of what is perceived as 'normal' society, is almost endless.

Many of these groups consist primarily of young people. Some are seeking through positive methods to change elements of our society; some are trying to confront, through direct action, central and local government policies and planning; others are a mixture of marginalised and excluded people who want a space to get on with their own lives with as little contact with the mainstream world as possible. And then there are the 'drongoes', called by this name in the alternative traveller-world, because they are virtually no-hopers, and are often the casualties of the 'straight' society. Their problems include mental health difficulties, extreme poverty, homelessness, drugs, alcohol, offending behaviour; many have been kicked out of institutions such as children's homes, prisons, hospitals and the armed forces.

Not all house dwellers are the enemies of the environment. And, not everyone in the counterculture is an eco-warrior. What Fiona Earle says in *A Time to Travel?* is relevant,

"I moved into a bus with a friend in '88, then got a trailer, then a truck. I am very aware of the advantage – I can move to where work is available, without worrying about accommodation; I am responsible for my effect on the planet; I can't live happily in urban areas; I have time, space and friends...I could go on.

Fiona is a qualified teacher. Sometimes she teaches in mainstream secondary schools. More often, she works for the Travellers' School Charity (TSC), co-ordinating the production and distribution of new, culturally appropriate resources for parents and teachers who live in the travelling community. Below are examples of the 'Children and their homes' series produced by Gubby and Fiona for the TSC.

This book is one of a series of ten based on children and their homes.

Through simple text and lively illustrations, the reader is introduced to the site and situation, as well as the general features inside the home. We have also focussed on aspects of particular interest to children, as well as alternative methods of providing basic needs.

The books can be used as readers; source material for projects linking with the National Curriculum; and as starting points for discussion.

We hope that you enjoy them.

MY HOME
I live in a tipi.

MY HOME
I live in a bus.

written by Fiona

illustrated by Gubby

MY HOME
I live in a bender.

written by Fiona

illustrated by Gubby

Gubby outside his bender

You've looked through the contents of the book through to this point and hopefully enjoyed Gubby's imaginative drawings. Gubby lives in a caravan in the winter and for the rest of the year in a bender he constructs wherever he has managed to find work picking fruit. His nomadic way of life doesn't mean that he doesn't work and the positive side of his lifestyle is that it gives him a very authentic view of the earth.

And, what is it doing here, in this Youth Action book?

The media and politicians mostly sees these groups as dangerous, delinquent, and a threat to ordered society. They are the folk-devils of 20th century, and like those of previous centuries, Robin Hood and Dick Turpin etc., the reality is a much more complicated picture than the myth and stereotyping which usually features in the media. The founders of the National Trust and The Ramblers Association were involved in a number of direct actions such as mass trespass in order to preserve areas of countryside like the Lake District as well as public rights of way. It will be interesting to see whether the actions of road protesters will be judged with the same reverence as Octavia Hill and Canon Rawnsley, leading lights in the conservation movement 100 years ago, are given today.

For instance, Maggie Thatcher's government likened the travellers to, "Medieval Brigands", and the travellers, animal rights activists, road protesters and ravers were lumped together as the main targets for the Criminal Justice Act, 1994. But these people didn't go away as a result of the legislation. And in the years between 1993 and 1997, they became more politicised, better organised and their numbers were swelled in what has become known as the DiY culture. That culture carries with it a mystique, and an increasingly loud n' proud image as the modern eco-warriors – the defenders of the environment. As a very disparate group they are presenting an increasingly heady mixture of Anger and Celebration. John Vidal, writing in the *Guardian* newspaper, under a headline which hailed Animal, Swampy and Co as heroes of our time at the Fairmile road camp, said,
> *"The camps have proved successful job training exercises. Greenpeace, Friends of the Earth, Transport 2000 and other blue-chip environment groups may be establishment and middle aged now, but they mostly have a radical past....so British protest today is throwing up tomorrow's leaders."*

They want the world to still be a place fit to live in after the new millennium dawns. It is for this reason that we have included some information under the heading, 'Alternative Lifestyles' in this book. The DiY culture makers of the late 90s remind us a lot of Sid Rawle, who was dubbed the 'King of the Hippies' at the time of the Battle of the Beanfield in 1985; his biographer, Jeremy Sandford (who, incidentally wrote, *Cathy Come Home*) says of Sid,
> *"You can like him or loathe him, but you can't ignore him!"*

Now, the increasingly large band of road protesters of Oxleas Wood, Solsbury Hill, Twyford Down, the M11, Newbury, Fairmile/Trollheim (near Exeter), and Pollok (on the outskirts of Glasgow), are much more closely linked with other Red-Green activists. These coalitions are involved with animal rights campaigns such as the port barricades at Shoreham in Sussex and Brightlingsea in Kent, hunt saboteurs, cycle campaigners, free festival and party groups such as the Exodus Collective in

Luton, squatters, environmental activist groups such as Earth First!, and the whole free information network.

To quote the editors of the *SchNEWS reader* (1995), one of the biggest circulation magazines of the counterculture, they invited the Home Secretary to their Ideal Squat exhibition, saying,

> "Your inspiration made us work closer together: Networking is happening across the nation – Road Protesters and Ravers, Gay Rights Activists and Hunt Saboteurs, Travellers and Squatters, and many more as we realise the strength of our numbers."

This move away from single issue direct action towards a broad-based grouping has given many young people their own cause, their own crusade and quest, and it is very much an environmental one. C.J. Stone, in his recent book, *Fierce Dancing: Adventures in the Underground* describes the travellers and road protesters,

> "When you live within the landscape, framed by it instead of framing it, breathing the air, hearing the breeze bustling through the trees, sleeping under the stars, cooking food on the open fire – acting out this ancient, almost nomadic way of life – something happens to you. It's as if the spirit of the land enters you. You become the landscape."

Within this whole 'movement', if that is what it has become, is a sense of urgency and outrage. Young people are critical of working within existing groups and the law. They want action on environmental and human rights issues such as:

- homelessness; and/or the right to travel and live in a home that is not necessarily a collection of bricks and mortar;
- why the government backs the need for more cars, more pollution and less public transport, when what is needed is support for cycles, car sharing and other more sustainable alternatives;
- farming methods, and in particular factory farming, genetic engineering, and the lack of small scale, organic farms;
- criminalisation and marginalisation of many people, especially those who do not share the dominant cultures of society with regard to race and sexual orientation;
- the right to celebrate and party;
- the need for alternative power sources;
- land ownership and land access;
- the value of cultural diversity, rather than conformity;
- and, above all, they want to participate in direct action for environmental change.

reprinted, with thanks to Earth First! Action Update

Youth Action and the Environment 117

The 'establishment' has not seen the development of this eco-radicalism in a positive light. The fact that local people have been protesting alongside the young road and animal rights activists is indeed a terrifying vision for many! In *SQUALL* magazine, under a banner headline of 'Green Terrorism?' the following was printed,

> "...no-one could have predicted a scenario where elderly ladies regularly take to the streets to 'subvert the authority of the state'...Seventy-nine year old Tilly Merritt was so angered by the harsher treatment meted out to so-called 'professional protesters' (at Brightlingsea) that she had her nose pierced and dyed her hair orange. 'The police just couldn't believe it,' she recalls, 'I said to them: 'See, I'm no different to these youngsters, they're just ordinary people just like me.'

and,

> "The loosely phrased Security Services Bill, currently making its way through parliament, gives MI5, with all its eavesdropping capabilities, 'the function of acting in support of the prevention of serious crime'..." which includes individuals and groups which are seen as 'environmental extremists.' "

Trollheim, Fairmile 96 (Matt Smith)

Merrick recently wrote *A Battle for the Trees,* about his friends and experiences at the Newbury by-pass protest camps. In it are many evocative descriptions of young and old people fighting together for a cause they feel passionate about. In environmental terms their successes may be small, but for them they are significant:

"On 29th March, the Secretary of State, acting through the Under-Sheriff of Berkshire, offered a reprieve to the 250 year old tree at Middle Oak on the A4/B4000 junction, which had been occupied by a similar camp. On Monday 1st April, the Under-Sheriff arrived here with several hundred security guards and police officers, and a full team of eviction bailiffs and chainsaw workers. He then offered the residents of Mary Hare camp a reprieve of the lives of trees in return for their immediate, peaceful voluntary vacation of the land. Once he had declared this in front of TV cameras, legal observers and dozens of witnesses, we complied.

Three trees in a farmer's field to be retained on the embankment of a dual carriageway is cold comfort set against the horrific destruction of delicate ecosystems in ancient woodland, water meadows and rivers only a few miles from here.

But it's a start. We made a stand, and we saved these trees. These three beautiful limes, which are much older than you and I, will live on. 'It's easy. All you need is love.' Join us next time. Imagine how much more we could do with you on our side too. Big love to you from the residents of Mary Hare camp, 1996."

Tree defender, Whitecroft, Solsbury Hill 94 (Matt Smith)

Alongside the protesters are Britain's travellers. Alan has already been involved with a lot of individual travellers and their organisations in publishing the book, *A Time to Travel? An introduction to Britain's newer travellers,* and is currently compiling a new book called, *No Boundaries,* recounting the experiences of new travellers across Europe in the last few years. He also lived for about three years in a narrow boat on England's rivers and canals, owned a converted Luton van and was a part of the travelling community for real.

Simon Fairlie, an editor of *The Ecologist* magazine and *Guardian* journalist, also happens to live with friends in a bender settlement in an area of Somerset known as Tinker's Bubble. This is also the area where Paddy Ashdown lives and is MP! However, rather than condemn this experiment in low impact dwelling and sustainable lifestyle, Paddy actually wrote the foreword to Simon Fairlie's book, *Low Impact Development,* saying:

> *"I have been fascinated by the Tinker's Bubble experiment. It is in 'my backyard.' It has generated considerable and powerful feelings, including in my own village. But my judgement is, that after two or three years of this experiment, the outcome has been to add, not diminish the quality of life as we have had to cope with different lifestyles and different ways of looking at the world."*

In this book, Alan and Howie, and the Council for Environmental Education, are keen that there should be a rich diversity of environmental information available for young people and those who work with them. So, in this section we offer some rather unusual (for a book aimed at youth workers, perhaps!) examples of what is going on in the DiY world of the counterculture.

The first is based on Alan's visit to the settlement known to many as Tipi Valley, near Lampeter in the South Wales valleys. Before that, since we strongly believe that young people should have information and knowledge on which to make their own decisions about how to get involved in environmental activity, we have put together a list of contacts of some of the groups, organisations and magazines that inhabit the DiY world. And still before that, here are two cartoon excerpts from Kate Evans, a young artist who has chronicled the traveller, road protest and party scene in graphic form. As you can see from the first cartoon, Kate's wry views of the protest movement stretch back to life as an 11 year old at Greenham Common. This was long before she ever dreamed of tree climbing as a radical activity! The second is an excerpt from *The Battle of Brynhenilys.*

GOOD MEMORIES

When I was 11 and my sister was 13 and my mum was 37 then we went to Greenham Common. We went to Violet Gate. The first time we brought firewood and packed lunches and we stayed all day.

1994. Kate Evans

Oh great! Firewood.

Would you like a cup of tea?

POLICE DOGS ON PATROL

The gate itself had a square hole in where the women had cut themselves a cooking grille.

Violet Gate is one of seven gates around Greenham Common U.S. Airforce Base. Also, there's Red Gate Gap which is a place near Red Gate where they haul the fence up and slip the lorries under it. They're sneaky buggers these missile convoys.

We realised that we weren't going to eat our packed lunches as they had chicken drumsticks in and maybe the other women wouldn't like us chewing animal legs around the fire. So we ate something from a big iron cooking pot on the fire. It had all sorts of vegetably beany things in that I would never have eaten at home.

do you want my kidney beans?

No. Do you want mine?

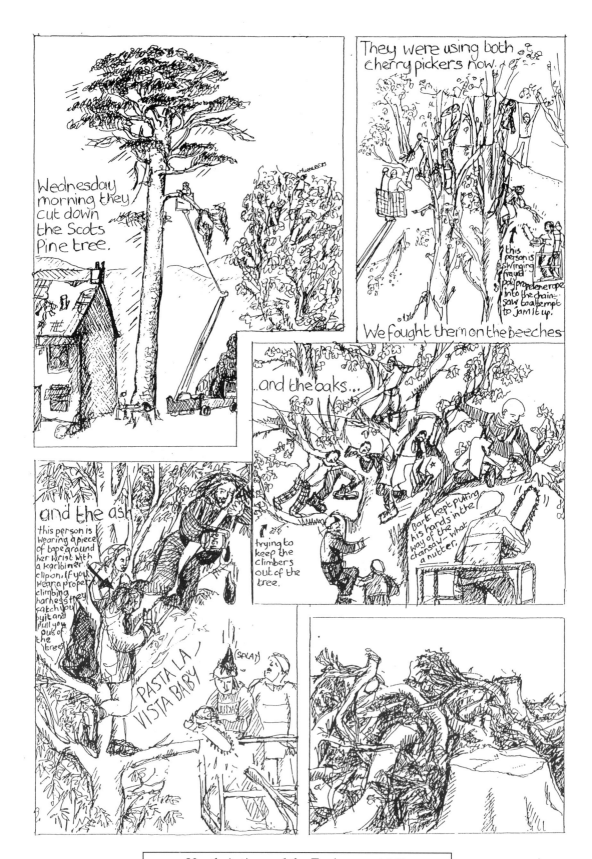

There were some people who stayed in the trees overnight so they had to use the cherrupickers and security to evict them. The rest of us went on the offensive and invaded Celtic Energy's Opencast site at Nanthelen.

I stood by one edge where the trucks go and I felt really weird, remembering back to the summer when I stayed at Brynhenllys... it was very hot and we went to a beautiful bathing pool, set between huge granite rocks and overhung by little trees... we took all our clothes off and swam, and made a rope swing which went out over the water... walked back very tired and ate pasta and drank crap cider... and we sang through the long summer evening. And now its an opencast mine.

Alternative lifestyles/travellers/road protest/parties contacts:
Charter 88, Exmouth House, 3-11 Pine Street, London EC1R 0JH
Conscious Cinema, PO Box 2679, Brighton BN2 1UJ
Diggers and Dreamers (communes UK and elsewhere) annual directory, PO Box 1808, Winslow, Buckinghamshire MK18 3BR
Dongas Tribe, 6 East St, West Coker, Somerset BA22 9BE
Earth First! and Reclaim the Streets, PO Box 9656, London N4 4JY
Exodus Collective, Long Meadow Community Farm, Chalton Cross, Sundown Rd, Luton, Bedfordshire
Festival Eye, BCM 2002, London WC1N 3XX
Freedom Network, PO Box 9384, London SW9 7ZB
Friends and Families of Travellers, Top Floor, 33 High St, Glastonbury BA6 9HT
Frontline magazine, Victoria Rd, Yarmouth, Isle of Wight PO41 0QW
Rainbow Circle Camps, Sampson's Cottage, Seven Leaze Lane, Edge, Stroud, Gloucester GL6 6NL
Rainbow International events, Eur-Asia-Bus, Postfach 4016, CH-8022, Zurich, Switzerland
Road Alert!, PO Box 5544, Newbury, RG14 5FB
SchNEWS, Justice?, PO Box 2600, Brighton, East Sussex BN2 2DX
SQUALL magazine (for sorted itinerants), PO Box 8959, London N19 5HW
Squatters Handbook, Advisory Service for Squatters, 2 St Paul's Rd, London N1 2QN
The Land is Ours, Box E , 111 Magdalen Rd, Oxford OX4 1RQ
Travellers School Charity, PO Box 36, Grantham, Lincs NG31 6EW
Undercurrents Videos, 16b Cherwell St, Oxford OX4 1BG
(see 'Issues around Food and Agriculture' section for some animal rights contacts)

Tipi Valley
What is it?

Now, that is some hard question to answer! Alan wrote to them about this book and Tom Gillespie wrote back saying that they would like to be included and enclosed the photo below of a rather wonderful circular, stone age-type building, amusingly inscribed, *Uncle Tom's Cabin* on the back! The Talley Valley settlers are a group of people who live in a fairly remote valley to the south of Lampeter in the Welsh valleys. Jill was one of the original purchasers of their land, along perhaps, with Chris, Stan and Cherry, Scott and Mandy, Clare and Rick the Vic. Local farmers sold the original settlers sections of agricultural land at agricultural prices, of then, three or four hundred pounds per acre. That was in about 1974/5.

They didn't have planning permission for living there then and only one or two have gained it in the intervening twenty plus years. A Welsh planning inspector recommended granting permission for a barreltop, caravans and tipis to be allowed to stay in the Tipi Valley, based on the law which makes it obligatory to award certificates of lawful use or development after ten years. But the Welsh Secretary only agreed to certificates for one barreltop. So, the settlement continues to exist *just* outside of the control and influence of the local and national authorities, on the extreme fringes of society. The residents of the valley have always been committed to working towards total sustainability, but perhaps as many as 60 per cent of the settlement still draw benefits. Their argument regarding this seeming

Uncle Tom's Cabin

hypocrisy is that it would cost that same state a lot more in unemployment benefit, housing benefit and family income settlement, if all the Tipi Valley residents moved back into the house-dwelling world.

A lady named Sonia sent Alan her own chronicle of some of the early years of Tipi Valley, under the title of *Tipi Visions.* Back then in the seventies, it was very much a time of gazing at stars and smoking joints. Some aspects of those early years remains. In the valley are tipis, some buses, trucks and vans, benders, a transportable yurt or two (a circular tent design from north east and central Asia) and low energy dwellings employing wind and solar power. A tipi is still often referred to as a lodge, and in the lodges life is frequently very much of a communal affair.

Life is a yurt, isn't it?

Charles Hoult visited the valley in 1990, and chronicled this and other visits to Green Communities throughout Britain in his book *Living Green.* During his couple of days amongst the tipis and other dwellings, Charles interviewed Brig Oubridge, one of the key figures in the valley and also an organiser of the more recent, Big

Green Gathering. Charles wrote,

"Brig described the village as a university of outdoor living, peopled by professors, researchers, postgraduates and freshers. Some stuck at it. A few graduated, made the village their home and carried on their own research. All sought the answer to living in harmony with the environment on a basis of minimum consumption. Live simply so others may simply live."

Alan spent a pleasant and informative afternoon in one of the lodges. Tom, Euan and Paul were his hosts. The people in the valley seem to enjoy talking on a variety of topics: the Mother Earth, the vital importance of water, fire, growing trees and small scale organic crops – all have a significance rarely sensed in even rural UK communities. Drumming, chanting, a pot of cha on the ever-lit fire, wood and water gathering, all still underlie daily life. The original hippie spirit of star-gazing hasn't completely disappeared, but it has at least evolved a bit!

Planning a settlement?

The 1996 Valley residents are no longer one or even two communities. Tom told Alan,

"It's a settlement, rather than a community....it is still made up of low impact dwellings, but there are lots of separate groups."

Euan, Paul and Tom are all in their forties or possibly fifties. They are weathered, and their tanned faces display the outdoor lives they lead. To an outsider they come over as an idiosyncratic, but not unpleasing group of eccentrics. All are able to recount their personal quests. Tom is five years into the creation of a small scale orchard of apple trees, using traditional grafting techniques. He is also planning to help organise a 1997 Rainbow eco-camp in Switzerland, based on the style of the Rainbow Circle camps in the UK. Euan, has moved on from early lives as a performance/anarchist in the Mutoid Waste Company and the Hackney Bus Garage with the Tibetan Mime Group. Now he is an ardent woodland conservationist. The posh word for his obsession is arboriculturalist. The local Carmarthen College uses him on an occasional basis as a consultant. Paul moves between the valley and a bricks and mortar dwelling in Bristol. He owns a bit of the land and sees that investment as an important aspect of the evolving nature of the valley settlement.

The reality facing the Tipi Valley settlers involves getting legal. That isn't at all easy, as Tinker's Bubble and the King's Hill communities of benders in Somerset have already found. A low impact dwelling such as a bender, yurt or tipi is still subject to planning regulations. And, as in Tipi Valley, a barreltop can be seen as more acceptable to the planning authorities than a more temporary and lower impact structure! Strange old world!

Owning a bit of land is not enough. Making a planning application after settling on a piece of land is pretty much 'up against the wall' stuff. But it can work and there are a number of travellers and settlers around the UK taking on the planning inspectorate teams at their own game. The trick seems to be learning to use regulations and guidance, such as the HMSO's Planning Policy Guidance 7 document, to support rural, sustainable developments. Simon Fairlie has written all about this aspect of alternative lifestyle development in his book, *Low impact development: Planning and People in a Sustainable Countryside,* Jon Carpenter Books, 1996.

Talley Valley Futures
There is a buzz going round the valley at the time of writing this report. There may be a £50,000 windfall on the horizon. The settlers have set up a Forest Fund and a Trustee Group. Tom talks of their need for more energy. He means money. The cash is earmarked to purchase two already cut areas of forest and one uncut area from the Forestry Commission. If this happens, some or all of the settlers in the valley will be able to push for their personal vision of the future. Euan dreams of a new woodland conservation scheme. Others see more land as a way of shielding the valley from the pressures of the outside world. There's even talk which echoes Conservative Party Citizenship or Labour's Stakeholding. Ownership and Trusteeship of the land is much discussed in and around the curling smoke of the Tipi Valley campfires! And this among a community which is described in *Diggers and Dreamers* directory as,

> *"We regard all our land as a nature reserve in which humans can live in integrated harmony with nature. Formal structure and organisation are minimal, verging on the non-existent, but we have a collective land fund to which all contribute."*

A bit of the valley

Perhaps the actual life in the valley isn't quite as idealistic. The people attracted to the settlement are extremely diverse. The level of caring, support and bonding is strong, but inevitably some fit in, and some may be regarded as a 'threat' by other members of the community. For instance, party people, and the use of heavier drugs have caused disagreements in the past.

One scheme which may soon come under scrutiny at a Circle Meeting in the valley is a potentially exciting one. I can imagine the elders, the Forest Fund Trustees, perhaps others, gathered around a crackling, wood fire in the middle of the Big Lodge. The Talking Stick is passed around as one person after another airs their views on the establishment of an Alternative Lifestyles Visitor Centre on the new land in the valley. It would probably be 'buffered' from the main settlement by a conservation zone. Ideas include:

- permaculture, arboriculture and reed beds;
- examples of alternative dwellings;
- workshops on how to build, tipis, benders, domes and yurts;
- workshops on woodland conservation;
- one day and residential courses on all aspects of alternative lifestyles and the DiY culture.

Interesting stuff, eh, for a bunch of self proclaimed eco-pagans? Tipi Valley PLC, 2000?

To contact the Tipi Valley, send a stamped addressed envelope to:
>Marchoglwyn Fawr
>Llanfynydd
>Carmarthern
>Dyfed SA32 7UQ

Words from the environmental counter culture

The next pieces have been included as examples of the powerful words and images which are being published in the direct action, DiY, environmental publications. The actions and activities they chronicle are a far more radical way of 'getting involved' than youth work can usually offer. We are not suggesting that all youth workers should immediately rush out and take part in a 'mass coincidence' bicycle protest or join the road protesters. However, direct action, travellers, communes, squatters and street parties are all part of the current day culture and political reality of environmental action – and it is important that young people are aware of their options.

The examples which follow are from *Road Alert, SQUALL* and *Frontline* magazines. We offer our thanks to them for freely allowing us the use of their material.

IN AND OUT OF THE PROMISED LAND

STORY BY C STOVOLD

Two years ago, two pairs of travelling parents decided to try and find shelter from the hectic turmoil of living on the road. Being flush at the time, they combined their entire collected wealth, to buy a 2 acre plot on the edge of the Forest of Dean. Young children needed a secure base, and as they moved in to settle, it was the start of a new dream......

Well for two days. A couple of days later, council enforcement officers came down to try and public order the travellers off. A week later they returned again informing Max, who's name the land had been bought in, that they couldn't park anything on the land at all, as it was a breach of the planning Act, and he faced 18 months inside and a £24,000 maximum fine. Thus started two years of constant hassles and protracted argument with the Forest of Dean District council. A new dream? Ha! if only. Since then, two other young families, one young couple, and a single bloke have bought into the land.

Claire and I turned up at the 'Promised land' after a mad two days of trying to get into the Seven Revels fayre in the Forest of Dean. It was a weekend of being pigged round and round the Forest, and when we finally arrived, exhausted and tired at the Promised land, we sighed with relief - this tranquil haven was safety at last. We were there primarily to visit Matt and Sylv whom we had grown to love a year earlier, when parked up in Brighton. Since then they had had a new son, Max, whom we hadn't yet had the pleasure of gurgling at and bouncing about on knees and sofas etc. Not knowing us from Adam, and even though the site was already chocka, everyone else on site was friendly and made us feel welcome, apart from one who we realised later, was suffering from the weight of his wad, which made him arrogantly, and grumpily unwelcoming. When you first arrive and walk round, the two things that stand out most are 'sorted' and 'children'.

The living vehicles are comfortably nestled in amongst the trees around the edge of the site, which in turn is surrounded by the 'outstanding natural beauty' of a Forestry farmed conifer plantation. There were no fences, and even though some owned more land than others, the land was shared, and the vibe of site remained.

Youth Action and the Environment 129

Festival of

Reclaim the Streets' biggest event this summer saw 10,000 people dancing on the M41. Pictures by **Nick Cobbing.** Lyrics by **RTS.**

"We live under a system in which walking and cycling have no economic or political value, because, unlike guzzling petrol, they involve no consumption and therefore make no contribution to economic growth. On the other hand, the gases belching out of an exhaust pipe are a visible manifestation of our gross national (waste) product. This begs an important question: what is the meaning of these economic statistics if they tell us nothing about the state of the earth... about our quality of life?"

"Have you ever watched the movements of bodies on the street? Ever seen someone breaking into a run halfway across a zebra crossing, one small human, embarrassed or uncomfortable about making a big car wait? Have you ever watched the elderly straining their bodies to get to shore before the lights change? Often left behind when the beeps go, they shuffle their frail bodies past the growling line of metal. It inches slowly forward."

Youth Action and the Environment 130

resistance

"With a metal river on one side and endless windows of consumerism on the other, the street's true purpose: social interaction, becomes an uneconomic diversion. In its place the corporate - controlled - one way media of newspapers, radio and television become 'the community'. Their interpretation of our reality. In this sense the streets are the alternative and subversive form of the mass media. Where authentic communication, immediate and reciprocal takes place."

"To 'reclaim the streets' is to act in defence of and for 'common ground'. To tear down the fence of enclosure that profit-making demands. The Street Party - far from being just anti-car - is an explosion of our suppressed potential, a celebration of our diversity and a chorus of voices in solidarity. A festival of resistance!"

ISSUES AROUND FOOD AND AGRICULTURE

In compiling this book we wrote to organisations working with young people in lots of different contexts. Pieces were written about the preparation of the book in magazines ranging from CEE's *EARTHlines,* through *Young People Now* and *Youth Clubs* to *SQUALL, SchNEWS* and *Schools Out* from the Kids Club Network. Literally thousands of other letters and information in magazines went out to individuals, representatives and organisations who had some level of involvement with the environment, young people, or both. The reason for mentioning this process at this point in the book is that food and agriculture produced some of the most conflicting responses and also some of the most animated. Some contributors, such as Common Ground, sent us material about rediscovering the delights of traditional British species of potatoes, pears and apples; some, like Alison Barlow, Divisional Youth Officer with Northamptonshire County Council, wanted more political aspects such as the Nestlé Boycott and the Baby Milk Campaign included. Alison pointed out, *"As a lifestyle issue, food and eating is an area (in which) young people have a direct involvement!"*

We also had to smile when, just before the New Year celebrations for 1997, an MP in Wales hit the headlines for seriously suggesting that young people in his constituency should work in the Welsh fields each autumn collecting wild mushrooms for the Netherlands export market. His problem was that he was talking about the common psilocybin mushroom, often referred to as Magic Mushrooms!

We heard from the Permaculture Association, Plants for a Future, and received material such as the Youth of Bath's Ethical Shopping Guide (see the Global Connections section) which showed exactly how young people can raise the profile of food related issues. Gubby, our artist, lives off the land for much of each year and contributed a section for us on wild foods which can be discovered by young people in the countryside (with the use of relevant, well illustrated, reference materials). Animal Rights activists sent us their magazine, *Arkangel*; the Vegetarian Society sent us their materials, and very much alongside this we received information from the National Federation of City Farms (NFCF).

Community farms

The ethics of farming, meat eating, pesticides, organic farming, permaculture, export of animals and food (the list could be a lot longer!) are closer to the heads and hearts of many young people than a lot of staff working with young people may think. Offering young people opportunities to make up their own minds about what they eat and how it is produced seems to us a perfectly reasonable youth work task.

NATIONAL FEDERATION OF CITY FARMS

One obvious place to stop off along this learning route about animals and farming is a community farm. At the time of writing, the NFCF had recently appointed

Karen Morris as their Youth Participation Officer. Karen told us,

"NFCF was established to provide support, advice and information for its members. Since the first farm started in 1972 young people have been very active members of the City Farm movement – there are currently 2,000 young volunteers on City Farms and Gardens throughout the UK. Recent funding from the Youth Programme enables us to develop more support, opportunities and training especially for young people.

City farms and gardens are unique community/environmental projects whose main strength is their diversity. They develop and grow to reflect the needs and interests of their lôcal communities - this is reflected in the variety of ways that young people are involved with projects. Some may be interested in working with animals and come to farms for experience; some attend farm clubs and may show animals as well as taking responsibility for general animal care; some are involved with gardening projects or developing adventure playgrounds on the site; other young people attend special clubs such as the girls' environmental youth clubs which are based at a city farm or garden. There are also 5,000 school visits made to city farms and gardens every year.

As founder members of the European Federation of City Farms, young people also get the opportunity to host and visit European projects."

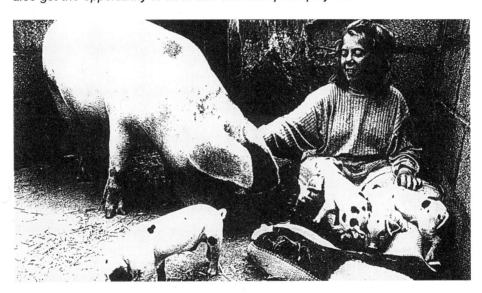

Sarah spent the night with the sow as she farrowed

The farms that exist vary considerably. Their size can be very small – 0.3 hectares right up to 38.88 hectares. All are managed seriously as working farms. Animals such as pigs, chickens, goats, turkeys, ducks and rabbits are commonly raised, and the farms sell the eggs, goat milk and cheese. Many also feature craft workers and teach skills such as building and carpentry alongside the food and farming techniques. Altogether there are 63 city farms and a further 116 farms which are attached to schools and provide practical experience of both food production and basic animal rearing. For many young people they offer the first experience of handling live animals apart from dogs and cats. Many of the school sites specialise in both keeping animals and growing food in a range of habitats and environments, with ponds, greenhouses, fields and indoor areas. This makes them useful for a variety of different subject curricula from biology though to design technology and information technology for record keeping. For instance, in Southampton 'Down to Earth' is an environmental education centre which was formed out of an amalgamation of Millbrook Community School Farm and Southampton City Farm. The school farming club meets four times a week and the resource is described by the school as a, *"Library of living material."*

At Kentish Town City Farm visitors find Maggie and Strawberry, the cows, and Julie the pig living happily right next to the busy railway line. It was the first farm of its kind and has been in existence for over 25 years. One of their specialities is offering a stables and horse riding tuition. The eight horses are a great attraction and the nearby Hampstead Heath is an ideal location for extensive rides. It's a community resource and many people with special needs as well as children and young people use it. The accent is on getting involved and mucking out and feeding the horses are seen as being just as important as the riding.

If you'd like to find out more about what goes on at city and school farms and arrange a visit to your local centre, contact Karen Morris at the national headquarters of the NFCF, the Greenhouse, Hereford Street, Bedminster, Bristol BS3 4NA. Tel 0117 923 1800.

Food growing and forest gardening

Many youth organisations have quite considerable amounts of land surrounding their buildings. The same goes for schools and many community organisations. Creating a garden or miniature forest is not that difficult to achieve and there are lots of resources and books to help reach that objective. For any group of young people, planning, growing and then utilising a garden which is based on edible plants can be an exciting and rewarding challenge. The benefits include:
* improving the community environment;
* experimenting with unusual edible plants and species, and re-introducing some of the 20,000 known species of plants which are in danger of disappearing;
* producing food and learning about alternative, sustainable farming methods.

Plants for a Future produce a number of practical leaflets on many aspects of growing and researching plants. Among them are checklists of edible trees and shrubs which are suitable for growing in the UK; and a fun leaflet called *The Edible Lawn,* which includes lots of ideas for growing a lawn which is rather different than the ordinary variety, and a leaflet on alternative food crops. Down in Lostwithiel in Cornwall, they also have their own 28 acre trial and demonstration ground, where, since 1989, they have planted over 1,500 species of plants including a woodland of over 10,000 trees and shrubs. They can give tours by appointment in return for some time and help or a donation towards their work and development. More important for many groups they also offer supplies of small plants. They keep their prices as low as possible, and in return they ask users of their services to keep them informed with information on how the plants have fared in different soils and environments. Krayg from PFAF was keen to encourage young people to get involved with their organisation and their projects. For a copy of their catalogue send a couple of first class stamps and an SAE to: PFAF, The Field, Penpol, Near Lostwithiel, Cornwall PL22 0NG, or phone 01208 873554.

Common Ground produce a range of beautifully crafted leaflets, newsletters and books on how monoculture can be fought against. Their materials on encouraging the re-planting and growing of fruit orchards are particularly stimulating. Even our local pears and apples have been replaced in the local supermarkets with imported varieties, frequently grown for uniformity and colour and not for taste and variation! Like most of the other Common Ground material, there's loads of hands-on information for sharing with any youth or community group. Common Ground are based at 44 Earlham Street, London WC2H 9LA.

Forest Gardens are primarily a different way of approaching the layout and tending of gardens. PFAF use a lot of their methods which drastically reduce the need for weeding through the use of perennial plants which grow year after year. SchNEWS say that,

> "Essentially a forest garden is a tiny imitation of a natural forest designed to achieve the utmost economy of space and labour. Like a natural woodland it has three layers of vegetation: trees, shrubs and herbaceous plants. Once established it requires minimal work and provides fruit, nuts, salads, herbs and other useful plants and fungi....What distinguishes a forest garden is that (everything) is grown together on the same piece of ground, one above the other."

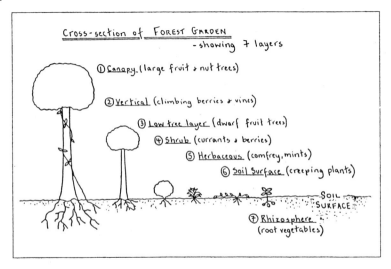

Source: *SchNEWS*

By moving away from the use of herbicides, insecticides and fungicides the semi-wild plants of the forest garden contain much higher vitamin, protein and mineral yields. There are some very good books on forest gardens including two from Green Books: *How to make a Forest Garden* by Patrick Whitefield, and *Forest Gardening* by Robert Hart.

Permaculture is defined by the Permaculture Association as, *"...permanent agriculture and permanent culture",* stressing the links between how we live, what we grow and what we eat. It is now one of the recognised methods for agriculturalists to design sustainable settlements, whether they are in youth groups, schools or a self-sufficiency enterprise. For more information, contact Permanent Publications, Hyden House, Little Hyden Lane, Clanfield, Hampshire PO8 0RU, with a SAE for their catalogue, which includes the regular *Permaculture* magazine. The Permaculture Association can be reached at PO Box 1, Buckfastleigh, Devon TQ11 0LH. The Centre for Alternative Technology is also very active in this field and the organic growing of plants and vegetables. Their poster/magazine on *Organic Gardening* by Peter Harper can be bought from them at CAT, Machynlleth, Powys SY20 9AZ.

Animal rights

The Vegetarian Society at Parkdale, Durham Road, Altrincham, Cheshire WA14 4QG, is a central source of a large number of publications and videos. As they point out in their publicity, *"Although there are now over 3 million vegetarians in the UK, we still slaughter more than 700 million animals a year!"*

The issues surrounding animal rights, vegetarian diets, health, environmental pollution, factory farming, live exports of animals, hunting and many other related issues are clearly made in their publications and videos. Many are specifically aimed at youth and educational audiences. Their magazine, *The Vegetarian,* includes a special youth *Greenscene* section and they have a junior membership section. The Vegan Society is based at Donald Watson House, 7 Battle Road, St Leonards on Sea, East Sussex TN37 7AA.

Animal Aid is a campaigning organisation fighting against all types of animal cruelty, and particularly the use of animals in experiments and the treatment of farm animals. Adult members receive their magazine *Outrage* and youth members, *Youth Rage!* Animal Aid is based at The Old Chapel, Bradford Street, Tonbridge, Kent TN9 1AW.

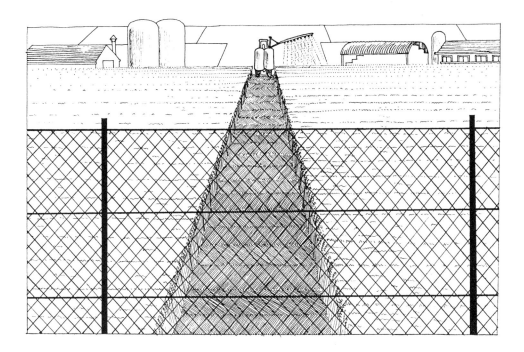

Where does your food come from?

To try to encourage young people to experiment with a vegetarian diet (as well as looking at the issues surrounding meat eating) why not try these two recipes for a bit of youth cookery? They are based closely on the material included in *Food for Life,* produced jointly by the Vegetarian Society and Animal Aid.

Veggie Recipes

Veggie Wedges
2 large baking potatoes, olive oil and sea salt
(amounts are based per two people – adjust for appetites and ages!)
1. Clean the potatoes and remove any skin blemishes. Cut each potato in half lengthways, and then each piece in half again, to make four wedges.
2. Place the potatoes in a saucepan with enough water to cover them. Bring the water to the boil, cook for a further 5 minutes, then remove them from the water with a slotted spoon.
3. Pour on a small amount of olive oil into a small bowl and place each wedge in the oil until coated. (or brush on with a pastry brush if you have one).
4. Place the oiled wedges on a baking sheet, or the grill pan and place under a pre-heated grill.
5. Cook for 10-15 minutes with the grill on high. (keep an eye on them to make sure that they are not burning!) The finished potatoes should be golden brown and cooked right through. Sprinkle with sea salt and serve with a variety of toppings.
(You can also add fresh herbs, toasted sesame seeds, home made tomato sauce or mustard, and why not try as an accompaniment, hummus (chick pea spread) or guacamole (avocado dip) or, just good old baked beans or cheese sauce!).

Veggie Sausage Casserole
1½ lb potatoes; 2 tbsp vegetable oil; 1 chopped medium onion; 2 chopped cloves of garlic; 1 bay leaf; 2 tsp thyme; 1 cubed cooking apple; 1 lb sliced carrots; 1 packet of veggie sausages; 10 oz of chopped tinned tomatoes; 1 vegetable stock cube dissolved in ½ pt boiling water; 1 tbsp tomato purée, and salt and pepper.
(designed for 4 people)

1. Put potatoes in a pan full of water for 5 minutes. (They need to be still quite firm). Keep on one side.
2. Heat oil in a large pan and fry onions and garlic for 2 minutes.
3. Add carrots, apple and sausages and fry gently.
4. Add tomatoes, stock and tomato purée. Bring to the boil and then simmer for 15 minutes.
5. Add potatoes and simmer gently for a further 10 minutes. Add salt and pepper to taste.
(Serve with rice, jacket potato, a green salad and crusty bread, or with guacamole and tacos (Mexican corn crisps).

For some other info on Animal Rights, info, campaigns etc. :
Barbara James, *The Young Person's Action Guide to Animal Rights,* Virago.
Annouchka Grose and Red Fox, *The Teenage Vegetarian Survival Guide,*
Vegetarian Society.
Mark Gold, *Animal Rights,* Jon Carpenter Books.

And, more controversially,
Green Anarchist magazine, PO Box 407, Camberley GU15 3FL.
Arkangel for animal liberation magazine, BCM 9240, London WC1N 3XX.
Juliet Gellatley with Tony Wardle, *The Silent Ark,* Thorsons.
Animal Liberation Front, BCM 1160, London WC1N 3XX.
Animal Rights Coalition, PO Box 339, Wolverhampton WV10.

Campaigns about the ethical and other standards in food production and distribution

Young people are naturally concerned about what they eat, how it is produced and what problems may exist. When Alison Barlow wrote to us concerning this book she enclosed two examples of campaigns which have been mounted following concerns about food. The first was from the Women's Environmental Network, Aberdeen Studios, 22 Highbury Grove, London N5 2EA, who were concerned about pesticide traces in chocolate; and a second international campaign concerned the encouragement by Nestlé of the use of infant formulas in developing countries, as a replacement for breastfeeding. The McDonalds' trial, which has been the longest libel trial ever in British courts, has also raised many issues which have been of interest to young and old alike.

Among the most frequently debated issues about food for the future are:
- the genetic engineering of animals and plants to produce the so-called 'best' product, usually as demanded by the supermarket chains;
- how to obtain organic and free range foods at reasonable costs;
- the protection of diversity in food, especially fruit and vegetables;
- 'fair trade' arrangements to give the workers involved in production just rewards;
- encouragement of reduced packaging in shops and use of re-usable containers rather than endless streams of plastic carrier bags;
- more accurate labelling of the contents of cans and packages to ensure that consumers know what they are buying/eating.

Youth workers and teachers might like to encourage young people to find out more about the current campaigns highlighted in the media.

Wild foods for free

Gubby, who has produced the large detailed illustrations in this book, spends more than half of each year living in a bender (a traditional structure of poles and cladding) and picking fruits (see also the Woodcraft and Alternative Lifestyles sections). Living closer than most of us do to nature and the bountiful supply of food for free, we invited him to provide some suggestions which can point the youth leader or young people themselves in the direction of making active use of the hedgerows and available foodstores.

Because this is a complicated and potentially dangerous subject, Gubby (and us) would urge you to use these suggestions as an introduction to the subject. A sortie into the countryside to collect wild foods, and especially fungi, requires using an authoritative, well illustrated guide such as the ones Gubby recommends. Happy foraging, and thanks to Gubby for his words of experience!

Over to Gubby, who says:
Going for a walk in the countryside?
Organising a stroll out in the woods, or out and about on your local bit of wasteland?
Nice views, and all that, but maybe you are short of things to do?

With a little knowledge, all the undoubted advantages of healthy exercise, learning about wildlife and the beauties of the local flora, can be supplemented with a nutritious and (probably) tasty meal from ingredients gathered along the way. It also means that your group is likely to pay a keener interest in the surroundings during your walk.

And there is much to be found. Generations of our ancestors would have been absolutely dependent on whatever they could find for their entire diet. Mind you, they did have a lot more countryside to hunt and gather in! I think that it is generally better for the casual collector to stick to the *gathering* aspect as the *hunting (and fishing)* involves a lot of specialised knowledge and equipment as well as being fraught with legal and ethical complications.

Gathering wild foods
By its nature this is a seasonal occupation. Apart from leaves and shoots, which are best picked young and succulent in the Spring or early Summer, late September and October is literally the most fruitful time of year. It also offers an interesting opportunity to contribute an unusual offering to local harvest gatherings and festivals.

Edible things to look for can be grouped roughly into: *fungi, fruit/berries,* and *leaves/shoots.* If you are based in a coastal region, you may also like to experiment with *seaweeds* as a food source. The first two are the most useful. Some roots can be edible but by and large taste of earth and aren't really worth bothering with. And now for the further word of warning. Most things are edible in the sense that you could eat them if you really had to, but only some of them actually taste good, and others are downright dangerous. So, ALWAYS cross check what you are collecting, ideally with someone who is experienced, or otherwise with a good book. Suggestions include:

Richard Mabey, *Food For Free,* Collins.
Frantisek Stary, *The Natural Guide to Medicinal Herbs and Plants,* Treasure Press.
John Wiseman, *The SAS Survival Handbook,* Harper-Collins.

The drawings in this section are by our friend, Marianne Gibson. Thanks!

Fungi

These come in a stunning variety of shapes, colours and sizes, from microscopic yeasts, to puffballs the size of armchairs, or root systems stretching hundreds of metres. They also provide some of the finest eating you could possibly hope for, however, many are too tough, slimy, rare, or poisonous – and are best left well alone!

A note on collecting and eating

Richard Mabey in *Food For Free* includes picking and cooking rules (with a few extra bits from us and Gubby) such as:

1. Use a good identification guide and try to be sure of what you've collected.
2. Avoid gathering on very wet days, since fungi soak up water and it spoils their taste.
3. Don't cut fungi with a knife, or yank them out of the ground. You need the whole stalk for full identification, and the fungi is the fruit of the plant which can be damaged by careless picking.
4. Don't pick any which are too old or beginning to blacken, since they will damage your good specimens.
5. Collect the fungi in an open, well ventilated basket.
6. Before cooking , again check the fungi to make sure of identification, and cut each one in half so as to avoid those containing maggots.
7. Fungi may require cleaning, but don't need washing or peeling unless specifically recommended in a text like Mabey's.
8. All fungi are best eaten within a day of picking.
9. With a really good crop, surplus can be pickled in brine (very salty water), or more easily, sliced thinly, threaded on cotton and dried somewhere warm and dark. These can then be excellent when used in stews or curries during the rest of the year.

The easiest mushrooms to collect tend to be found on grassland, though there are many woodland varieties worthy of the cooking pot. But, many of the really bad ones are to be found in woods; of these the *amanita* family are worthy of special note. Amongst these is the *fly agaric,* with its white spotted red cap, familiar from illustrations in many children's story books.

A typical member of the amanita family showing the cup (volva) at the base

The amanitas all have a cup at the bottom of the stem and many have white gills, so always look for this, and tell your young gatherers never to touch anything that has a cup like this.

One of the easiest mushrooms to find and identify is the *field mushroom,* which are almost identical to the mushrooms available from your greengrocer, apart from a slight ring halfway up the stalk. These are found on grassland, usually where the grass is long enough for you to end up with soaking wet socks!

A close relative is the *horse mushroom,* which is very similar to the field mushroom, but bigger and more crudely shaped. It has a pleasant, slightly almondy smell, and they taste even better than field mushrooms.

The only dangerous fungi that could be mistaken for either of these is the relatively rare *yellow stainer,* which though not fatal can cause nasty bellyache. They have a much larger ring, more like a skirt really, and a funny iodine smell. To be absolutely sure, slice one lengthways and within a couple of minutes it will develop yellow blotches, especially at the bottom of the stem.

At a distance, the *common puffball* looks a lot like the field mushroom, but when picked, you'll realise that it has no stalk! It's just like a little round football. They are quite edible, but a bit slimy; not as nice as the *giant puffball,* a truly spectacular fungus, like some weird alien space thing, nestling in scrub grass. They can grow up to a metre in diameter. To cook, slice them into steaks, add butter in a pan, then fry quickly. They're greasy, but scrumptious.

The puffball

The *common* or *shaggy inkcap* is easy to spot on wasteland in the late summer, with their very distinctive tall caps, they also cannot be confused with anything dangerous. They lack body in cooking but make a lovely peppery sauce.

Parasols are another common fungus, especially on pasture land, that make for good eating. Fried, the whole top of the fungus can be put in a bun and eaten just like a burger. Amongst woodland fungi are some quite valuable varieties including the *chanterelle.* This is a beautiful egg-yolk yellow, trumpet-shaped fungus that smells of apricot and very highly esteemed in the French cuisine. The underground *truffle* is worth an astronomical amount of money, should you or your group find any, but realistically you would need trained dogs or more traditionally, pigs, to be successful.

Beefsteak fungus is an edible variety of *bracket fungi,* the hemispherical growth jutting out from tree trunks, particularly in birch woods. These are rated by many as the best of all fungi for eating, and as the name implies, to the carnivorously inclined, both in its blood-red flesh and its flavour, they are surprisingly meaty.

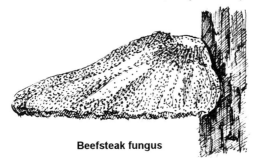

Beefsteak fungus

The *boletus* mushrooms found in beech woods have a good texture and taste good. They have pores like a sponge, rather than the usual gills and are safe as long as you avoid any with red or purple bits on them.

Fruits and berries

I suppose the most familiar and widely collected wild food has to be the *blackberry*, even if merely from plucking a few from the hedgerow on the way to school. The first berries, picked from the very end of the branch are the sweetest and are known as brambles. These are the best for eating raw or using in jam. Later in the season, the larger berries from further along the branch are larger and richer and are particularly good for puddings and wine-making.

Almost as common is the *elderberry,* though these are much too seedy to eat raw, and are best used in wine. In the Spring, elderflowers have a wonderful aroma and flavour, and can be used in puddings (try them battered or fried) or for making elderflower champagne, one the most refreshing beverages you can possibly imagine. For use as a youth club activity, you'd better check out on the ethics of home/club wine making as a youth activity, but it's actually not illegal!

On hills and moorland the low growing *billberry* is a good find, and in hedgerows, *sloes* can be used to make a jelly which requires a fair amount of sugar to counteract the tartness and acidity. *Crab apples* are the common ancestor of all modern apples and may appeal to those who enjoy bitter tastes. Due to the high pectin content they are useful as an additive for setting jams.

Wild strawberries

And, if you are really lucky you may find *wild strawberries* which though tiny are ten times nicer than their commercial relatives! Berries to watch out for and avoid: most especially the *deadly nightshade,* which though not common, do look delicious, like a large luscious blackcurrant, but very, very poisonous. *Lords and Ladies* also look quite edible, but while not as lethal as deadly nightshade, will give you severe stomach cramps, so watch it!

Nuts

These are some of the finest of wild foods and often ignored. They have a very high protein content and a range of pleasant flavours. If your group collect enough they can also be worth some money if sold.

Especially in the South of England and Wales, the *hazel tree* is very common in the hedgerows. The nuts can be collected in late September, early October as they drop, but the race will be on between you and the squirrels! Try baking some in the oven for half an hour (shell 'em first, mind).

Hazel nuts

Beech nuts, known as mast, make good eating, but the triangular nuts are quite fiddly to peel. *Sweet Chestnuts* baked in their skins are a good, traditional eating on cold nights, but don't bother with conkers *(horse chestnuts),* which are poisonous, or *acorns,* which are far too bitter, though apparently pigs love them!

Leaves and shoots

Should your country ramble take place in Springtime or early Summer, young leaves and shoots provide the bulk of available wild foods, though many tend to be bitter and taste at best a bit like cabbage, which is all very well if you like cabbage, but....

Wild garlic

I think the very best is *wild garlic* the leaves of which are very tasty indeed. Do not be put off if you or your charges don't like garlic. These are much milder and more oniony in flavour. The distinctive smell makes it very easy to locate in woodlands. It grows in clumps. The leaves can be used as a herb or as an alternative to spring onions or garlic in salads and cooking.

The furry leaves of *comfrey* plants are quite palatable, especially when cooked in a batter. Do not confuse with *foxglove* which is poisonous and not furry! It is better known, however, for its medicinal properties, known as knitbone, which can be rubbed onto bruised areas as you would with *dock leaves* after a nettle sting.

Young *beech leaves* can be eaten straight from the tree. *Dandelion* leaves may be used in salads, and *nettles* if picked young make a very nutritious base for soup, using plenty of butter for the frying. I wouldn't recommend any of the stories about grasping the plant firmly to avoid stings – use gloves!

Seaweeds
Alan currently lives by the seaside in Dorset and seaweeds of various types are common on the local beaches and rocks. He added in this bit!

Being rich in vitamins and minerals seaweeds are one of the best known survival foods. Whenever possible they should be thoroughly washed in freshwater before preparing for eating. By and large they are best eaten raw sliced thinly in salads, boiled lightly as with 'greens', or stir-fried with oil and Soya sauce. They are a popular ingredient in traditional Chinese cookery.

When going gathering, collect only growing weed, not bits washed up on the beach. For eating it is best to experiment with small portions at first. None are poisonous, but some are very acidic. As with fungi etc., do try to use a well illustrated reference book for identification purposes.

Sea Lettuce, Laver and *Kelp* are amongst the most popular varieties eaten in the UK. Indeed, in the south-west of Wales, kelp is still regularly collected by residents and sold in shops in purée form – it forms part of a breakfast consisting of fried bacon and laver bread, which is the purée rolled in oatmeal.

HOME-MADE PERSONAL CARE RECIPES
Introduction
Plant materials have been used for cosmetic purposes throughout history. Early cultures used these materials to preserve and decorate the dead, and later on for religious and ceremonial purposes. It was the ancient Greeks who developed the use of plant materials for the range of cosmetic uses we are familiar with today.

The Romans extended the use of cosmetic and herbal remedies and many recipes were gathered together in book form. This awareness of natural remedies and preparations remained after the fall of the Roman Empire and were handed down through the generations.

Industrialisation led to the mass manufacture of beauty preparations; a visit to any supermarket or chemist shop today will give you an idea of how big this market is. Globally it runs to billions of pounds, and of course much of this is spent on advertising, marketing and expensive packaging. The preservatives, synthetic perfumes and colourings added to many of these preparations have contributed to the rise in allergic reactions among those who use them.

As we approach the millennium there is an increased public awareness of the 'downside' of many of these preparations, not least that animal testing is still used by major manufacturers. The wisdom about the properties of natural remedies and cosmetics which has been passed down through the generations is now supported by research findings which prove the remarkable properties of herbs and plant materials. Consumer demand for products containing natural ingredients has rocketed and manufacturers are now responding by creating 'natural' and 'herbal' product ranges.

Making your own preparations

Encouraging young people to make their own cosmetics has several advantages, quite apart from the fact that they will cost a fraction of commercial products. For a start, they will then know exactly what the ingredients are, where they came from, and how fresh and pure they are. They can experiment with preparations to find out what suits their exact needs, for example, the kind of hair or complexion each person has.

When using the following preparations, bear in mind that no preparation can claim to be non-allergic, as there is always the possibility that some individual will have a reaction to it. However, by getting young people involved in making their own preparations they should be able to easily identify what has caused an allergic reaction and change the recipe accordingly. For individuals who have experienced allergic reactions in the past it is sensible to test for this before using a preparation. This can be done by putting a spot of an ingredient on gauze (or on the gauze of a sticking plaster) and then fixing this to the inner arm (between wrist and elbow) for 24 hours. Any reaction will be evident within the 24 hour period.

Cosmetic preparations are generally simple and quick to make, although some may require heating and blending. A fair amount of mess can be involved so your group will need access to a sink and plenty of towels and tissues. The recipes which follow can be photocopied onto sheets and then laminated (a helpful hint from users of CEE's earlier *EARTHworks* publication, who found that non-laminated sheets disintegrated under the assault of avocado, cucumber and melon!)

We can only offer a few simple recipes here, but if your group wants to investigate more sophisticated preparations then consult the bibliography for useful publications (e.g. Lesley Bremness's *The Complete Book of Herbs*).

Be sure to read the following 'Tips' section before making or using any of these preparations.

The illustrations for this section have been provided by Alan's friend Claire Erryn. Thanks, Claire!

TONERS AND ASTRINGENT LOTIONS

Birch leaves – Put a handful of young leaves into a pint of boiling water. Strain when cold.

Tomatoes can be sliced and smoothed over the skin.

Rosewater Astringent – Blend the following ingredients in a bottle and shake well before using. Gently boil just over ¼ pint (160 ml) of rosewater, allow to cool; then add 6 drops of glycerine; and just under ¼ pint (140 ml) of witch hazel. This preparation suits dry skin.

CLEANSERS

Potatoes are good when sliced thickly and rubbed, raw, over the face. Wipe with a damp tissue when you've finished.

Camomile Cleansing Milk – Heat ½ cup (125 ml) creamy milk with 2 tbs. (30 ml) camomile flowers, dried or fresh, in a double boiler for 30 minutes. Don't let the mixture boil or form a skin. After heating, leave it to infuse for 2 hours and then strain. Keep refrigerated and use within one week. Apply with cotton wool and remove excess with tissues. This preparation suits dry and sensitive skins.

Buttermilk and Fennel Cleansing Milk – Use ½ cup buttermilk and 2 tbs. crushed fennel seeds. Prepare and use as for Camomile Cleansing Milk. This preparation suits oily skins.

AFTER SHAVES

Coriander seeds should be as old as possible for this recipe – over a year if possible. Simmer 2 ounces of seeds in a pan with 1 tbs. of honey and 1 pint of water for 20 minutes. Cool and add 1 tbs. of witch hazel. Strain into a bottle and keep cool for best effect.

Elder is also useful. Pour 1 pint of boiling water onto 2 large handfuls of elder flowers (shake off any insects first!) Soak for 12 hours, strain and bottle. Keep cool.

MOISTURISERS

Avocado – Mix the flesh of an avocado with 1 tsp. honey, 1 tsp. lemon juice and natural yoghurt to make a stiff cream. Cool for 30 minutes then massage on until it disappears. Leave on overnight.

Cucumber soothes the skin. Blend a small peeled cucumber with an equal amount of natural yoghurt or cream. Cool, then massage on until absorbed.

Egg Yolk is good for normal skins. Mix a yolk with 1 tbs. almond oil and 1 tsp. honey. Work in with a cotton wool pad, leave for 30 minutes then rinse off with warm, then cold water.

Water Melon is very relaxing in hot weather. Cool some melon, slice and then squeeze some lemon juice over it. Place on the face and neck and leave for 30 minutes, lying down (preferably in a darkened room).

EYE TREATMENTS

You can use eye treatments at the same time as you are lying down with a face mask on! **Try slices of Cucumber, Teabags and Water Melon.** After this, bathe the eyes using an eyebath and one of the following:

- You can buy **Elderflower** water from chemists, but to make it, infuse 2 large handfuls with 1 pint boiling water for 12 hours. Strain and keep cool.
- You can also use **Cornflowers** (1 handful to ½ pint of boiling water) and **Fennel** (simmer 1 oz. fennel seed in 1 pint of water for 20 minutes).

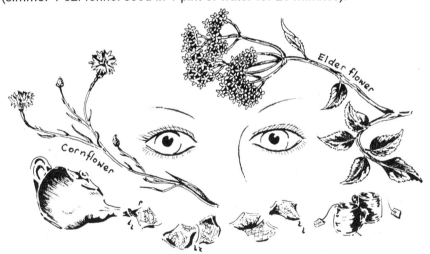

Eye Compresses – these herbal tea bag compresses will refresh tired eyes. Make 2 cups of **Camomile** or **Rosehip** tea, using 2 tea bags, and brew for 3 minutes. Remove the bags and cool. Place the tea bags over your eyes for 15 minutes, put your feet up and rest.

MOUTHWASHES AND TOOTHPASTE

Blackthorn Leaves and Cornflowers make good mouthwashes. Infuse them in boiling water and use once cool.

Fresh Parsley, Watercress or liquidised Nettle Leaves can be chewed to sweeten the breath.

Strawberries can be squashed and brushed on the teeth. Leave for a few minutes and then rinse out with a teaspoon of bicarbonate of soda dissolved in water. Now dust a toothbrush with bicarbonate of soda and brush the teeth. Rinse well.

A **Sage Leaf** can be rubbed over the teeth and gums to make them feel polished and clean – or peel a twig of **Flowering Dogwood**, chew the end to create a brush, and rub on the teeth and gently on the gums.

To make **Peppermint Toothpaste**, take 1 tsp. (5 ml) bicarbonate of soda and 2 drops essential oil of peppermint. Add enough drops of water to make a paste. Mix and use.

FEET AND HANDS

Use **Rosemary** as a footbath. Infuse it in boiling water and when cooler, soak the feet. Massage with olive oil afterwards.

To refresh tired feet, use **Bay, Lavender, Sage, Sweet Marjoram or Thyme.** Put a large handful of fresh flowers (or a ¼ cup of dried herb) and 1 tbs. (15 ml) of sea-salt in a basin of hot water.

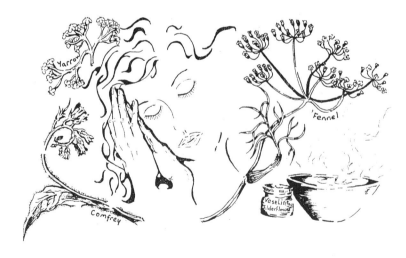

Elderflower is a useful hand lotion when several handfuls of fresh flowers are added to a pot of petroleum jelly (vaseline) that has been warmed gently until melted. Leave for 40 minutes, reheating as it cools, then sieve and store in screw topped jars.

To soften and soothe hands, soak them in an infusion of **Lady's Mantle, Fennel, Comfrey, Yarrow or Marsh Mallow.** Calendula or Camomile flowers are also effective.

FACEPACKS

These can be a really luxurious experience and are fun to use. Use every month or so for a great complexion!

Bananas should be ripe. Mix with an egg cup of Almond Oil and 2 egg yolks. Smear over face and neck, leave for 30 minutes and rinse off with warm water and lemon juice.

Tomatoes are also astringent. Sieve 2 or 3 ripe tomatoes and mix with a small carton of yoghurt. Stir this into a bowl with oatmeal that has been boiled for 20 minutes to give a smooth paste. Cool and apply thickly to the face (protect the eyes). Leave for 30 minutes and rinse off with cold water.

HERBAL BATHS

Hang a few herbal teabags of your choice from the hot water tap, or put a small herb filled tea infuser in the bath.

Relaxing bath herbs include Camomile, Jasmine, Hops, Meadowsweet and Valerian.

Stimulating bath herbs include Basil, Bay, Sage, Eucalyptus, Lavender, Mint, Pine, Rosemary and Thyme.
Healing bath herbs include Calendula, Comfrey, Spearmint and Yarrow.

RECYCLING

Recycling is a brilliant idea in principle – in practice it is actually quite difficult to develop successful recycling schemes. The most common ones in the UK (glass, newspaper, aluminium cans) work because there are substantial energy savings to the manufacturers in using recycled materials, and they are therefore prepared to pay a good price for this. However, if the market price drops, e.g. because of a glut, it can become uneconomic to collect the material. Central co-ordination is needed to get the economics of recycling right and avoid such problems. The most pressing issue, as recycling gains momentum and 'new' materials come to market, is how to persuade manufacturers to use them in their products and consumers to buy them. At the end of the day, it may require government action to stimulate large scale use of recycled materials in manufacturing.

Despite the difficulties, many governments and communities world-wide are at last getting their act together. In the UK most people now have access to some recycling facilities, either near home or at the workplace, and the range of materials which can be recycled continues to increase – but the UK does lag behind in some areas. For instance, why can't we recycle our batteries! In Italy and Germany, for example, you can find collection bins in shops selling batteries. Much more remains to be done, particularly in the area of educating the public about the tangible global benefits of recycling.

Youth groups and clubs are obvious places where a recycling culture can be created through adults setting good examples and stimulating recycling ventures – either for their own sake or for club fund-raising. Most young people will have some knowledge of domestic recycling but may know nothing about the problems associated with industrial and agricultural waste and recycling. This presents opportunities for action research by young people in both urban and rural settings.

Quite apart from reducing waste, and therefore demand on landfill sites, recycling can help reduce the demand for resources, particularly finite ones like oil (from which most plastics are derived) and metals. Other benefits are reductions in poisonous fumes when factories use recycled materials.

Of course if we reduce the amount of waste we accumulate in the first place, this will mean less recycling and waste disposal. This has coined the notion of 'precycling' – buying selectively to avoid bringing too much rubbish into the home in the first place. Simple strategies can all help, such as:

- using refill packs;
- buying products with a minimum of packaging;
- and taking boxes for carrying goods away from supermarkets, rather than using lots of plastic bags.

This can become particularly effective, where schools, youth clubs and other organisations co-ordinate the effort and help to create a strong community 'anti-waste' mind set. Unbelievably, almost two-thirds of all litter in the developed world is discarded packaging.

Recycling is a complex issue in itself, and also needs to be considered alongside the related concepts of reclamation, reuse and repair. Reuse or repair are the preferred forms of recycling, as little energy is needed to make such items fit for use again. Where this is not possible, recycling (adding or substituting reclaimed materials to make another product) can be used.

Some facts about the UK
20 million tonnes of solid domestic waste is produced annually. Although over 60 per cent of this is potentially recyclable, the UK only recycles around 6 per cent of household waste. Most of this waste ends up in landfill sites with only a small amount being incinerated. If you think of the difficulty posed each year by millions of discarded Christmas trees alone, you can begin to appreciate the scale of the landfill problem.

The UK relies on a voluntary approach to promote recycling whereas some other countries legislate to ensure that it happens. The government has now set a target of recycling at least 25 per cent of household waste by the end of the century. British Glass is committed to 50 per cent recycling by the year 2000. However, despite the 'success' of bottle banks, we still bin 5 billion of the 6 billion glass containers used annually in the UK. Arguably, we still have so far to go in the UK that there is plenty of scope for organised groups to have significant impact at local level in promoting recycling.

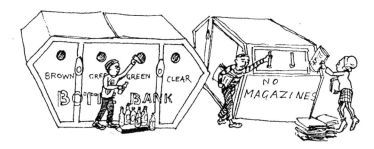

How a few other countries are doing
Italy uses legislation to control the kinds of packaging used and there are separate collections for a range of materials. Plastics are collected from bins in supermarket car parks and manufacturers must recycle 40 per cent of plastics used in containers. Batteries and medical waste are collected separately and Italy is a world leader in composting techniques for organic waste (see *Reuse, Repair, Recycle* by Jan McHarry).

SCRAP METAL

BROWN GREEN GREEN CLEAR
BOTTLE BANK

NO MAGAZINES

Denmark excels in implementing European directives on reuse and recycling of household waste. A target of recycling 40-50 per cent by the year 2000 has been set. Disposable drinks packaging was banned in 1979 and 400 million bottles are returned for refilling annually. Only a small amount of waste ends up in landfill. Incineration, with energy recovery, is favoured and accounts for over 60 per cent of the country's wastes.

China, with 20 per cent of the world's population but only 7 per cent of the arable land, has a long tradition of recycling animal and human waste for agriculture. There are separate collection systems for domestic and industrial waste so that non-hazardous wastes can be used for composting. Many things are salvaged for reuse and municipalities organise collection and payment schemes.

The *USA*, with only 8 per cent of the world's population, consumes a third of its resources and creates almost half the world's non-organic rubbish. Most of this goes into landfill disposal and has created an epic problem. However, action is now being taken and virtually all US cities now have either established or are piloting kerbside recycling schemes. Many 'buy-back' centres have also been set up by private operators and charities. The US is responsible for many innovative initiatives, including the garden and community composting programmes currently developing, often as a response to a ban on garden waste in household rubbish.

What you can do

Aluminium cans are the classic material to recycle, as so much energy is saved (95 per cent). World wide, we still throw away 50 per cent of the aluminium cans we use, so there are loads of opportunities to recycle more. The UK only recycled 16 per cent of its cans in 1992, as against Sweden's 85 per cent and over 60 per cent in the USA. Try to find alternatives to cans whenever possible, such as refillable glass bottles. Aluminium foil and packaging can also be collected for recycling, but it needs to be clean.

Baths and showers – baths use twice as much water as showers, so shower whenever possible. Put a brick (or a plastic bottle filled with water) in your toilet cistern to reduce the amount of water used with each flush.

Cardboard and paper make up about a third of household waste in industrialised countries. Reuse what cardboard you can. Boxes make good containers for children's toys and other items, and can also be cut down to make filing boxes for paper and magazines. Schools and playgroups have many uses for boxes. Store boxes flat to save space before taking them to a recycling centre.

Cartons pose a particular problem – because most of them contain a mixture of materials such as paper, plastics, waxed laminates and aluminium coatings they cannot be recycled. It's best to avoid buying them if you can, or wash empty cartons and use them for freezing foodstuffs.

Charity shops are often able to accept a wide range of materials for resale or recycling. This should be your first choice for the disposal of old or unwanted clothes, as they are likely to be reused.

Compost could be made using around a third of the organic matter in the average wastebin. This is a very important process, as it enables gardening to be carried out without the use of chemical fertilisers. Home composting is common in the US and some European countries, and kerbside collections are increasing.

Dyeing can rejuvenate old clothes, but avoid black, navy blue and dark shaded metallic dyes as they are not biodegradable. Other coloured dyes are not a long term hazard. Where you can, use plant and vegetable dyes, or make your own from blackcurrants, coffee beans, marigolds etc..

Use recycled pulp, for example, *egg cartons* instead of plastic ones, which are difficult to recycle and are not biodegradable.

Plastic foam is used in huge quantities for packaging. Polystyrene in particular is very difficult to recycle, so avoid using foam packaging and cups.

Glass bottles should always be returned, reused or taken to a bottle bank.

Use *jumble sales* to raise money for your youth group or favourite charity and to get rid of items you would otherwise be tempted to throw out.

The UK uses *landfill* for 90 per cent if its' waste, compared to 20 per cent in Switzerland, 30 per cent in France and 65 per cent in Italy and Germany. Countries with low landfill rates typically use incineration and reuse/recycling schemes. Keeping hazardous materials out of landfill is a priority, because of the potentially dangerous leachate produced when organic matter decays. By using rechargeable batteries we can keep some of the most toxic materials from reaching landfill sites.

Use energy saving *lightbulbs* where the light tends to be left on for three hours or more at a time. Although these bulbs are initially more expensive to buy, they last eight times longer than ordinary bulbs and produce very considerable savings on electricity bills.

Mosaic has been used as an art form for thousands of years. You can use weathered glass collected from beaches, together with shells, pebbles, seeds and broken china or tiles to make your own mosaics. You can also add other things, like wheels and springs from old clocks or watches. (See section on the Seaton Mosaic Project).

Always try to find alternative uses for old *newspapers*. They can be used for animal bedding, to protect floors when painting and decorating and you can buy special machines to turn them into 'bricks' for burning in open fires or stoves. Newspapers can even be shredded and added to your compost heap.

Plastic is not necessarily an environmentally unfriendly product in itself. It is so light, for example, that considerable savings on transport costs are made when plastic bottles are used instead of glass. The disposal of plastic waste is still problematic, but plastic bottles, in particular, can now be recycled and collection banks are available in many supermarket car parks. At minimum we should be reducing the amount of plastic packaging in the goods we buy. Plastic shopping bags are a tremendous waste where they are thrown away after a single use. World-wide we use many billions each year, so avoid using them wherever possible. Reuse or return them to collection banks in supermarkets. They can also be donated to market stall traders, jumble sales or charity shops.

Making patchwork *quilts* is an excellent way to reuse unwanted rags. Give any you cannot use to playgroups, schools, jumble sales or charity shops for reuse. As a last resort, take them to a rag bank for recycling.

Finding uses for old vehicle *tyres* is a major environmental problem. We discard 25 million in the UK each year, and it is ten times this amount in the US. Fewer tyres are now being retreaded, as manufacturers claim that modern tyres are being used much harder, rendering them unsuitable for retreading. Alternative uses are being developed, such as incorporating shredded rubber into surfacing materials for roads pavements and children's playgrounds.

Ultimately, it is up to each one of us to make our own contributions where we can. Many little actions, taken together, can have major impact. Some manufacturers have admitted that it was constant pressure from children – organising themselves in schools, youth clubs etc. – which persuaded them to take a more environmentally friendly approach. As consumers we *can* be powerful, particularly when we organise together.

Further information

WasteWatch
Gresham House
24 Holburn Viaduct
London EC1A 2BN
Tel: 0171 248 0242

Tidy Britain Group
The Pier
Wigan WN3 4EX
Tel: 01942 824620

POLLUTION SOLUTIONS
Background
While we were compiling material for this book, both Friends of the Earth Trust in London and their Scottish organisation contacted us with information about campaigning work they were involved in with young people. Both are members of the Friends of the Earth International Network. Their member organisations have been active at the forefront of global and local campaigning on environmental issues since the organisation was established in the 1960s in America. (In England, FOE was set up in 1971).

Throughout the UK many young people have become involved in environmental campaigns as a direct result of the FOE. They are involved in many different aspects of the environment, but combating pollution is one of their priorities, and the recent *Fuming Mad Campaign* has offered opportunities for campaigning against air pollution caused by cars. FOE is a membership organisation and publishes quarterly magazines, *Earth Matters* (England, Wales and Northern Ireland) and *What on Earth* (Scotland) which are sent automatically to all members. Curiously, membership for young people and students costs one pound less in Scotland per year!

Friends of the Earth, England, Wales and Northern Ireland, 26-28 Underwood Street, London N1 7TQ
Friends of the Earth, Scotland, 72 Newhaven Rd, Edinburgh EH6 0JL

Wanstonia, Cambridge Park eviction, No M11 Link Road Campaign, East London 93 (Matt Smith)

Action on Car Pollution
The following ideas are based on information from the FOE *Fuming Mad Campaign* and other sources.

What's the fuss about?

- The number of children admitted to hospital with asthma has more than doubled in the last 20 years. Children are particularly vulnerable to pollution because their bodies are still growing and absorb toxic substances more quickly.
- Up to 90 per cent of the carbon monoxide in the atmosphere is generated through car emissions. Carbon monoxide replaces oxygen in the blood and puts a strain on the heart.
- In the last 20 years the number of motor vehicles on the UK's roads has risen from 17 to 26 million.
- Cars use a lot of energy. A full car uses about seven times more energy than a full double decker bus.
- Motor vehicles are the fastest growing source of air pollution today.
- The Government plans to build more than 350 new motorways and main roads costing around £13 billion. The Government predicts that there will be a further 10 million cars on UK roads by 2025.
- Fewer cars equals fewer new roads being built and that means less of a threat for wildlife.

Taking Action: What can young people do?

Friends of the Earth and many other organisations such as Greenpeace and Earth First! are totally committed to a future which is more energy efficient. Encouraging people to use their cars less and pressuring the Government to provide better public transport are just part of the way forward. Some of the specific ideas which FOE asked young people and adults to put into action during the *Fuming Mad* campaign are worth considering in your own area. They include:

1. Encourage drivers to leave their cars at home two days a week by placing photocopies of *Fuming Mad* parking tickets underneath the windscreen wipers of cars in a car park. We suggest that this is best done by a group of young people who should be responsible about their action, since some drivers may get annoyed!

Be a Friend of the Earth

Leave Your Car at Home

Traffic fumes are putting more and more children with asthma into hospital, causing cancer, and killing an estimated 10,000 people every year.

You can help make a difference. Leave your car at home two days a week. Walk, cycle or travel by bus or train instead. You'll be helping everyone breathe more easily.
No choke!

FRIENDS *of the*
earth
for the planet for people

Published by Friends of the Earth England, Wales and Northern Ireland, 26-28 Underwood Street, London N1 7JQ

The Fuming Mad Campaign

Don't be a litter bug. If you don't want this ticket, please put it on somebody else's car!

2. Campaign for better public transport and a reduction in vehicles in your area.
3. Lobby the local council(s) for more cycle lanes, special cycle tracks and safe bike parks (see section on Sustrans: the National Cycle Network).
4. Encourage car sharing.
5. Write to your local paper with your views on air pollution. Enclose a photo or drawing to illustrate your points. For example, you or friends may be asthmatic; ask a friend to take a photo of a person using an asthma inhaler by the side of a busy road.
6. Become a dirty diesel spotter! Report smoky diesel lorries, buses or coaches to the Vehicle Enforcement Group at your local Traffic Area Office. They'll need to know the vehicle registration number, and the date, time and place, so carry a pen and pad with you or possibly a camera.
7. If a young person or their family are thinking about buying a new vehicle look for small, fuel-efficient models, preferably with a catalytic converter, which produces less harmful emissions.

Obviously, the list of lobbying and campaigning which young people can engage in is almost endless. For some, the relatively PC (politically correct) nature of some agencies' lobbying tactics may not seem enough. Then it is the turn of organisations such as The Land is Ours, Road Alert, the Third Battle of Newbury and Reclaim the Streets (see Alternative Lifestyles section for contacts), which offer options for direct action. As authors we are neither condoning nor condemning, but young people should be offered choices and information regarding the organisations working to offer more sane and ecologically sound alternatives to the headlong rush towards what FOE call 'Carmageddon.'

SOURCES OF ENERGY?
A bit of background
We own up very readily to having had some difficulty in getting our own 'heads' around options regarding sources of power. We have visited the Centre for Alternative Technology in Wales and delighted along with other visitors over the range of wind, solar (sun) and water powered exhibits. On the World stage, other renewable power sources such as geo-thermal power, tapping the energy from inside the Earth's crust, are being developed. At that level, it is hard to explain to any non-geothermal scientists, young or old, or to translate into a local context!

Much more hands on, the Croissant Neuf stage at the Big Green Gathering 1996 festival, had a substantial circus-style tent powered entirely by solar panels and wind – enough to keep a 5,000 watt sound system functioning all day and lots of coloured lights! There and at the Green Field at Glastonbury we have helped pedal power dance sound systems and have seen a number of performance shows for young people, which have employed the youngsters to power their own entertainment – a graphic way to bring home the message that not all power has to come from the national grid!

One of the performers to use pedal power as part of the message in his work with young people is Prof. Des Kay, whose Heath Robinson-type pedal machine is a converted ice-cream tricycle. This is used in a half hour Agenda 21 show about recycling, sustainable power and all things 'green'. (Des and the Green Roadshow can be contacted at 8 Crescent Road, Kingston, Surrey KT2 7QR)

Prof Des Kay and the Green Roadshow

Some of the dilemmas

In terms of international development, there is a tragic conflict between the rich countries of the Northern hemisphere and the economically poorer countries of the South. In the early 1970s around 5.5 billion metric tons per head of carbon dioxide was released into the atmosphere – now the figure is approximately 7 billion tons. The environment globally is suffering, and now, almost too late, the industrialised nations like the UK are awakening to the potential of environmental catastrophe. However, as was made clear at the Earth Summit in Rio de Janeiro, which led to the adoption of the goals of Agenda 21, the poorer countries need economic growth as well as protection of the environment. Indhira Ghandi expressed in a stark way when she said, *"Of all the pollutants we face, the worst is poverty. We want more development."*

Youth Action and the Environment 162

Another global issue which relates particularly to the large multi-national companies is the exploitation of the World's limited non-renewable sources of energy. Even at the Earth Summit, the USA wanted to prevent the multi-national companies, many of which are North American, from being subject to any further international control. This at a time when many nations blame those very same companies for exploitation and some of the worst environmental disasters and pollution. In its own way, the movement towards sustainable – renewable energy sources, is the key to future developments. Much of the World's population is still in need of economic growth and development. To achieve this we are entering what history may call the **Environmental Revolution**, a period of change of perhaps more profound importance to future generations than the Agricultural or Industrial Revolutions, since it is of global rather than national importance.

Agenda 21, Chapter 9 stated,
> *"Governments must get greater energy efficiency out of existing power stations and develop new, renewable energy sources such as solar, wind, ocean and human power."*

The three major problems which are related to the atmosphere of the planet are:

- **Ozone depletion** – often referred to as the 'hole' in the protective filter (ozone) that surrounds the earth (primarily caused by the use of chloro-fluorocarbons (CFCs) in aerosols, fridges and air conditioning units.
- **Acid rain** – rain which kills trees and can kill fish in lakes – is directly caused by releases of sulphur dioxide and nitrogen oxides from factories, especially electricity generating stations.
- **Global warming** – sometimes called the greenhouse effect – carbon dioxide is being produced in increasing quantities, particularly through the use of coal and under fossil fuels. This prevents a proportion of the Sun's rays bouncing back from the Earth, leading to a gradual warming of the planet which may result in the melting of the polar ice caps.

It is this third area around global warming that has prompted individuals and governments to try to develop both energy saving policies and new sources of energy which are sustainable and renewable. Electric and solar powered vehicles exist in varying forms of efficiency, but may offer one solution to the lack of energy sources and the problems of pollution.

Project idea:
The Centre for Alternative Technology sells some interesting and cheap solar cell, photovoltaic kits. Starting at about £10 these can be used to power small motors which in turn can be used to power a model boat or pump. They come with a good set of instructions and ideas for making models from scrap materials.

An Energy handout or notes for a presentation
The following is a useful set of material developed by the Network for Alternative Technology and Technology Assessment. It can be effectively used with younger groups, as a story or presentation to give them, through the dinosaur story, a bit of information about the danger of using up all the non-renewable sources of power.

The Dinosaurs' Revenge
<u>Why</u> we can't carry on burning fossil fuel

Most of the energy we use comes from 'fossil' fuels – coal, oil and gas, which we get from deep underground. These fuels were created millions of years ago when the dinosaurs reigned and took millions of years to create – from the remains of plants buried gradually under layer and layers of rock and soil. Some dead dinosaurs no doubt also got involved. We've only been raiding the Dinosaurs' graveyard, by extracting coal, for a few hundred years, and oil and gas only more recently – but we've already used up a lot of the reserves, especially of oil and gas, which look like they will run out in a few decades.

At one time people thought that the mining-out of these fuels was the main problem – that was the so called 'energy crisis' of the 1970s. – it looks like we <u>won't</u> be able to – or <u>shouldn't</u> – use up what remains – because of the effect of burning it on the atmosphere. The problem is what's called the <u>greenhouse effect</u> and it's caused by a gas called <u>carbon dioxide.</u> It's tasteless – it's what's in the bubbles in soft drinks. It's also what you get when you burn fossil fuels – which are basically <u>carbon.</u> Carbon plus oxygen from the air gives you carbon dioxide and heat. That's what <u>burning</u> is all about. Basically we're burning off all the carbon from the fossil material laid down millions of years ago.

The trouble is, when you push more and more carbon dioxide gas from burning fossil fuels into the atmosphere, it begins to have an effect on the <u>sunlight</u> that we receive. The gas acts like the glass in a greenhouse, allowing the Sun's rays to come in but blocking the escape of heat. So <u>very</u> gradually the whole planet warms up.

The actual average worldwide temperature change is quite small – less than a degree or so in a 100 years. But we are burning more and more, so the rate of temperature rise may increase. And remember, the temperature change that caused the Ice Age was only four degrees or so.

If we persist in burning off the rest of our fossil fuels, we could face another similar change in average temperatures – but this time an increase – and that could mean widespread flooding, more desert areas, crop failures and a lot more. The last couple of years' erratic weather in the UK – hot summers, windy winters, could only be a small sample of what we might expect. And worldwide it could be worse. Millions of people could be affected – around the world – made homeless, losing their food supplies and livelihoods...

Not a pleasant thought: the **_Revenge of the Dinosaurs_** if you like...

Are there any ways out?

Basically we have to stop burning so much fossil fuel.

We can do that first by stopping wasting so much of the energy we currently have to produce and second by using other types of fuel which don't produce carbon dioxide.

Energy saving first – currently we waste more than half of what we produce, with badly insulated houses, inefficient machines, lighting and cars. A lot can be done to avoid this waste – and to save money.

Second, the **alternative sources**. Nuclear power was for many people the great hope, at one time – a clever way of twisting the tail of dinosaurs to get power – stealing the dragons' secret if you like. But it's turned out not to be cheap and many people are worried about the risks: again the dinosaurs may get their revenge. Also the reserves of the fuel it needs are not infinite: there's only around 50 years worth of uranium known to be available if we carry on using it as at present – and if we tried to expand nuclear power to take over from coal, we'd use the reserves up even faster. Of course we might be able to find some more uranium and develop ways to use it more efficiently – like the so called Fast Breeder Reactor. But all that does is put off the day when we have to find a long-term, reliable alternative to raiding the dinosaur's lair. Something which will last.

In the end, the only real alternatives are the World's natural energy sources – wind, wave, tidal and solar power. These will continue to be available as long as the planet exists and tapping into them does not use them up. They are naturally replenished – so they are called 'renewables'.

We already get about 20 per cent of the World's electricity very cheaply from hydro-electric dams, but eventually we could supply about the same from each of the other renewables: enough for all we need from a mixture of wind, tidal, wave, and solar powered systems, without producing any carbon dioxide or any other pollutants.

Of course, no technology can be entirely without impact – windmills may be thought to intrude on the landscape for example, and big Tidal Barrages across estuaries will obviously have some local impacts on wildlife. But then the greenhouse effect – or a major nuclear accident – would have much more dramatic impacts. So it's a matter of choice – and renewables are increasingly looking like the cheapest option. Windmills, under some conditions, for example, can generate electricity at half the cost of conventional power plants – and there are now thousands of them in use around the world. These are not primitive low-tech devices – but the very latest in advanced technology – as in the US and the UK Windfarms.

Britain is very well placed to develop many of the renewables – we have amongst the World's best wind, wave and tidal sites. And the Open University (OU) is doing its bit to help develop some of them – for example the OU Energy and Environment Research Unit has a major wind power project and is looking at biofuels and solar energy. We're also looking carefully at the problems of renewables – like their environmental impact. But the message that's emerging is that, given careful design and siting, renewables are very well suited to the UK. So, maybe, we will soon be able to leave the dinosaurs and their graveyard in peace...

Dave Elliott

The above analysis is very much Dave's, and should not therefore be taken, necessarily, to reflect the views of the Open University. Dave has used the 'dinosaur' concept in a geologically light hearted way , and the 'dragon' graphic produced by Tam Dougan, is obviously mythological. But, according to myth, the dragon did guard hidden treasure and wreaked terrible vengeance if disturbed.

For further information on *renewable energy* contact NATTA, the independent national *Network for Alternative Technology and Technology Assessment* c/o Energy and Environment Research Unit, Open University, Milton Keynes, Bucks., MK7 6AA.

CENTRE FOR ALTERNATIVE TECHNOLOGY (CAT)

There is a sense of excitement and wonderment from the very moment that a visitor, young or old, arrives in the car parking area below the steep rocky incline up to the Centre for Alternative Technology in the Snowdonia area of Wales. The wooden chalet-style reception cabin leads directly to the 180 ft trackway on which the water-balanced railway cars take groups of visitors up to the CAT site. It is the start of a fascinating quest of discovery around all things environmentally friendly. Already dubbed as Europe's leading Eco-Centre with over 30,000 young visitors per year, the Centre is an obvious facility to take groups of young people to.

The seven acre complex is not connected to the national grid and as such offers a living example of how a lifestyle can be sustainable through consideration of factors such as:
- power
- food and agricultural methods
- energy efficient building design and construction
- low impact lifestyles
- composting, recycling and reusing of materials
- the relationship with the environment and nature.

The site is well signposted with an array of different interactive features, especially involving for young people including:
- a maze which confronts the user with difficult problems about transport use, road building and vehicle ownership;

- the Mole Hole, an underground cavern where the 'beasties' of the underworld have mysteriously grown to the size of small humans; lots of buttons to press which explain the 3-D scenes of underground activity;

The Water-balanced cliff railway

- the 'smell me' and 'taste me' flower and herb beds – full of delicious smells and exotic tastes, ideal for livening up a salad or meal;
- a wild bee observation hive;
- displays and examples of solar voltaics, solar water heaters, wind, water and wave power, many of which are interactive and 'hands on' to show exactly how much power is being generated by different types of power source;
- examples of composting with a variety of equipment and methods including tyres and worms;
- compost toilets and a sewage system using reed beds for filtration;
- the bookshop which has books on just about any conceivable 'green' subject plus activity kits including equipment to build a solar powered boat, lamp or propeller ;
- and, of course, a small, but enjoyable adventure play area!

Solar and Wind power at CAT

From the STAR QUIZ SURVIVAL TEST
(there are actually 100 questions in the full version)

A score of 75-89 is officer material and 90 or more puts the contestant on the bridge! So, in our scaled down version, people should try to get about 8 questions correct. Spaceship Earth is careering through space on a particularly perilous stretch of its eternal journey. It needs a new crew. Are you fit for the task?

Energy:
1. The sun is the source of all life (as we know it) on Earth.
True ☐
False ☐
2. What percentage of Britain's electricity comes from nuclear power?
a) 85%
b) 50%
c) 25%
3. Solar cells are used to generate electricity from sunlight. What are they made of?
a) sand (silicon)
b) aluminium
c) cardboard

Pollution:
4. What is the link between fast food cartons, fridges, aerosol cans and holes in the ozone layer?
5. We can obtain a useful gas from sewage and rubbish dumps?
True ☐
False ☐

Recycling:
6. How many trees does one person use for paper each year?
a) 2
b) half a tree
c) 6
7. What percentage of the contents of the average dustbin can be recycled?
a) 20%
b) 50%
c) over 75%

Organic growing:
8: Human urine diluted with water is a great fertiliser.
True ☐
False ☐

Energy conservation:
9. Which is cheaper to have on for one hour?
a) a colour TV
b) a one bar electric fire
10. What percentage of your body's heat do you lose through your feet?
a) 0%
b) 60%
c) about 15%

Reproduced with grateful thanks to the Centre for Alternative Technology

Young people using the CAT questionnaires

For groups of young people visiting CAT there are also options for a guided tour and various photocopiable materials including quizzes, which can be used as visitors go around the site or afterwards. For adults, the Centre organises specialist courses on a range of subjects including solar and water power; self-build and energy conservation houses and organic horticulture. For student accommodation there are Eco-cabins, the Self-build house and hostel-type rooms above the restaurant.

If you are working with a group of young people in your own area it is well worth sending off for their publications lists which include a lot of CAT publications along with books from other publishers. Of particular relevance are:

Watch Out! Things to do about solar power and *'learning by growing'* books for 8-12s and 13-16s
Activities for Children for Key Stages 1 and 2
Star Quiz Survival Test (part of which is reprinted next as a useful exercise to use with a youth group).
A complete catalogue of environmental books and products on offer is available for five second class stamps.

The Centre for Alternative Technology
Machynlleth
Powys SY20 9AZ
Tel 01654 703409

A bit more about CAT and the CAT people!

In 1995 a glossy A4 book entitled *'The CAT Story: Crazy Idealists!'* was published. It is a lively, colourful (in all senses!) and intriguing peep behind the scenes of the Centre and the many people who have lived and worked there in the 20 years since the disused slate quarry was acquired by the founder, Gerard Morgan-Grenville. With a background of radical environmentalism, the succession of workers embodied a blend of ideals and practical knowledge which effectively traced a development of eco-counter culture from the Levellers and Diggers of the 16th century through to the counter culture of the 1960s and beyond of hippies, communes, spirituality, intermediate technology and environmental action groups.

Pete Harper from CAT was the person who coined the phrase 'Alternative Technology' to embrace a variety of sustainable approaches to living and working alongside nature. En route to the CAT of the late 1990s, the CAT people have shed a lot of their hippy, and uncompromising political attitudes, yet kept a pay structure that has everyone paid the same annual salary. They are a lot more pragmatic about a future which involves being on the information superhighway with a Web site already up and functioning, along with providing enthusiasm and specialist professional advice for individuals, organisations and companies who want to adopt more sustainable practices. Internally, this has meant that whilst they operate as a community, they don't expect everyone to agree on all aspects of the organisation. For instance,

"At times I've gone round the Quarry and I've felt it's almost too polished and conventional. More recently, I haven't felt that so much. It still has a lot of chaos in it."

Tim Kirby

"The organisation is still bohemian in temperament and appearance, although we now enjoy dressing up and do a nice line in snazzy suits. We have accepted that skills are precious and require specialisation to make the best use of them."

from The CAT Story

"I would like to see a change of emphasis towards a much more politically radical approach. I believe now, even more than I did at the start, that we are governed by people without vision who are rather incompetent and self seeking."

Gerard Morgan-Grenville

And of the future,

"The high-tech vision is surely right in that there will be a lot of high-tech, perhaps higher than we can now imagine. But it is right too, in a more fundamental respect that thoughtful green theorists are coming to accept: for all the ecological significance of the land and countryside, towns and cities must be the basis for any sustainable future.

But eco-cities will have Arcadian qualities. They will take living systems, not machines, as their touchstone. They will appreciate the creative disorder of nature. Their technical emblems will be the computer, the bicycle and the tree."

from The CAT Story.

LEADHILLS SCHOOL ENERGY PROJECT

It's fair enough to call this a 'school' project as the class from Leadhills Primary School carrying out the project was a composite of Primaries 4, 5, 6 and 7! Leadhills is a very small village in South Lanarkshire, not far from Wanlockhead – at some 1,500 feet above sea level, it is the highest inhabited village in Scotland.

The implications of this remote location gradually became apparent to Howie one cold November morning, as he slithered several miles along very snowy roads which had rather nasty sheer drops on one side! In fact, the conditions were such that the school might have been shut for the day had most of the children and staff not struggled in quite early on. Howie quickly became intrigued to see how a small rural school tackled a major environmental topic like 'energy', and was suitably impressed by the wide range of activities undertaken by the class, including visits to three different types of power station.

The teacher had prepared the topic thoroughly, and in the process discovered some excellent 'fun' resources and practical projects for the children to use. Aimed at younger children they could be adapted for use as part of a youth group visit or for primary schools. The resources included:

Energy 'Snakes & Ladders' game available from:
Energy House
Snakes & Ladders game
British Gas, Room 818
326 High Holborn
LONDON WC1V 7PT
Tel: 0171 242 0789 X 3452

A third world 'Wind Aid' project, involving the design and construction of a working windmill to draw water from a well for an African village. This utilises an engineer to help the class. Details from:
Exciting Science & Engineering Project
Chemical Industry Education Centre
Dept of Chemistry
University of York
Heslington
YORK YO1 5DD

Plans to make a working water wheel model, available from the Centre for Alternative Technology – see Centre for Alternative Technology section for details.

The questionnaire and quiz included below can be used to get your own groups started, or can be adapted to fit in with your own energy project. Since you will have to make it appropriate for your own area and resources, we haven't offered any answers!

The aims of the Leadhills energy project were:
• To look briefly at where our energy comes from and how we use it, for example to keep warm.

- To give the children a clear idea of what energy forms there are, where they come from, what are their uses, what are the consequences of their use, why we need to conserve energy and how to do this.
- To provide the opportunity for practical experiments with wind, solar and water power, through making working models and using these.
- To explore the part played by natural and manufactured energy in myths and legends from different parts of the world and work out why these forces feature in so many cultures.
- To investigate the history of energy use, e.g. gas lights on streets, cooking on fires; and energy use in different cultures.
- How the sun operates as our primary energy source.

ENERGY STARTER QUIZ

Work as a group and choose someone to read questions aloud and one to record clear answers. You may take turns for these tasks if you wish but don't waste time and energy discussing how you do this for too long!	*Possible Points*
Neat work	*1*
1. What is energy?	*2*
2.	
a). What do we need energy for? Give at least 4 examples of which only one may be a sport!	*4*
b). Put your list in order starting with the activity using most energy and ending with that using least.	*4*
3. Why do young people need more energy than older people	*2*
4. Where do we get our energy from?	
a). Give the name beginning with N for this group.	*2*
b). What two groups of living things can we use stored energy from?	*2*
5. What two things that we eat do not give us energy?	*2*
6. How is the energy content of food measured?	*2*
7. Which food group do we mostly get energy from and which other two groups give us some energy?	*3*
8. Give two examples of each of the three groups named in 7 above.	*6*
	30

WIND and WATER

1. Look carefully at the shape of the wind turbines and the water turbines so you can draw them on your return to school and explain why they need to be different.

2. When does A) the wind energy become electricity?
                B) the water energy become electricity?

WIND SECTION
3. How are the wind turbines monitored or checked for damage?
4. What is a met mast and what is it used for?
5. Find out all you can about the computer system which controls the Wind Farm.
6. What is an electricity substation?
7. Check for any concerns about Wind Farms.
a) You might listen for noises at different distance.
b) Would the noise be greater on a windy day?
c) What are your views on the Wind Farm?
d) Are there any other concerns ?

WATER SECTION – HYDRO ELECTRIC
8. What happens to fish in a hydro scheme ?
9. What water is harnessed on the Clyde near Lanark ?
10. How are the turbo generators protected against overloading ?
11. Make a mental note of any other things you learn on the trip to write about at school.

OPENCAST MINING

A few years ago, Howie's friends, Claudia and Michael, moved to an isolated cottage in Lanarkshire to get away from the noise and pollution in London. Shortly after moving in they discovered to their horror that an opencast mine was planned for a site near the bottom of their garden. This, apparently, is not an uncommon experience and many families have found that their dream home has been ruined by the noise and pollution of opencast mining. Since that time Claudia and Michael have been actively involved in opposing opencast mining and in presenting evidence to a number of enquiries.

We wanted to include information about opencast mining in the book because it affects many areas throughout the UK, and has been a growing phenomenon since the demise of deep mining. In many senses it has 'crept up on' communities since that time. Also, it is an obvious blight on the landscape with high profile effects such as dust, noise and vast numbers of heavy lorries. At the CEE national conference in 1996, Alan showed part of the *Undercurrents 5* video about the Selar opencast site in Wales, where local villagers joined forces with young direct action protestors from around the UK. (Undercurrents Productions, 16b Cherwell Street, Oxford OX4 1BG.)

RIP Selar, opencast mine protest, Wales 96 (Matt Smith)

We were very pleased to hear about the study carried out by Mark McCrorie, a fourth year pupil at Inverkeithing High School in Fife. In it, Mark shows the way he was able to identify how local communities can harness support in opposing this kind of mining. Mark put a lot of hard work into his study and we hope that it will act as a stimulus for other groups interested in finding out about opencast mining or about how communities can organise themselves. The material can be photocopied and used in a number of ways, for example to stimulate discussion, or, a couple of people could use it as a basis for making a presentation to the rest of the group. What follows is a précis of Mark's study – the full submission is very substantial!

How successful were UCAD in fighting against opencast mining in the Crossgates area? *Mark McCrorie*

Introduction
I chose to do my fourth year modern studies individual study on opencast mining in the Crossgates area. I chose this topic because I want to find out more about opencast mining (and my Aunt's involvement in the pressure group 'UCAD'). My aunt is the chairperson of UCAD (United Communities Against Drumcooper) so she will be a good source of information. I think it is an interesting topic to pick for a study but involves a lot of time and hard work. It has also given me quite an insight into people and their attitudes.

Aims
(Mark established nine aims which he then investigated.)

Methods
Method 1. Interviewing Maureen Cuthbertson (Chairperson of UCAD) and Alex Falconer (Euro MP for Mid Scotland and Fife). Doing this will give me information to help me in my study.

Method 2. To write to different people e.g., Dr. Gordon Brown MP, Alex Falconer MEP, Rachel Squire MP, SOAG., the Planning Department at Glenrothes and the Prime Minister, Mr John Major. These letters were written to get information from everyone listed and to get their views on opencast mining.

Method 3. Obtain newspaper cuttings and photographs all about opencast mining. Obtaining these two things will give people an idea how big an opencast site can be, what it looks like and what the newspapers think about the opencast.

Method 4. A questionnaire to find out what the people in the surrounding areas of Crossgates think of opencast mining. Doing this I will get the views of people in the areas of Crossgates, Mossgreen, Coaledge and Fordell.

What Mark found out
AIM 1. How coal is made?
Coal is one of the most natural types of fuel in the world. Coal is one of the most expensive fuels to obtain. Coal was made millions of years ago, before humans lived. The earth was covered with seas and forests. In the seas lived fish and other creatures. The forests were very hot with damp places. The trees and plants in the forests would grow very quickly because of the heat. After a few months they would die, fall to the ground and rot. More plants grew on top of the dead ones, but they would also die and rot; soon the ground would be covered with thick piles of dead trees and plants.

At times the surface of the earth would move. The forests would drop and water from the seas would come in and flood the forests. This would form swamps. More trees and plants would grow, die and fall into the water and then rot. The earth moved again, letting more water into the forests. The water would carry things like rocks, sand, clay and cover the dead plants, this would build up a lot of pressure which then squeezed everything together. The squeezing slowly made the pile of rock, sand, trees, plants etc. turn into coal. The process of creating coal takes thousands of years.

AIM 2. The differences between opencast mining and deep coal mining
Deep Mining
At one time deep mining was the main employer in the Fife area. Thousands of people worked in the mines from the age of 13 to the age of 65. Deep coal mining has been in operation for hundreds of years now. Villages usually sprang up around these mines. The housing was owned by the mine owner and he rented them to his workforce. Deep mines kept these villages and their families in employment for many years, as generation after generation became miners.

Opencast Mining
Opencast mining has been in Scotland since the 1940s. It was introduced at the end of the war to supplement deep mining, until the mines returned to normal, after the men returned from the war. It was not envisaged that it would become, what action groups like UCAD consider it to be, or the abhorrent industry it has mushroomed into. It is claimed that opencast mining is cheaper than deep mining coal. It is stated to be 35 to 40 pounds per ton of deep mining coal as opposed to 15 to 20 pounds per ton of opencast mining coal. Opencast coal is cheaper because very few people are employed to operate even the largest site. When deep mines were closed thousands of men were out of work. In contrast, only 12 to 20 of these people will be lucky to get a temporary job on the opencast site which is replacing deep mining. Opencast mining can be environmentally damaging and is being imposed upon many areas against their will, all over the UK. It is damaging for a number of reasons:

- Dust problems may arise through the handling and the amount of minerals, plants and vehicles over the working area. The amount of dust will vary according to the time of year and time of day.
- Moisture content in the soil, the temperature and the weather. The dust can travel up to two miles away from the site, so it affects people and animals very much. Noise on site arises through blasting, drilling, crushing, maintenance and operation of machines and also transportation of the minerals and associated materials. The reversing sounds of lorries and their beepers can be extremely intrusive for residents living near these sites.
- Heavy lorries on the road are also an intrusion in villages and communities. Heavy lorries driving past your door everyday, sometimes as many as 120

journeys a day, making a lot of noise as they pass, can be very upsetting and can destroy the enjoyment of your home.

- Ecology. Opencast destroys all the landscape meaning that the soil will be bug free for about 5 years after the opencast has stopped. That means no wildlife, no worms, spiders etc.. Nothing will grow on that land for up to 7 years after the opencast mining had stopped. Regeneration can take up to 15 years.
- Opencast mining deters tourism and makes it very hard for people to sell their houses if they need to move out of the area.

AIM 3. The pressure group UCAD

UCAD is a pressure or action group opposing opencast mining in the Crossgates area.. UCAD stands for United Communities Against Drumcooper. UCAD is made up of four communities – Mossgreen, Fordell, Crossgates and Coaledge. The name UCAD was formed because there were four communities involved in opposing the opencast application, so they were united together in their fight against this. Plus Kier Mining are right CADs for what they are doing! UCAD first began when people in the areas realised the imposition this development would have on their lives and their environment.

AIM 4. How UCAD went about stopping the opencast
A group of interested individuals agreed to form an 'Action/Pressure Group' and liaise with the local Community Council, who were also opposed to the proposed development. They applied to Dunfermline Council for recognition as an interested party to this application and also to be consulted on all aspects of it. A survey of the villages was undertaken by UCAD and the Community Council which showed clearly that the majority of residents were opposed to further opencast operations.

The villages have been surrounded by opencast sites for nearly 25 years on one side of the village or another. After this survey a detailed, lengthy document was produced by UCAD listing their objections to the application. This was submitted to the Planning Authority, along with a further detailed objection from the Community Council and all the letters of objection from individuals in the community.

AIM 5. Involvement of my aunt (Maureen Cuthbertson) in UCAD
My aunt is the chairperson and spokesperson. She also types up the reports and collects all the information. The others who are associated with the group support her in obtaining information, and collecting and delivering leaflets and surveys in the communities. Once this has been collected they also contribute with their views on the content and the layout of the presentations etc..

AIM 6. The pressure group SOAG
I have chosen to investigate SOAG, a pressure group which has much the same aims as UCAD, the group I have choosen as my main study. By studying SOAG it gives

me the chance to form other views on another action group. SOAG stands for Scottish Opencast Action Group. SOAG supports individuals and communities threatened by opencast mining. The aim of the group is:

"To develop a national network of groups and individuals committed to protecting and improving the quality of communities, living on coal, or near opencast sites. The association's objective being to protect the environment generally and wildlife and their habitats in particular, for the present and the future."

AIM 7. Help provided by the MEP

For my investigation, I wrote to Alex Falconer searching for information on opencast mining. I also wrote for an interview to record his views on this subject. He was very quick to reply to my letter and very willing to do an interview. This interview was held at his office in Inverkeithing. The interview contained topical questions about opencast mining and UCAD. In the interview I first asked Alex his views on the industry. He stated that he was totally against opencast mining and he qualified this by stating:

"Why close hundreds of mines, leaving thousands of people out of work, to save a few pounds on a ton of coal? The closures will raise the unemployment rate and force more people to turn to crime, in an effort to support their families."

Alex helped UCAD by writing letters to different people involved in opposing opencast mining and asking for information about fighting opencast.

AIM 8. Views of people in the surrounding areas

The people of the communities are very worried about the final decision for the opencast at Drumcooper Farm. Most of the residents bought their houses because they thought Crossgates, being a rural area, would be peaceful and quiet and a great environment to raise their children in. Some newer residents to the village, when they bought their houses, did not know about the pending application which had been ongoing for the last two years. There were many new residents I met on my travels around the village, who stated:

"We were never told about any opencast development when we bought our house".

I carried out a questionnaire in the area on opencast mining containing nine questions and those approached were extremely helpful and co-operative towards filling it in.

Mark McCrorie

In addition to this, Mark included a lot of other information in his study drawn from newspaper articles, submissions to the enquiry and various other sources. Many thanks to Mark for allowing us to use his material.

INTERNATIONAL ACTION

Introduction

Young people are often very concerned about global environmental issues such as rainforest destruction, but it is the sort of thing that individuals in a country such as our own, far way from any direct experience of these problems, can feel powerless to influence. A good way to help is to support environmental organisations such as WWF or development organisations like Save the Children, Oxfam, Action Aid, Christian Aid or the Red Cross, who are working generally to help communities, and help protect threatened areas. However, this may not give young people the sense of personal involvement they want with a particular issue, area or community.

One suggestion for young people to get involved is through building a relationship with a small-scale project working on the particular issue or locality that is of concern. Some of these projects are part of other international campaigns, others operate independently, perhaps with government and voluntary agency support. In this way, young people can choose to get involved in work with a community struggling to develop more sustainable food crops; wildlife conservation; irrigation; alternative employment; housing issues or work with communities suffering from the effects of war. Young people can then get to know exactly what problems are faced by aid organisations, the dilemmas and decisions, and see how their money and efforts get used. As Bud Simpkin at CEE puts it,

> "Young people involved in global youth work are often inspired to become more concerned for environmental issues in their home region and understand the links between the two – the local and the global."

In this book, we have tried to include some interesting examples of international action, including the work of Children's Aid Direct, Tools for Self Reliance, the Water 4 Life project, and in the next part of this section, the Caquetá Rainforest Campaign in Colombia and the work of Homeless International with the Sadak Chaap of Bombay. There are literally thousands of small and large projects like this around the world. Some are initiated by individuals, like the Caquetá Campaign, others grow from the support of community groups, local or national/international environmental organisations or youth groups. It is worthwhile for both young people and those who work with them to look out for local 'support groups' operating in the community, or build on links made through cultural and school exchanges, or the work of lively local individuals.

The youth worker or teacher role in this process can be to help individuals and groups of young people make contact with relevant projects, and help clarify what the aims of the project are; the ethics of the project; the reasons why young people might get involved, and how their enthusiasm can be translated into action. **REMEMBER, ALWAYS CHECK THE VALIDITY OF ANY PROJECT INDEPENDENTLY, IF YOU OR YOUR YOUTH GROUP INTEND TO SUPPORT ITS WORK.**

Sadak Chaap – the Bombay street children project

Background

In India, the Society for the Promotion of Area Resource Centres (SPARC), was formed back in 1984. It is what is called an NGO, shorthand for a non-governmental organisation. Since 1989, SPARC has been working with 'Sadak Chaap', a self-help organisation of street children which it helped to establish. Their organisation's name means, 'Stamp of the Street'. In the Indian city of Bombay, over 2,000 children live rough on the street. These children are mostly boys who are fiercely independent. Many earn their living by rag-picking, which is sorting out the recyclable or reusable waste from other refuse at the City tips. Out of necessity, the street children have got used to fending for themselves and supporting one another. But, the authorities in Bombay viewed the street children entirely as a problem; young criminals on the rampage.

What happened next.....

Sadak Chaap identified their own greatest need as being shelter. A safe place to eat and sleep and be with their friends without constant harassment or adult interference. With help from SPARC, they promoted themselves to Bombay Municipal Corporation as an, *"...asset to the City",* but in need of somewhere to erect shelters. This led to the subsidised leasing of two areas of land under footbridges to the Sadak Chaaps. Each area was big enough to build a shelter big enough to house 300 children. Adult help was provided for the shelters, but they are run on the terms dictated by the Sadak Chaaps: No Rules! It seems to be working, and now, SPARC together with the Sadak Chaaps, have established a set of longer term aims. Most seem to be about empowerment, rather than getting the Sadak Chaaps under 'control'!

Inside and outside the night shelter

Some of the Sadak Chaaps

How you can get involved
The initial three year project is estimated to cost £137,853. The organisers are looking for support from people in the UK and elsewhere. Homeless International is co-ordinating fund-raising and contact with the project from the UK. (Homeless International, Guildford House, 20 Queens Rd, Coventry CV1 3EG. Tel 01203 632802).

So, if you or your youth group wants to get directly involved, you can help them to:
- build more night shelters for the Sadak Chaaps and cover their running costs;
- develop educational and employment training opportunities for the street children;
- promote positive publicity about the Sadak Chaaps both in the national and international community about the problems they face living on the very edge of the society;
- develop inter-city street children networks, which will support children who travel between cities, or come to the city, to have a better basis for survival.

Caquetá Rainforest Amazonian Campaign (CRAC)
Help save the Colombian Rainforest
The story so far............
As we were writing this book, Rebecca Garcia, the daughter of Colombian eco-campaigner, Jenny James, wrote to Alan, with the following words,

> "I think your idea of youth groups 'adopting' Jenny's projects in Colombia is great.....Energy and original ideas is exactly what is needed and the forest is in great danger; 'waiting' to do something is _too late._"

So, exactly what is Jenny James about? We'd heard of her work in Eire, establishing and 'mothering' a commune in Burtonport, Co. Donegal for the last 20 years, which still exists today, but may be sold to raise funds for further purchases of the rainforest. John Kelly in the Irish Press, described her,

> "We should be grateful for the presence of the phenomenal Jenny James in our midst. And perhaps we should be aware of her criticism of the new society we are breeding, the 'grab all – give nothing' type of consumer."

Rebecca Garcia and a Colombian friend, Magdalena, in Burtonport, Eire

In 1987, feeling the encroachment of what she saw as European restrictions, Jenny, Ned, Bill, Fred and her three small daughters set off to Colombia in South America. By the mid-1990s they had established a 500 acre forest farm high in the mountains of Caquetá. In her own words from her regular newsletters to friends and potential friends throughout Europe,

> *"I left my country, England, 20 years ago, in disgust and forever, to see the 'natural world'. I have found the natural world and it is bleeding, screaming. I am over 50 years old, and I have maybe 15 years of active life left yet. At the moment I am travelling around the hot, flat lands of Southern Caquetá where the great rivers are half the size they were a few years ago, and where the only wild animals one sees are stuck on people's walls as trophies, and I am making vegetable gardens for anyone who will let me.*
>
> *I have an idea. I always hated giving to charity, thinking what horrible bureaucrat is going to waste this? Yet, financial aid is the most obvious, the most rapid and the most potent thing that the average concerned European can give. I want small green groups in Europe to adopt small local projects here, keeping in direct personal contact with problems and progress, completely bypassing all government interference and control, visiting whenever you like, receiving hospitality on our farms and with local communities who are trying to reverse the terrible tide of false 'development'; that is engulfing them."*

'What next' was a beginning, but by no means an end of Jenny's dream. Jenny stopped travelling and started organising in the Caquetá area. She worked closely with the Spanish speaking local farmers to try and encourage them to get organised and try to prevent further cutting down of forest trees, and to learn about alternative crops. The reality is not for the squeamish. It's a political situation, and one well removed from our cities and communities, road networks, satellite TVs and fast food stores.

And it continued.................

> *"The guerrilla force which rules the countryside in many parts of Colombia has banned, if you please, the Green Party. This is not as catastrophic as it sounds as they have not banned 'green work', in fact they are supporting it, doing their best to educate the country people on preservation, and have prohibited further*

forest cutting in key areas....This is Colombia, ergo, all things are possible, both excellent and atrocious.

We are starting to over produce deliberately, so that we can take fresh vegetables – unheard of in the countryside! – for sale, barter and giving away to neighbours, local settlements and villages. This is excellent propaganda, and the people are touchingly impressed and show an unexpected openness to being taught how to use such 'exotic' items as watercress and kale.....Having coped (after just one year on this farm) with our own food needs, we are now branching out into tree-seeding, that is, nurseries for baby trees which we will offer free to anyone willing to replant. This is only symbolic because of the scale we are operating on – but we can only be as big as we are!"

Gradually, Jenny and her European farmer friends began to understand how the world around them actually worked. The FARC, (the Communist guerrilla force) is perhaps surprisingly to us, *"...disciplined, coherent and highly principled."* It acts as a mix of local bobby and the marriage guidance service, sorting out domestic disputes and curbing drunkenness when it turns to violence. The next letter from Jenny contained a stark reminder of cultural differences operating in Colombia.

"This 'Green' letter comes to you edged thickly in black. I have just received the news that my friend and colleague in the tiny emerging green movement of SE Colombia, Luis Erasmo Arenas Hurtado has been murdered. Luis was 62 years old, strong and healthy. Ironically for me, he was Conservative, an ex-police officer, a straight, determined, highly educated man. His crime: efficiency in leadership of green community work in the little river port of Milan, Caquetá, and the massive surrounding coca-growing area. Three hours before his death he wrote to me.......(saying) he was delighted to hear that members of the Irish Green Party might want to visit and offered his home 'unconditionally' to anyone who comes. (This offer remains open with his family).....At 8.15 p.m. an unknown man (a 'sicario' – a hired killer) entered the room with a machine gun and filled Luis with 19 bullets. He died instantly."

So why are we communicating all this to a 'green' European audience? Because the death of Luis is much bigger than Luis, great as he was. ......We must make sure that those who saw the murder as the way to create SILENCE, find that what they have brought about is the most unholy NOISE."

Luis's brother-in-law joined in the fight and called on the international green community to condemn the killing as a political crime, and furthermore pointed specifically to the fact that Luis had been spurred to action by the cocaine traffickers who were 'pitilessly' deforesting the jungle, causing rivers to dry up and filling the countryside with the stench of desolation and death.

But, even in the wake of Luis's murder, Jenny continued her struggle. She immediately leapt into action when her closest neighbour, Ricardo, said he was going to sell his 500 acres of land for £6,000, even though Jenny's family had first option on it at £4,000. After another fervent plea in her green letter to supporters, there was good news!

And the struggle.......still continues

This last letter really did produce the 'goods'. By March 1996 Jenny was able to write:

> "Two wonderful unknown friends in England, Mr and Mrs Bullough, immediately sent £4,000 for the farm, and after much hassle with Ricardo, our neighbour, we have finally come to an agreement whereby he keeps the part of his land already opened and sells us every inch where there are trees – this includes a huge mountainside above us where you can actually see the damp mist and clouds forming just before it rains on us. To Mary and Colin Bullough, 'thank you' is a weak word for what we feel."

Jenny also continues to receive smaller donations of money and seeds from other supporters, including Unwin's and Fothergill's in the UK and more recently seven kilos of seeds from the 'Known-you' seed company in Taiwan. And she struck up a friendship with Cliomedes, Camilo and Roberto, in nearby Chorreras, who with a donation from Jenny's supporters of one million pesos, look set to become the environmental enablers for developing new forms of agricultural practice in the region. Jenny has also helped Camilo bring the 'green' message to the local school he runs, where they now have a vegetable garden and a growing resource collection of environmental materials. Meanwhile, Ricardo has even started his own vegetable garden using Jenny's seeds, so the 'word' is spreading!

There's still plenty to do, and Jenny and her family and friends in Colombia, and Rebecca, co-ordinating the campaign from Ireland would be delighted to hear from any groups of youth organisations who would like to find out more about CRAC and possibly get involved.

All questions, queries, doubts, suggestions, please send to:
Jenny James, El Movimento Verde, Apartado Aéreo 895, Neiva, Huila, Colombia, South America, or, her daughter, Rebecca Garcia, An Droichead Beo, Burtonport, Co. Donegal, Eire.

To help, Jenny suggests that you can do any or all of the following things:
1. Jenny is always pleased to hear from you in a letter. She will translate what you say for the local people. You can also ask to receive a copy of Jenny's regular newsletters.
2. Financial aid, however small. The smallest amount of European money goes a long way here. All projects and use of money can be checked by direct contact, and would in any case be under constant vigilance by use here.
3. The campaign is also always looking for more seeds for vegetables and further information on how they may best be grown in the Colombian situation. Jenny and her group are learning, by trial and error!
4. Visits from anyone from Europe are always welcomed, from anyone who is willing to come and see and touch the problem, and talk to the people here.

WATER 4 LIFE PROJECT
Emmanuel Youth Project, London, building water tanks and a dam for the Kola people in Kenya

Background

Whilst over 70 per cent of our planet is covered in water, many communities do not have clean water for drinking and sanitation. Education and training in water use, storage, hygiene issues, pollution control, sewage treatment, and agricultural use for irrigation are all essential parts of the 'answers' to water related problems. This is an account of a youth work initiative which enabled self-help solutions to combat water shortage.

The Kola district of Kenya is one the areas of Kenya worst affected by drought and poor water supplies. Many of the local people have to walk up to eight miles to collect water from river beds and water holes which is not really fit to drink. The result is a vicious circle of famine, poverty, reduced food production and for some even death. In the Forest Gate area of London, staff and members of the Emmanuel Youth Project (EYP) have made a significant to contribution to help change the situation for a substantial number of the Kola shambas (farms). The idea behind the project arose from Tracey Hemmerdinger, the senior youth worker. She had been involved in a similar project as a team member when she was a teenager. In 1993 she took a holiday in Kenya and visited Kola. As a result of that visit, she realised that Water 4 Life, *"...was not only a possibility, but for the villagers of Kola, an essential project."*

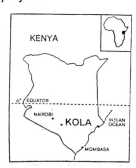

Emmanuel Youth Project is a detached youth work project, and part of Emmanuel Church. At the time of writing it has two full time workers, a part time worker seconded from Newham Youth Service, a part time administrator and several volunteers. The focus of the work is on,

> *"Developing relationships and encouraging participation particularly with those who are vulnerable or at risk....youth workers go out and meet young people on their own territory, streets, parks, arcades, cafes, playgrounds or even homes."*

The following is an extract from the appeal letter entitled 'Nothing comes for free', in which the young people who formed the Water 4 Life team explain their aims.

Nothing comes for free

We don't want 'nothing' and we're not looking for your help 'for free'. We are a group of young people aged between 16 and 21 from Forest Gate, East London. Between us we share many cultures, backgrounds and experiences. Some of us have been homeless, some refugees, some unemployed, some in trouble (until now) and some low achievers (until now).

We want to help a village community in Kola, Kenya. By working together with the villagers we will build 20 water tanks, 15 roofs for houses (to collect water for the tanks) and a sub-surface dam. These can ensure a year round supply of clean water which will improve food production and health, so enhancing the quality of life for the whole village.

This doesn't happen for free. The villagers are providing 10% of the cost of materials (reduced from 20%) because of drought and famine. We have to pay too: 50% of our air fare and three weeks of hard work, blood, sweat and tears.

By supporting our work you have the opportunity to make a lasting impact on two communities in one go. The villagers will have clean water. We will live and work in a different culture and learn new skills. We will change our own lives and those of others, thereby improving our ability to contribute to our community.

'Nothing comes for free'. Please help us turn 'nothing' into something of lasting value.

Thanks for your time

The Water 4 Life team
N.B. the attached leaflet sets out our plans.

The EYP team members

Project funding and preparation

The elements of the planning and preparation for the trip to Kenya fell into distinct phases.

1. The screening of a slide show about the plight of the Kola villagers. This meeting generated the interest and enthusiasm amongst the young people involved with Emmanuel.

2. The various phases of fund-raising at national and local levels, included sending over 600 letters to potential sponsors, including the Prince's Trust, Barclays and Hambros banks, Landrover, the Royal Victoria Dock, Rank Xerox and the British High Commission in Nairobi. Use was made both of a list of previous donors to the Harambee 1985 project which Tracey had been a part of and the Directory of Grant Making Trusts. Local fund-raising events ranged from a quiz night hosted by Tony Anstis from the BBC, through sponsored slims, 2,000 canoe rolls, a summer fair, and two friends of the team, Peter and Andrew, walking from the lowest point in Britain (a mine in Yorkshire) to the highest point (the top of Ben Nevis) in under 24 hours. In all they raised over £45,000.

3. Four in-depth training sessions for all the team members to build team skills, identify specialist team skills required, including building skills, catering and to learn about Kenyan culture and customs. This raised interesting questions about what team members felt was the sexist nature of Kenyan society which insists that women keep their bodies covered even when doing hard physical work. In addition, there were special courses for individual team members on book-keeping, photography, motor vehicle maintenance, first aid and tropical medicine. From the UK there were 16 members of the eventual EYP Water 4 Life team, including four staff. Clive Wells, the 17th, was the team's contact in Nairobi, and on writing the report, the group felt that he should be included as a team member, since the entire venture would have been virtually impossible without him.
   Each person was a member of one or more work groups which were: *fund-raising, catering, publicity, photography, water, transport, grants, report editing, medicine and hygiene.* The work groups were organised in such a way that there were males and females in each group; groups possessed strength and resilience, and that team members would get on together.

4. A reconnaissance trip to the Kola area to ensure that everything was prepared and that contacts were properly established. Joshua Mukusya established the Utooni Development Project back in 1978 and was involved with all the three Harambee projects. (Harambee means literally 'pulling together'). Especial emphasis was placed on ensuring that the site locations for the water tanks was well planned.

5. The trip itself.

EYP in Kola, Kenya

This account you are reading is based on the EYP's own report of their trip. The team members agreed in advance to keep a diary which everyone contributed to. The following offers a unique glimpse into their trip to Kenya. It particularly illustrates the commitment of the team members and the skills and confidence which they gained as a result of the project. For the local Kola residents, the final project provided 25 water tanks, 15 roofs, 2 sub-surface dams and I barrage (a smaller water dam designed to slow the flow of water).

Dam and tank building in Kola

Extracts from the diary reports:

(of the journey via Sofia in Bulgaria)
"We discovered that nine of our tickets had the wrong departure date on them, but Niall came to the rescue. Tracey meantime panicked......The flight so far has been awful. Ayo cannot return home!! Her return ticket from Nairobi to Sofia was taken out by mistake: luckily for her this was spotted at Sofia (unlucky for the rest of us!)."

"I'm surprised that we're still alive. The food if you can call it that was indescribable, cardboard chicken, bland vegetables and some other muck. It got to the point where we were pretending to be asleep to avoid the food (on the plane). The no-smoking section was obviously full of smokers, so waking up at 5 am in thick smoke was wonderful. We had to stop in Cairo, spending over one hour in the plane without air conditioning."

(after arriving in Kola)
"The welcoming ceremony was amazing, there were lots of long speeches, dancing, singing and delicious food. Group members mingled with the villagers and a great time was had by all. The Health Centre where we would be staying was a lot better than people had been expecting. The group has its own fan club – the local children who come and stand by the fence to watch us for hours and hours. We are their entertainment."

(work begins)
"We were supposed to start working on three tanks today, but unfortunately when Joshua arrived at 7.30 pm he told us there had been a death last night and we couldn't start work in the area. We got to the dam before 8 am to find very few people – it appears that Kenyans have a problem with Monday mornings too! This also reminds you that people working on the dam are also tending their shambas before and after work."

Passing cement down the line

"The women stand in a loop with the cement at one end and the dam at the other, Small trays like prospecting pans, are filled and passed down the line to empty in the dam. I can't describe the feeling I have seeing the co-operation, joy and achievement of the people......I've no doubt the hard work is creating indelible lines in our memories!"

"Today was the second day of the tanks. Tired is a word that has lost any meaning at the moment. (we've all never worked so hard)."

"Turned out to be a rather hectic day. It was Mustafa's birthday and he was taken breakfast in bed. We also had a surprise for him, but this was not too much of a success as the day was not a happy one for him. Fathia and Simon had to deal with a girl in her early teens who had been brought to the clinic next door. After being unable to find a doctor in the area willing to treat her and finding her extremely ill, they were told that the baby she was carrying was dead. her condition worsened and she fell unconscious. Simon drove to the nearest hospital with Mustafa, Rhoda and the girl and her parents. Sadly, the girl died before reaching the hospital. Many people were obviously shocked and distressed."

".....such happy faces"

"While we were at one of the houses painting a tank, we were found by a group of children.....who started singing and dancing...it was really nice to see such happy faces."

"This is our last day in Kola. We didn't work. The leaving party was very good.....It made me realise how much I am going to miss this place. During the three weeks we argued, worked and laughed, but it was something different. I think we will appreciate it more when we are in London and are able to reflect on our time here......I would like to say I had a great time and say thank you to the leaders, especially Tracey. She had lots to put up with."

Afterwords

Here are a selection of comments from the team members once they had left the Kola area of Kenya.

"It was annoying to watch the local women doing most of the work while the men watched."

"Seeing the difficulties the villagers have to deal with made me realise how lucky I am."

"It was difficult coping with the cultural differences at times, but both our group and the Kenyan villagers learnt a lot about each others way of living."

"When can we do it all again?"

For further information about the project in Kenya, contact:
Emmanuel Youth Project
Emmanuel Church
Romford Rd
Forest Gate
London E7 8BD
Tel: 0181 519 5922

ENVIRONMENTAL NETWORKING
Communications of the future
The Internet is fast becoming the environmental network of the present (not the future anymore!). And in many cases it is young people who have got themselves connected and are teaching the adults in their lives, whether it is parents, teachers or youth leaders, how to get the greatest benefit from visiting worldwide sites. Many environmental and youth work agencies are developing Web sites and Conference facilities, where visitors through the Internet can browse, download material, or leave messages. The number is growing all the time and includes many of the major organisations as well as the fringe organisations. RSPB, Friends of the Earth, The Land is Ours, Greenpeace, the Third Battle of Newbury, the World Wide Fund for Nature and the Green Generation Service are all online. Many of the sites also offer useful links to other sites with similar aims.

Look out also for sites which can link you to a whole variety of environmental organisations. These include: GreenNet, ENDS Environmental Links and Environlink. We are not reprinting a long list of Web site addresses, since they are continually changing as users change server networks, but the following two examples help to give a flavour of what is being developed.

Green Generation Service
The Green Generation Service is being established as a multilingual, environmental facility on the Internet, specifically aimed at children and young people and those who work with them. Why, you might ask, the Internet? Despite the fact that only a few youth organisations and schools really understand it yet in Europe or in many other parts of the world, it is undoubtedly the medium which most fascinates young minds. Shame that these authors – despite being 'online' for the past few months – are among the uninitiated! On the other hand, many parents have faced big phone bills as their teenager goes surfing the Web on a worldwide search for information and international contacts. Used well as a tool, it opens up a host of extraordinary possibilities. As an example, indigenous people the world over already have a wonderful network, and are helping one another around the globe, by means of the Web.

Susan Cerezo, who is based in France, has worked for the past few years through the small, Green Hope Association, trying to inform and encourage young people to get involved in environmental issues and activities. Basically the organisation is trying to:
- share environmental information aimed at young people on a worldwide basis;
- encourage young people to contact one another and join together in engaging in imaginative environmental projects;
- use the online services of the worldwide web to motivate young people, reduce isolation and work together at a global level.

On one side there are glorious projects being tried out, imaginative ideas, experiences of all sorts undertaken by schools, youth groups, children on their own around the world. On the other, the majority of motivated children around the world feel alone, uninformed, unguided, absolutely lost. They have no idea others are doing anything, that children have a big role to play, and that there is a lot of hope.

The Green Generation Service is designed to give them that hope, as little by little they get online. To break through a few more barriers, they will be working in four different languages.

The work of setting this service up is being done in partnership with youth organisations and schools worldwide. Each one is invited to make a particular contribution and to take responsibility for a particular area of activity. This is a real and vital form of networking at its most practical. Relevant and worthwhile information is collated, and with some help from the central organisers, the Internet and any other means is used to sort this information into useful 'packages' and to make it accessible. The process entails active participation from everyone involved – in essence, everyone is learning about the environmental information, how to set it up on the Web, and then keep it alive and up to date.

The process has started, but there is a long road still ahead. It should lead to some fascinating collaborations, across national boundaries and cultures, and environmental, technological and language constraints which will provide a unique and valuable experience for the young people involved.

The story so far...
The initial list of themes, and an introduction to the project is up on the Web already, on pages generously hosted by the University College of Aberystwyth, University of Wales. The Internet address is:
http://www.aber.ac.uk/~grewww/index.html

The initial youth groups and schools involved cover a very varied range of ages and experience. Some are very Internet-experienced; others are at the beginning, taking their first faltering steps. The Green Generation Service is especially looking for some youth organisations and schools who have a reasonable level of Internet knowledge. Some children, in the US particularly, have been using this technology for some years already.

Susan Cerezo told us,
> "What we are looking for is basically: youth groups and schools, youth workers and teachers who not only care very much about the planet, but who can encourage young people to take positive action...They also have to see the benefits of this kind of technology, and have the Internet at their disposal. Unfortunately, those things don't always come together! We are looking for adults who love communicating, collaborating with others, and who want young people to think and act independently.
>
> In a few years time this technology will be common currency among our young. We hope it will largely be THEY who will be running their Service. Green Generation is not meant to be static. It will develop, grow and change whenever necessary. We are starting with a simple, easy to use base. We hope that growing out from there in endless branches and sub-sections, it will link up with all that is exciting and inspiring, eventually including all parts of the world."

At a very personal level, Susan explained to us why she saw the Internet as the medium for the future,

> "It is very difficult to imagine how it works before really experiencing it, and I had no clear picture of how it worked. Having been online and getting used to it for some months, I am absolutely convinced that we have a remarkable tool here. There are the most wonderful projects...schools and youth groups, sometimes award winning activities, already on the Web itself. But it needs hours of 'surfing' to find them. They are written about in all sorts of far distant corners, and one has to be very persistent to find them. Our service will be there for young people and the adults who work with them to link into what is online, as well as talking about projects and ideas that are not to be found online."

Green Hope is an entirely voluntary organisation. France Telecom has recently offered them a partnership, paying for their phone and Internet bills, and the free page space from Aberystwyth has been an enormous help in getting them started.

Green Hope and the Green Generation Service would be very happy to hear from anyone interested: youth groups, schools, play centres, local community environmental initiatives, in fact, anyone who would like to take part. Specifically they would like to receive:

- any ideas and experiences of youth action that they can write about and share on the Web;
- offers of help with translations, especially in German and Spanish...we can cope with French etc.

By the time you are reading this in the book, the network should have developed still further!

Susan Cerezo,
Association Green Hope,
692 Chemin de Clodolio,
06790 Aspremont,
France
Tel/fax: +33 93 0408 03 09 (to be checked as we are in for new numbers again soon) e-mail: gr.hope@mail.micronet.fr

The World Wide Fund for Nature (WWF)

This is one of the many environmental organisations that are making extensive use of the Internet. A recent example of this is a National Scholarship Scheme for Science and the Environment. This is a partnership project between WWF-UK, NCVQ and Tioxide Europe Ltd., a leading international manufacturer of titanium dioxide – the white pigment used in most of our paints, plastics and papers.

This exciting project offers opportunities for GNVQ Science students to develop an environmental dimension to their mainstream GNVQ assignments and coursework. As part of the project young people get direct involved with the environmental and sustainability issues relating to the white pigment manufacturing industry and personnel at Tioxide. Consequently, young people gain a valuable insight into the difficulties involved in making decisions concerning industry and the environment. (See the 'Useful Addresses' at the back of the book for their contact details).

CHILDREN IN WAR
Is this an environmental issue?
When the Council for Environmental Education first talked with Alan and Howie about compiling this book, one thing became apparent early on. Everyone agreed that positive responses to environmental concerns must range a lot wider than, 'plant a tree and recycle another can', important though these are.

In recent years a number of new agencies in the UK have become involved in providing direct aid in war-torn areas throughout the world to children, young people and communities. War Child, the Serious Road Trip, Action Aid and the organisation, Feed the Children, now called Children's Aid Direct are amongst the best known. They have now joined Oxfam, Save the Children and the International Red Cross as major providers of aid in damaged communities.

Tragically, each new day brings news bulletins with fresh tales of death and extreme hardship and suffering; the consequence of war, drought, flooding, or any other calamity. The effects of man made and natural catastrophes are often the most profound forms of environmental disaster. For youth leaders, playworkers and others who work in social education networks it is hard to know how to involve young people in a practical and helpful way. The following material comes from Children's Aid Direct, whose Executive Director, David Grubb, felt that inclusion in this book on *Youth Action and the Environment* was entirely appropriate.

Children's Aid Direct in action
This organisation is one of the fastest growing and most dynamic direct aid organisation working from the UK. They have developed local networks of support and DARTs – Direct Action Response Teams, which have worked in many countries throughout the world, including Rwanda, Bosnia, Georgia, Croatia, Azerbaijan, Northern Iraq, Albania, North Korea, Sierra Leone, Kusovo and Haiti. At the time of writing, after six years existence, they have grown in size to a point where they have now delivered over £40 million worth of aid that includes:
- food
- clothing
- hygiene
- medical supplies and 'baby boxes'
- footwear,
- toys and play equipment,
- school equipment and materials, and
- seeds for growing new crops.

They describe themselves as a 'People to People' charity. Their local field co-ordinators ensure that the aid can get to the people in the greatest need in the particular country. In addition, they supply skills enabling healthcare, agriculture and community regeneration. Central to this is their hard work building up local self-help initiatives in order that distribution chains operate fairly and support ways in which people can create sustainable futures. When tragedy strikes, they are equipped to take action fast, which is often the only way to save lives. Especial emphasis is placed upon ensuring that:

- food offers appropriate nutrition for each child and their carer;
- immediate first aid is made available as required;
- shelter and water requirements are catered for as adequately as possible;
- training in medical aid and preventative programmes are established in the local communities;
- education programmes are established/re-established.

The above list combines both immediate, short term and medium term objectives.

"It's been eight months since I was found and brought to the transit centre run by Children's Aid Direct. They take good care of us; we even go to school. They have tracing teams who try to find our families. My best friend left last week. I was happy for her but I miss her."

"My parents were killed but I have a brother. They haven't found him yet. I know they are trying. I'm happy to be here, They are nice, they care."
Esperance, age 8, Taba Transit Centre, Rwanda.

"Children always suffer the most in war. Air raids and sheliing are not for children. We get caught up in it. It's the older people who do the fighting, you know."
Dubrovka Milovish, 14 years, refugees in the republic of Sprksa.

The Work continues

David Grubb says that the work of the organisation is aimed at helping children and young people to move from, *"...survival to revival"*. He adds that, *"Children are the most needy and most vulnerable...the needs of children and the response of their carers to these needs are the catalyst of recovery for the entire community."* Children's Aid Direct estimate that in 1980, six million children were affected by war. This figure had escalated to 24 million in 1996, and by the end of the century that figure is likely to be 31 million.

The work focuses on the need to be sensitive to local circumstances and to build and reinforce local skills and services, rather than replacing or disempowering them. Another central aspect of the work is to protect the childhood of young people who are caught up in conflicts or the aftermath of war.

Funding

The financial wherewithal for Children's Aid Direct comes from individuals, local community groups, companies and statutory donors. For instance:

Since 1991 over 700,000 pairs of children's shoes have been distributed by the organisation. These have been donated by customers at many of the Clarks Shoe shops up and down the country, and at the Clarks Village in Street, Somerset where they are now aiming to collect a further 100,000 pairs of shoes per year.

Local youth clubs and schools regularly organise sponsorship and fund-raising events for Children's Aid Direct. These have included:
- *challenge events such as: bicycle rides, mountain climbs, haircuts, fasts and parachute jumps;*
- *fund-raising events such as: lunches, dances and discos, jumble and bring-and-buy sales and street collections.*

Children's Aid Direct is a flexible and dynamic organisation. They are keen that young people in the UK and elsewhere get involved in the future of their work. Raising funds is a part of that involvement, but 'spreading the word' about the crisis situation faced by young people around the world is another very important aspect. Many facets of their work have been written up in field work reports and they have a publication entitled, *A Children in War Campaign Pack,* price £6, including post and packing. This includes a *War Report* performance script and a 'practical response' booklet which, in David Grubb's words, *"Makes the situation real."*

To find out more about their work and to get involved:
Children's Aid Direct,
82 Caversham Road,
Reading,
Berkshire RG1 8AE
Tel 01734 584000

LANDGRAB
Bringing homelessness to your own doorstep: An activity for you to try in your own area

The background
Since 1992, Homeless International have been organising this activity as both a consciousness-raising and fund-raising event. The activity involves building a temporary shelter on a piece of land 'grabbed' for the day/night.

The **consciousness bit:** throughout the world there are many millions of people with no proper home. They live on the street, in temporary shelters, slums and inadequate accommodation. Unhealthy, overcrowded and lacking in any basic amenities for sanitation, cooking, water supply or hygiene, this is among the most extreme example of environmental deprivation. There is also a problem which is social and political. People in nearly every part of the world are denied access for land on which to live, or even roam through (see Land Access section).

In the UK, squatting, temporary shelters and hostels, living in tipis, benders, vehicles and caravans, are all symptoms of homelessness and lack of land access for thousands of individuals and families. (see section on alternative Lifestyles). In many cases it is as much a rural problem as an urban one, as young people either can't afford local accommodation in the communities in which they were brought up, or cannot find employment to financially sustain them. Homelessness can affect just about any section of society, and is a condition which further marginalises and excludes people who are poor and in need of support, rather than rejection.

One Landgrab, WHAT, at Crystal Palace, taking shape

This activity can't make the problem go away, but it should help to raise awareness of how difficult it is to survive outside without a secure form of accommodation.

The **fund-raising bit:** Homeless International, Guildford House, 20 Queens Rd, Coventry CV1 3EG (Tel 01203 632802) have been using the activity to raise funds every year since 1992. The Landgrab event takes place each June, but it can be organised locally at any time of the year. It is an ideal opportunity to raise money in sponsorship and to involve the local media in publicising the event itself and the issues around access to land and shelter, and the right to build, which it raises.

Organising the event

Since the idea is to raise funds for Homeless International or another local organisation working with homeless people, squatters, Travellers or whatever, make sure you allow enough time to publicise the event and get the maximum media coverage. A youth club, school or environmental organisation can be the ideal base for putting on the event.

What you need. The usual format for a Landgrab event, is that each team either uses waste material or has a maximum team budget of £20 for materials to build the temporary shelter. Depending upon the local politics of your organisation, the land can be literally 'grabbed' – a disused site or a public space such as a corner of a car park or a playing field, or part of your organisation's land.

To participate in a Homeless International Landgrab, you require:
- *One or more teams of enthusiastic and creative participants.*
- *Assorted waste and gleaned building materials (used cans, plastic, cardboard, metal, and imagination applied liberally).*
- *Each team of at least five members designs and builds their temporary home on their Landgrab area. They then test the quality of the construction by spending the night in it!*
- *All the team members persuade friends, relatives and colleagues to sponsor their intrepid and creative endeavour.*
- *We'd add that for use with youth groups, each team should have at least some adult advice available, and during the sleep-out, there should be adequate adult supervision to avoid potential hazards and dangers, for instance from drunks, unwarranted hassle from the police or local authority personnel.*

Outcomes

Even one night in a temporary shelter brings home the realities of not having somewhere secure and dry to live. It also demonstrates in a graphic way, how much most of us rely on facilities that many people in the world don't have. Comments from previous 'Landgrabbers' include:

"We were excited, tired, fed up; all those things during the one night." John.
"We're pretty confident we can put up something waterproof. Whether it would pass the building regulations is quite another matter!" Maureen.
"Our shelter was somewhat improved on last year's attempt to build a water tight shelter out of cardboard boxes! So much fun was had by all." Lorraine.

The money raised by Landgrab events has been used by Homeless International to provide funds for self-help housing and impoverished communities in Asia, Africa, Latin America and the Caribbean.

Of course there are other organisations working on behalf of the homeless which this activity, or something similar such as a 'sleep-out', could also be used to support, including organisations working with homeless people in the UK, such as Shelter and Crisis.

GLOBAL CONNECTIONS
Is it youth work?

Cultural exchanges of information and people are a vital element in environmental education. In 1996, the National Youth Agency published *Changing the World: a Directory of Global Youth Work Resources* by Marianne Flood and Doug Bourn. Earlier in the same year the British American Arts Association brought out Jennifer Williams' *Across the Street Around the World: a Handbook for Cultural Exchange*, and the Commonwealth Youth Exchange Council organised *Mind Your World* conference. There's obviously something stirring out there on the international youth work stage!

The first two are publications about making connections and getting things started. Resources including information, lists of publications, videos etc., and contacts for youth exchanges and volunteering are an invaluable first step towards young people getting involved in international activities.

One of the major challenges today is how to manage and promote diversity as a positive force, so that the recently released energies of ethnic identification and solidarity serve as catalysts for creativity rather than destruction, for concord rather than division.

Raj Isar, UNESCO

from Across the Street Across the World

In this book we are not going to repeat the information contained in these and other useful resources; rather this is a signpost towards some of what is waiting to be discovered. In the next part of this section, we are offering:
- some information about some of the resources available;
- a couple of 'taster' excerpts from existing publications,
- two examples from the field: the Youth of Bath's *Ethical Shopping Guide* and Jennifer Hurd's report on the *Mind Your World* event.

Especial thanks for providing this information go to Jennifer Williams, who is the founder of the British American Arts Association, Doug Bourn, who is Director of the Development Education Association, Jennifer Hurd a participant in the *Mind Your World* conference and Libby, Marg and Bud at the CEE.

Across the Street Across the World

> *"Recent years have seen a dramatic growth in the recognition of diversity in modern societies. Advances in communication technology, the opening of previously closed borders, and increased migration of peoples have all contributed. The need for deeper understanding across religious, ethnic, national and other barriers – real and imagined – has never been greater."*

In many ways the above is a good description of the framework for all environmental work with young people. Jennifer's book describes arts and cultural exchanges, but many of the processes with regard to planning and evaluation are vital for any youth group working on an environmental project, if it involves a specific movement of bodies from one country to another. We felt that it is reasonable to see **all** cultural youth exchanges as having potential for improving the global environment. Understanding, tolerance and an exchange of information and ideas are essential steps towards a sustainable global community.

The **planning section** suggests that workers should,
"ask themselves:
- *Why is contact/dialogue being sought in the first place?*
- *Why is an exchange the appropriate programming choice?*
- *What can an exchange offer as opposed to other alternatives?*
- *What are the contexts in which the exchange will occur?*
- *What are the primary motives for organisers and participants?*
- *What short and long term benefits are expected for each party in the collaboration?*
- *Is it a project that could involve new partners?*
- *What measures are used to evaluate different benefits?*
- *What are potential opportunities and dangers for the participants?"*

In her **evaluation section** she suggests using,
"a questionnaire asking:
- *Was the work presented in an understandable context?*
- *Were there problems with any part of the exchange?*
- *Did the project reach its target audience?*
- *Did the exchange bring together different communities?*
- *Were each of the participants sufficiently involved?*
- *Is there a possibility of continuing contact with the visitors?*
- *Did the funders understand the goals and results of the exchange?*
- *Did the visit contribute to sustaining the discussion about diversity?"*

At the back of the book are two very useful, hands-on sections. The first is a selection of case studies from exchanges from around the world. The second is the contacts lists which includes: arts councils, exchange organisations; information organisations, and networks throughout Europe and the rest of the world.

A short excerpt from one of the case studies: *A Journey to Serendipity*, admirably captures the spirit and enthusiasm of a successful cultural exchange. This one involved the Crucible Youth Theatre from Sheffield visiting Sri Lanka – a very different environmental experience!

> *"The core of our work centred around exploration of the central theme of the exchange: how does our culture shape our perception of our world? We arrived at the Institute of Aesthetic Studies, a sprawling complex encased by jungle...somewhere between Colombo and Ratnapura. We never did discover exactly where; it didn't seem to matter too much, to be 'here' – 'now' was enough. We worked together on an open stage. Days started early, fuelled on a breakfast of rice and curry. Slowly we began to exchange our ideas, feelings and responses as we built bridges through and around conventional language. Gradually a piece of theatre began to emerge from our enquiry, shaped by our journey, by our being there together.*
>
> *Word of mouth alone conjured an audience from the darkness. They sat waiting on grassed terracing before the stage. Fireflies pulsed points of light around their heads, our house lights the moon. All the conventions of Western theatre were missing – it was wonderful! To illuminate the play a large fire of powder wood and coconut torches blazed. The flames breathed life into the space. No need for 'calls' or 'bells' – one could feel the moment of performance approaching. It arrived and we'd begun, no one seemed to dictate this moment. It just happened. The drama unfolded and a story was told."*
> Brian Jones, Director, Crucible Youth Theatre, Sheffield.

The British American Arts Association is based at 116 Commercial Street, London E1 6NF. Tel. 0171 247 5385.

Global Youth Work

The Development Education Association describes itself as aiming, *"...to bring about local awareness of global issues..."* The DEA's work has been very influential in supporting youth workers and others involved in promoting development education, which is defined in their report *A World of Difference* (1995) as,

> *"...educational methods and outlooks concerned with tackling global inequalities and giving people the knowledge and skills to take action and secure change."*

From that same report, Doug Bourn and his co-author, Ann McCollum, made some interesting observations about environmental youth work and development education work.
They said,

> *"There are three ways in which this concern [for environmental issues] can be translated into action: through action taken by environmental organisations, action by young people themselves and finally the youth work approach. They are not mutually exclusive, but as with development education, they raise issues of whose agenda young people are working to."*

The report then goes on to explain that most youth sections of environmental organisations are predominantly focused on conservation and are seen as being white and middle class. And, interestingly, it described the closure of Earth Action, the youth section of Friends of the Earth, which in 1993 closed through financial cutbacks and a conflict and tension between the demands of the youth section and the parent body.

A World of Difference also touches on the perhaps controversial question of how acceptable direct action by young people through organisations like Earth First! and Reclaim the Streets is, and how it relates to the youth work approach, embodied in publications like the CEE EARTHworks (1990 and 1992) book and the follow-up three year training programme. Hopefully, this book you are now reading takes up the challenge. Youth workers should be able to ensure that youth work offers young people a number of routes to empowerment, including taking their own direct action. This seems to be embody the spirit of the CEE approach which sees participation, empowerment and equality of opportunity as good practice in environmental youth work.

The Changing the World (1996) directory from the NYA/DEA provides some of the much needed, international information about organisations and resources available to youth workers and similar. The range of entries is sometimes a little strange, lumping the National Youth Agency together in a list with Youth Hostels Association and the International Broadcasting Trust. The resources list is more coherent, describing books, packs, videos, audio tapes and games which have some global elements, including useful references to well-loved resources such as: the Trading Game (1982), from Christian Aid, which is described as, "...a lively game which will help the participants understand the international trading system."

Doug Bourn also supplied us with a project report from the innovative development education project in Bath, entitled, Communication Breakdown (1994). It was aimed at youth workers involved in social education with young people, who have an interest in exploring international, environmental development initiatives. The original report was published by the Bath Development Education Centre. The following is based on that report, written by Paul Adams, Emma Cray and Paddy Nesbett and illustrated by Tim Benton, plus material from CEE's EARTHlines 3 and Young People Now (issue no 14, August 1993).

Doug Bourn and the Development Education Association are based at Third Floor, 29-31 Cowper Street, London EC2A 4AP. Tel. 0171 490 8108.

Ethical Shopping Guide

The Youth of Bath (wryly called the YOBs in their acronym!) are a group of young people who have worked together, on and off, for nearly five years in the south-west of England. Back in 1994, they described their focus as being to, "...explore and raise awareness of development education issues." Their first project was very much an active one. They researched and produced an 'ethical shopping guide' to the city of Bath. We thought that it might serve as a useful example, an ideas exchange, if you like, for other groups. Entitled Shopping with Awareness, it looked at:

- recycling policies of companies and waste disposal;
- whether their products were tested on animals;
- access for people with disabilities;
- provision for vegetarians;
- consumer voting – how every consumer can support or boycott a product on the basis of its ethics;
- CFCs and HCFCs;
- policy on refusing entry on grounds of dress and appearance;
- exploitation in the workplace;
- links with other countries;
- facilities for parents;
- irresponsible marketing of baby milk in developing countries;
- trading and environmental policies of national chainstores and supermarkets.

Some short extracts from the foreword to the guide captures the approach of the YOB group,

"*In order to solve the problems facing **all** of us at the moment, i.e. human rights, the environment, poverty, AIDS etc., we must learn to think of ourselves as belonging to a world community. The larger your boundaries and the terms in which you think of yourself, the more chance we have of surviving as a planet.*

By thinking of someone as foreign, or not belonging to the same groups as you, it allows you to abuse or discriminate against those people far more easily. It is an attitude that is growing in popularity, and could be associated with the rise of the extreme right wing in various places. In contrast, if you put all people in the same group as you – the group labelled 'us', it is far harder to abuse them or kick them around."

Cartoon by Stan Eales from the *Ethical Shopping Guide*

During the preparation of the guide, the group used questionnaires and visited shops throughout the Bath area. The publication of the guide, nicely typeset and with some smashing cartoons from Stan Eales, was the outcome, but it also provided a wonderful shared learning process for the group members. They also managed to use it as a stepping stone to further work. In the following 14 month period, further bulletins were issued by the group. These focused on themes such as 'Whaling', 'Transport', 'Rainforests' and 'Freedom'. A number of the bulletins were accompanied by campaigning events. For instance, to accompany the publication of the 'Transport' bulletin, the group organised a 15 minute cycle (very slowly) round one roundabout to slow up traffic and bring attention to transport policies and solutions.

A bit more about the YOBs
The YOBs were not affiliated directly to the Youth Service. The group was formed following the proactive intervention of the Communication Breakdown Youth Project, which was a three year project in the Bath area, funded by the EC. To quote from the *Communication Breakdown* Report,

> "The target group was young people aged 16-25, specifically outside of the youth service...The publicity referred to issues such as human rights, sexism, homelessness and so on, to avoid jargon such as 'development education'. Therefore, young people with some level of interest in these sorts of issues were the ones targeted."

With access to photocopiers, computers, phone etc. in the Bath DEA Centre, the group met for discussions, planning and meetings, but their focus was always very much about action. Over the years they maintained a core group of about ten, with people joining and drifting away. After their production of the *Shopping with Awareness* guide, the YOBs turned their attention to making a video called *The A to Z of the Environment.* In both ventures, members of the group had to take on the roles of researchers, interviewers, editors and writers. In the *Communication Breakdown* report, it says that among other skills the group members acquired learning outcomes...

- critical thinking skills;
- communication skills;
- networking skills at local, national and international level;
- public relation skills;
- groupwork and facilitation skills.

During the years of the Communication Breakdown project, all the young people had access to a good range of media equipment and advice. This included video, photography, magazine production and drama. But, essentially the YOB group grew through mutual exploration and activity around specific concerns and issues. This is relatively unusual in a lot of youth work, where skills-based sessions are seen as an end in themselves.

The Bath Development Education Centre sadly no longer exists, but individuals who were involved with the YOBs are still very active in environmental campaigning.

Mind Your World – *breaking barriers through global connections*
This was the title of an exciting three day conference held in July 1995. The event, with 50 participants, was planned and run by eight young people aged 16-22 who were brought together by the Commonwealth Youth Exchange Council (CYEC). The following extract was written by Jennifer Hurd, one of the eight young people involved in the planning committee.

Starting out
I got involved with CYEC while participating in an exchange between Staffordshire's Duke of Edinburgh's Award Scheme and Ghana's Head of State award in 1993/94. In September 1994 I was contacted by CYEC and asked to be on the planning group for another conference whose aim was to link youth exchanges with the environment. In the first meeting we all sat with blank sheets of paper and it was hard then to believe that we would ever achieve what we have.

Over a series of one day meetings and a residential weekend things gradually started to come together. One thing that amazed me was that we actually had to make all the decisions ourselves, work out the programme and sort out the finances. The CYEC staff kept us going with advice and they did most of the boring administration work but they left the rest entirely up to us. Finally, after hours of planning, lots of hard work and our fair share of setbacks, the weekend of the conference arrived. We were fortunate enough to have people attending from two schools in Tanzania, one of them for the blind and partially sighted, a school and a YMCA group from India, as well as people from the UK. This created a good cultural mix.

The first activity involved splitting the delegates into six smaller 'home groups'. One of the main aims of the conference was to share experiences, so these groups were a mixture of people from environmental groups and those currently undertaking exchanges. The first home group session was an introduction to the conference and an opportunity for the delegates to mix with new people. Each group was led by one of the planning group members. On the Friday evening we had hired a drama group to perform a short play and run environmental workshops. The workshops were a brilliant ice-breaker and really got the conference going.

Saturday morning was taken up with two short presentations by groups attending the conference. Each group then made a mini display of their projects and there was a chance for people to look at and discuss each other's displays. In the afternoon. Kevin McCullough from Christian Aid, ran the Trading Game simulation for us, which turned out to be one of the highlights of the conference. The young people then chose one workshop from six, ranging from ecotourism to fair trade. Two of the workshops were run by planning group members and the others by people from outside organisations.

A highlight – playing the Fair Trade game

New ideas and future plans
Sunday's focus was to discuss future action that delegates and CYEC could take to encourage youth exchanges with an environmental theme. Each home group came up with a set of proposals directed at CYEC and at their individual organisations. The groups then presented their ideas to the whole conference in a feedback session. The main theme which emerged from all the presentations was the need to raise awareness.

- *For the environmental organisations, this involved making greater international connections with environmental issues, including promoting youth exchanges, so young people from different countries can work together on environmental issues.*
- *For the organisations already undertaking youth exchanges, it was to incorporate environmental themes into their future exchanges, so participants not only have personal gains from the visit, but are also able to benefit the country they are visiting.*

At the end of the session it was clear that the delegates were all going to take future action and the conference had given them ideas to move forward with.

Sense of achievement
Coming home I felt a great sense of achievement that the aims we had set out a whole year ago had been fulfilled. Through the conference we had given young people the chance to discuss how they felt about important issues, which turned out to be the same concerns for young people throughout the world. At the end of the weekend the young people were empowered to do something about these issues for themselves and not just be an observer.

Comments from the evaluation forms *illustrate this feeling:*
"Brilliant! - I've thought more in the past two days than in the past six months."
"...we were encouraged to participate at every level."
"In the end, it seems hard to believe that what started off with a blank sheet of paper could ever have become **Mind Your World***..."*

For more information contact: Commonwealth Youth Exchange Council, 7 Lion Yard, Tremadoc Road, London SW4 7NF. Tel. 0171 498 6151.

TOOLS FOR SELF RELIANCE
Background
Alan first became aware of Tools for Self Reliance (usually known by their acronym, TFSR) about a year ago. He then met some of their workers and volunteers at the Big Green Gathering in Wiltshire, and subsequently got to know more about the organisation and how young people can get involved. Judith Barrett and Sam Platt are their Group Support Workers, who kindly provided the following outline of the work which the organisation is involved with. It seems a straightforward and very logical example of getting involved in global issues, which also happens to reuse equipment in an eminently sustainable way! And, easy enough for youth groups and individual young people to get involved with!

In a sentence, TFSF acquires, refurbishes and then distributes good quality hand and craft tools from the throw-away, leave-it-to-rust, cultures of the Northern hemisphere to Africa and Central America in the Southern hemisphere. Good on them!

Judith Barrett and Sam Platt told us,
"Basic tools are essential for all kinds of trades – carpentry, blacksmithing, tailoring to name just a few. Here in the countries of the North most of us take power tools for granted and buy disposable saws which are used for just a short while and then thrown away. Yet the costs of key tools are prohibitive for many in the South – and that's if they are even available. At the same time, thousands of hand tools lie unused and rusting in sheds and garages all over the UK. That's where TFSR comes in..."

Tools for Self Reliance
Essentially TFSR works through small local groups in the UK to collect tools

together, making them as good as new, ready to be used again. They are careful to send only tools which are requested and try to match supply and demand. They also try to encourage the use of old, often better quality tools, to be reused in our own UK community.

In Africa and Central America, TFSR work with individuals and groups offering technical training, credit schemes and establishing resource centres, where tool maintenance and even manufacture can also be learned. The workers at these centres then assess local needs, which in turn provides the basis for requests to the UK for tools. Hand tools are versatile, low cost and environmentally friendly. In skilled hands, they can make a significant difference to the community in which they are used. For instance, in rural Africa a carpenter may make desks for school children or an ox cart for a farmer to be able to transport his goods to market.

Local youth action
Young people have been involved with TFSR in a number of UK locations. Two recent ones are *Tonbridge Youth Action* and *Lowestoft Breakout.*

Tonbridge Youth Action
This is a Voluntary Service Unit based in the Design and Technology Department of a girls' school. Helped by professional staff, following a visit to the TFSR main workshop near Southampton, the group now meet weekly to refurbish tools. They also get involved with the issues around why they are doing it and where the tools will eventually be used. Samuel Masakume, from one of the Zimbabwean partner organisations, recently visited the girls' group and explained, first hand, how useful the tools could be in his country and some of the uses to which they could be put.

One of the girls at the Tonbridge TFSR programme

Ruth Corner, a volunteer with the Tonbridge group said,

> "It's good to be able to do something for other people as individuals which is not going to fade away."

Lowestoft Breakout

Very different from the Tonbridge group, Breakout exists for young people who have left school unsure of what they want to do. Most of the young people have few academic qualifications, and Breakout enables them to develop useful woodworking and restoration skills. They are also personally involved in the collection of handtools from the local area. Like the Tonbridge group, members did their initial training at the TFSR main workshop. Now they are ready to distribute their first tools to Africa. David from the group said,

> "It's good to be helping someone else to become self-sufficient – in this case a group of carpenters in Zimbabwe."

TFSR can be contacted through their Groups' Office at 10a Bishop Street, Leicester LE1 6AF. They have produced a handbook (price £5) which provides lots of practical information to stimulate the establishment of a TFSR group. They also have posters, slides and leaflets to publicise the work in a local area, from tool collecting through to renovation and distribution.

AN ALTERNATIVE BARTER SCHEME: LETS
What is it for?

Young people are among the most vocal critics of money systems, so it is natural that it is amongst the young, the innovative and the artistic, that alternative economic systems have tended to develop. Where Alan is based in Dorset, locals have banded together and created their own LETS (Local Exchange Trading System) scheme, using 'Cobbs' as the unit of currency, named after the local harbour. The idea is that a local system of (non-monetary) exchange encourages people both socially and economically.

Young people are, and should be, encouraged to be idealistic. And that is exactly what LETS is all about. It relies on trust and participation. It is principally a way of letting people help one another and choose how much they value their time or expertise. The person receiving goods or services can then 'owe' all the other people in the LETS system an agreed amount of the LETS currency.

In primitive societies, barter; exchanging services or goods directly without using a measurement of exchange (money) was the norm. For instance, the hunter would swap meat for the grain produced by the farmer. But, because of money markets and international exchange rates and agreements, the import and export of commodities can often wreak havoc with the economy of many local communities. Widespread unemployment and poverty can be the result. As compilers of this book neither of us know enough about economics of global exchange to argue that LETS schemes can change the nature of our society, however, on a local basis, *it can assist members of a community to trade even if they are poor or socially disadvantaged.* Within a LETS scheme, it is impossible to have people making money out of trading in money. Peter Lang in his book *LETS Work: Rebuilding the*

Local Economy, says,

> "LETS is a community resource, it is not a design for a private business, and there is no need for a system to be 'owned' by an individual or company, it is unlikely to work effectively if it is."

How to introduce it within a youth group

Money was traditionally regarded as a measurement of the *value* of services or goods. Take it away and people have to find a new way of valuing those same exchanges. For instance, if Delia repairs a bicycle for David, the LETS system allows Delia to suggest how much value in the LETS currency she wants to charge. In a system where the LETS unit is worth about £1, this might make a smallish repair be worth £5. David then owes the community system *not* Delia individually, the equivalent of £5 worth of his own goods or labour. Peter Lang says in his book about LETS,

> "LETS may mean fewer disaffected youths around on street corners. It could mean youth workers running clubs for LETS, and more young people having somewhere enjoyable to go....Employing young people for LETS on environmental projects can reduce vandalism."

As youth workers we think that this is a bit simplistic, but there is something of relevance and value for youth work in the system. To work successfully it relies on people spending (using services or goods). Being in debt doesn't mean that the person has to have any currency to start with, they just need to be willing to offer services or goods to someone else who is part of the local network.

Unfortunately, we can't quote from a youth group which has actually used the LETS system, but if used it might operate as follows:

1. A Youth Council or group of young people decide to start a LETS scheme. A meeting is held and they establish the name of the scheme and the unit of currency. Often the name of the unit and scheme reflect some aspect of the local community, so Malvern has Beacons and Newbury, yes, you've guessed it, has New Berries!
2. The way LETS works is described to all the potential members. For instance, some of the original aspects of LETS, as it originated in America, are: it is non-profit making; there is no compulsion for anyone to trade; information about the balances of member accounts is available to all members, and no interest is charged.
3. The local LETS group creates a list of members which could be just youth group members or could perhaps include their families. Then a directory is created of the services, goods or whatever they want to sell or exchange with other members. This is easier these days with simple computer databases, which can easily be up-dated. In some of the flourishing community LETS the range goods and services is enormous. One member may offer aromatherapy, another, car repairs, a third accommodation. In a youth club or group the services might range from typing and Internet time through to services such as baby sitting, hairdressing, craft goods and dog walking.
4. The service gets into gear. Members start using the goods and services available. By going into debt, they encourage other people to make use of services and goods available within the local barter network. Unlike simple

barter, the exchange of goods and services rarely takes place between just two people.

5. Early on, the LETS group needs to make sure it has a small team of efficient administrators. They don't own the system and they do not receive pay, but they do usually receive recompense, either in Sterling or units of Lets, for their expenditure on things like stationery, printing, stamps and telephone. They are responsible for making sure that the following exist and are regularly up-dated:
    - the directory of goods and services;
    - accounts and possibly issue of chequebooks;
    - publicity;
    - and, a secretary and treasurer to act as the main points of contact for members and other people in the local community.

Is it legal?

We haven't tried to cover every aspect of the ways in which the system develops. Some possibilities are definitely illegal, for instance, a 14 year old setting up a brewery business might be popular, but it would be might prove likely to put the LETS scheme outside the law! There are also complications regarding people who are obtaining benefits. If a person is working for many hours each week on LETS work they may very well not be seen as unemployed and available for work. The Department of Health and Social Security have indicated that some LETS members may infringe their Income Support entitlements and other benefits by earning credit through LETS, but there really hasn't been a clear ruling. The tax situation is equally tricky, but since it seems to be confusing the Inland Revenue, many might argue that the more confusion the better!

Peter Lang, *LETS Work: The Rebuilding of the Local Economy* (1994) Grover Books.
LetsLink, the national UK grouping of LETS organisations, 61 Woodcock Rd, Warminster, Wiltshire BA12 9DH.
National Council of Voluntary Organisations, Regents Wharf, 8 All Saints Street, London N1 9RL.

CHILDREN'S RIGHTS

There was much debate, as we carried out the planning for *Youth Action and the Environment*, about whether this was an issue which could or should be considered 'environmental'. We were aware of populations of children whose life chances were very poor due to endemic disease in their environment – 14 million children under five die each year in the developing world, mostly from disease and malnourishment. The financial cost of enabling these children to live is infinitesimal in comparison, for example, to the vast sums of money which most countries spend on armaments.

The more we thought about it, it did seem to us that children's rights were a fundamental environmental issue, simply because so many children die because their right to a clean, disease-free environment is not respected. Even if we look closer to home, we can find many examples where the rights of children are subjugated to the primacy of the industrial culture, with its attendant pollution. Britain allows the sale of fruit which has been sprayed with chemicals banned in other countries because they are suspected of causing cancer; the breast milk of British mothers contains 100 times more dioxin than the government's recommended safety guideline; and there is now little doubt that many respiratory diseases in children are caused by local air pollution created by industry, power plants or motor vehicles. Unbelievably, almost half the households in this country are still supplied with water through lead pipes.

At a global level the third world *debt crisis* places intolerable stress on poor nations as they struggle to maintain interest payments. In fact, when all factors are taken into account, third world countries give far more to the developed world each year than they receive in aid. The knock-on effects include reductions in health spending in these countries; in the 1980s health spending per head dropped by over 50 per cent in the 37 poorest countries of Africa and Latin America. During the same period, spending per head on education dropped by 25 per cent. Unsurprisingly, military budgets did not suffer significant reductions in the same period. In 1990, half of all third world government spending was on debt repayment or on the military. Military spending by these governments totals $125 billion every year. UNICEF has estimated that if one week of this spending was used to augment existing resources each year then most of the deaths of under fives in the developing world could be prevented.

Pollution and young people
Pollution of all kinds affects children more than adults; infants have higher metabolic rates so they inhale more pollution per unit of body weight than adults. Also, they have very little body fat (which can store pollutants quite effectively) so pollutants circulate for longer, causing more damage. Their rapid body and organ growth makes them vulnerable, particularly to toxic chemicals as they cannot 'process' the pollutants the way that adults can.

Motor vehicles and their pollution demand special attention as they inflict more damage on the global habitat than any other single commodity. The tragedy is that, even with full knowledge of their polluting effects, particularly on children, governments effectively subsidise their use. The car has such a tenacious hold on the psyche of humankind that it will take a gargantuan effort – or God forbid, a gargantuan disaster – to force change. Change, though, is inevitable as the traffic flow in most of our major cities approaches gridlock.

There is the argument, too, that our inaction in the face of *global warming* may have created an unstable and dangerous world for future generations. Few countries have as a first priority the fulfilment of children's social, psychological and physical needs as outlined in the 1989 UN Convention on the Rights of the Child; yet it is only through the active implementation of such undertakings that we will begin to properly respect our own children and their rights, let alone future generations.

Child Protection
Even in 'civilised' developed countries like our own there are glaring transgressions of the UN Convention. Howie has been an active worker with EPOCH, a campaigning organisation working against corporal punishment. He argues,

"For example, the child's right to the protection of its physical integrity is incompatible with allowing parents to hit their children in the guise of 'reasonable chastisement' as happens in the UK. There is also much evidence that condoning violence towards children (remember that this kind of violence is not tolerated against adults!) actually teaches children and adults that violence is an acceptable problem-solving device and therefore contributes to the overall levels of violence in society."

The UN Convention includes many articles which have relevance to young people and the environment. For example, they have a right to protection from exploitative work, and from drug abuse and sexual exploitation. An article which will strike a chord with many British children is the right to play – many young people feel that they have no safe, accessible areas in which to play. Another important agreement is 'Agenda 21'; this commits governments to set up ways to promote dialogue on the environment between young people and government at all levels. Agenda 21 is discussed in detail elsewhere in this book.

Save the Children's education unit produces a series of activity packs called 'Spotlight'. One of these is on children's rights and the environment and can be obtained from the address shown at the end of this section. We thank them for permission to reproduce two useful exercises from the activity pack which can be used to stimulate young people's interest in the issue:

What would happen if everybody did that?

It's quite likely that young people have met a disapproving adult who argues against any mildly unorthodox behaviour with the words,
   'What would happen if everybody did that...?"
You might regard it as a rather pointless response – after all, not everybody is going to do that. But it can raise interesting questions for discussion starters. Especially if you play it fast and initially with not too much seriousness (that can follow later).

Prepare some questions, on cards if you like, and encourage a young person to select one at random and shout it out. Then the group gives their initial response – just saying whether it would be a good or a bad thing 'if everybody did that'. Use questions such as:

* if everyone turned vegetarian;
* if everyone worked a maximum 30 hour week;
* if everyone demonstrated against a bypass;
* if everyone used public transport;
* if everyone lived in a city;
* if everyone bought fairly-traded goods;
* if everyone voted for what they believed in.

And throw in the odd 'if no-one' question as well:
* if no-one recycled anything;
* if no-one used pesticides;
* if no-one used a bike.

Once you have been through a few of these imaginings, take one or two that seem to have created most interest (or disagreement) and explore them in greater depth. Don't just follow the pressure group or fashionable line, though. Seek all interested opinions. The Vegetarian Society will tell you that the world will be a better place if we were all vegetarian. But the National Federation of Meat Traders will have a different view. Write and ask them. Look at the negative effects as well as the positive.

Two images from the anti-Criminal Justice Bill demos (Graeme Strike)

Do not just accept what the tree/road protesters are saying about the bypass. Seek out views from local politicians and interest groups who are in favour of the new road. What might young people in the area think? Search out the full story.

Who has greatest say?

Explore what young people think about their right to a voice. These polarised cards should stimulate discussion. You could have each one copied onto a card and have one young person read out the view to the rest. Invite discussion. If your group is into role play and acting, they could develop the characters and improvise a short scene, perhaps with the two characters meeting, brought together by an environmental problem.

Once you have discussed these, no matter what the balance of opinion among the group, you can explore different ways in which young people can have a say. What voice do young people have in their immediate environment – at school or youth club? There are some examples of good practice around – in all countries and at all levels. They can range from individual participation projects, to local youth councils and youth parish councils in the UK, to the children's world summits that have operated at United Nations level.

View One

Children and young people are idealistic and caring. That is good. But they simply do not know enough about the world to make useful decisions about it. They do not know how the real world works, they do not appreciate the importance to the economy of industry. They do not understand the financial implications of their impractical visions. They campaign against roads and get pious about traffic fumes. But they would be the first to complain if they couldn't get their fashion clothes, sports goods, American cola or their beefburgers. All those get here by road and lorry, manufactured by very efficient multinational companies to keep the costs down.

Young people should take an interest in the environment, but they cannot take a part in decision making until they have achieved the balanced outlook that comes with maturity.

View Two

Children and young people have a moral right to a say in important decisions about the environment. They are much closer to the day to day reality of life than adults. They are more vulnerable to the damaging effects of pollution, and to accidents like Chernobyl and Bophal. They will have to live longer with the results of the decisions than the people who are now making them.

Young people are less likely to take short term or politically convenient decisions than adults, and they are quite able to take a broader perspective. It makes me angry when I hear people saying that young people do not know about the real world. We do know about the real world – and that is why we care about saving it. When adults talk about the real world they really mean their own money-making businesses. They don't really care about the environment, they only act when their own interests are threatened.

And if young people have a strong view, get them to articulate it. There are plenty of local opportunities, letters to newspapers and radio phone-ins, where they can air their voice generally on the environment or on a specific issue that matters to them.

Two young people from Whitecroft, Solsbury Hill 94 (Matt Smith)

The whole issue of children's rights, and the wider one of human rights should be a key focus in work with young people. Not only does this educate young people, in a very personal way, about issues of personal and collective morality, but it encourages a broader vision of the world and a respect for what (with all its imperfections) used to be called the free world.

If we really did think about our children and their heritage – and it was this which drove key political decisions – we would be creating a very different world from that which we appear to be heading towards today. Enabling children's voices to be heard, to touch our conscience, is arguably the single most powerful thing adults can do to recognise their rights. In stimulating their interest in all matters environmental, youth workers and teachers play a crucial role in focusing their concern and creativity.

FURTHER INFORMATION

Save the Children
17 Grove Lane
London SE5 8RD
Tel: 0171 703 5400

Contact the education unit if you want to receive the magazine *RightAngle* and future editions of *Spotlight*. If you are wired visit the HOT SAVVY web page on http://www.oneworld.org/scf/youth

BIBLIOGRAPHY

The following is a mixture of reference material used in compiling the book, plus other books and publications, which either the authors or the CEE felt might be useful to those working on environmental action issues with young people. Some publications have been republished in a number of editions. Others like *Diggers and Dreamers* and *SchNEWS* are intended as annual publications.

Brief Glossary of acronyms

BEN is the Black Environment Network
BTCV is the British Trust for Conservation Volunteers
CAT is the Centre for Alternative Technology
CEE is the Council for Environmental Education
CFC is the abbreviation for chlorofluorocararbon
CYEC is the Commonwealth Youth Exchange Council
CRAC is the Caquetá Rainforest Campaign
DEA is the Development Education Association
DFY is Drive for Youth
EF is Earth First!
EYB is the Emmanuel Youth Project
FFT is Friends and Families of Travellers
FOE is Friends of the Earth
LETS is the Local Exchange Trading System
LGMB is the Local Government Management Board
NAOE is the National Association for Outdoor Education
NATTA is the National Association for Alternative Technology and Technology Assessment
NCH Action For Children is National Children's Homes Action For Children
NCVYS is the National Council for Voluntary Youth Services
ND indicates date unknown or undated source
NGO is a Non-Governmental Organisation
NIF is the Neighbourhood Initiatives Foundation
NFCF is the National Federation of City Farms
NT is the National Trust
NYA is the National Youth Agency
PFAF is Plants for a Future
RA is the Ramblers' Association
RSPB is the Royal Society for the Protection of Birds
RSPCA is the Royal Society for the Prevention of Cruelty to Animals
RTS is Reclaim the Streets
SPARC is the Society for the Promotion of Area Resource Centres
TFSR is Tools for Self Reliance
UNED-UK is the United Nations Environment and Development UK
WWF UK is the World Wide Fund for Nature UK
YCUK is Youth Clubs UK
YHA is the Youth Hostels Association
YOC is the Young Ornithologists Club of the RSPB

Publications

Adams, Paul *et al.* (1994) *Communication Breakdown* Bath Development Education Centre

Advisory Service for Squatters (1996) *The Squatters' Handbook* Advisory Service for Squatters

Allaby, Michael (1989) *Guide to Gaia* Optima

Allaby, Michael ed. (1989) *Thinking Green* Barrie and Jenkins

Allen, Paul and Todd, Bob (1995) *Off the Grid* CAT

Angel, Heather *et al.* (1981) *The Natural History of Britain and Ireland* Michael Joseph

Bourn, Douglas (1994) *Delivering the International Curriculum for Youth Work* DEA

Bourn, Douglas and McCollum, Ann (1995) *A World of Difference: Global Connections in Youth Work* DEA

Bremness, Lesley (1990) *The Complete Book of Herbs* BCA

British Trust for Conservation Volunteers (ND) Series of practical handbooks including: *Footpaths; Hedging; Waterways and Wetlands; Trees and Aftercare,* and *Dry Stone Walling* BTCV

Bronze, Lewis (1990) *The Blue Peter Green Book* BBC Books

Brown, Maggi (1996) *Growing Naturally: A Teacher's Guide to Organic Gardening* Southgate Publishers

Budgett-Meakin, Catherine (1992) *Make the Future Work: Appropriate Technology – A Teachers' Guide* Longman

Bunyard, Peter and Morgan Grenville, Ferm, eds. (1987) *The Green Alternative Guide to Good Living* Methuen

Button, John (1989) *How to be Green* Century Hutchinson/FOE

Calouste Gulbenkian (1995) *Children and Violence* Calouste Gulbenkian

Centre for Alternative Technology (1995) *Crazy Idealists! The CAT Story* CAT

Centre for Alternative Technology (ND) *Activities for Children (Ecology and Sustainable Development)* CAT

Centre for Alternative Technology (ND) *Organic Gardening* CAT

Centre for Alternative Technology (ND) *Watch Out! Things to do with Solar Power for 8-12s, and 13-16s* CAT

Chandler, David *et al.*(1992) *The Environmental Indoors: A Guide to Indoor Meetings* RSPB

Christian Aid (1982) *The Trading Game* Christian Aid

Clayton, Caroline (ND) *Causing a Stink: The Eco Warrior's Handbook* FOE

Club of Rome (1972) *Limits to Growth*

Coates, Chris *et al.* eds. (1996) *Diggers and Dreamers 96/97: The Guide to Co-operative Living* D & D Publications

Common Ground (1994) *Celebrating Local Distinctiveness* Common Ground

Common Ground (ND) posters: *Tree Dressing Day* and the *Alphabet of Celebrating Local Distinctiveness* Common Ground

Community Service Volunteers (1990) *Spring Green Motorway Game* CSV/CEE/Transport 2000

Cornell, Joseph Bharat (1979) *Sharing Nature with Children* Exley/InterAction

Cornell, Joseph Bharat (1987) *Listening to Nature* Exley

Cornell, Joseph Bharat (ND) *Journey to the Heart of Nature: A Guided Exploration* Deep Books

Council for Environmental Education(1994) *The Story So Far: A Brief History of Environmental Youth Work* CEE

Council for Environmental Education (1995) *Good Practice: Criteria and Case Studies* CEE

Council for Environmental Education (1995) *The Environmental Agenda: Taking Responsibility (Higher Education Curriculum)* Pluto Press

Croall, Stephen and Rankin, William (1982) *Ecology for Beginners* Writers and Readers Co-op

Dearling, Alan and Armstrong, Howie (1994) *New Youth Games Book* Russell House Publishing

Dearling, Alan and Armstrong, Howie (1995) *World Youth Games* Russell House Publishing

Dearling, Alan and Armstrong, Howie (1996) *New Youth Arts and Craft Book* Russell House Publishing

Duckworth, Sue (ND) *Be Your Own Recycling Expert* Richmond Council Recycling Section

Durrell, Gerald (1982) *The Amateur Naturalist* Dorling Kindersley

Earle, Fiona and Gubby (1996) *My Home Series of 10 Culturally Friendly 'reader' for Traveller Children* Travellers School Charity

Earle, Fiona *et al.* (1994) *A Time to Travel? An introduction to Britain's Newer Travellers* Enabler Publications

EDET Group (1992) *Good Earth keeping: Education, Training and Awareness for a Sustainable Future* UNEP-UK (now UNED-UK)

Elkington, John and Hailes, Julia (1985) *The Green Consumer Guide* Victor Gollancz

Emmanuel Youth Project (1996) *Water 4 Life Report* Emmanuel Youth Project

Esso (1996) *Treewatch Survey and Action Pack* Wildlife Watch/Esso

Fairlie, Simon (1996) *Low Impact Development: Planning and People in a Sustainable Countryside* Jon Carpenter Publishing

Fetwell, John (ND) *Recycling: A Practical Guide for the School Environment* Learning Through Landscapes Trust

Flood, Marianne (1996) *Changing the World: A Directory of Global Youth Work Resources* NYA

Friends of the Earth (1990) *How Green is Britain?* Hutchinson

Friends of the Earth (1991) *The Recycling Officer's Handbook* FOE

Friends of the Earth (ND) *Going Green at Home and School* FOE

Girardet, Herbert (1996) *The Gaia Atlas of Cities: New Directions for Sustainable Living* Gaia Books

Gellatley, Juliet and Wardle, Tony (ND) *The Silent Ark* Thorsons

Godwin, Fay (1990) *Our Forbidden Land* Jonathon Cape

Gold, Mark (1988) *Living Without Cruelty* Green Price

Gold, Mark (ND) *Animal Rights* Jon Carpenter Books

Green Guide (1997) *The Green Guide for London* Green Guide Company Ltd.

Greenpeace (1987) *Coastline: Britain's Threatened Heritage* Kingfisher

Grigson, Geoffrey (1982) *Geoffrey Grigson's Countryside* Ebury Press

Grose, Annouchka and Fox, Red (ND) *The Teenage Vegetarian Survival Guide* Vegetarian Society

Groundwork (1996) *SiteSavers Report* Groundwork Trust

Grundy, Lisbeth and McLeish, Ewan (1994 and 1996) *Educating for a Sustainable Local Authority* and *Local Agenda 21 and Young People* Local Government Management Board

Hardy, Ralph *et al.* (1985) *The Weather Book* Michael Joseph

Hart, Robert (ND) *Forest Gardening* Green Books

Hawken, Phil (1994) *The Ecology of Commerce* Weidenfield and Nicholson

Henshaw, David (1989) *Animal Warfare: the Story of the Animal Liberation Front* Fontana

Hinde, Thomas (1985) *Forests of Britain* Abacus

Hogan, Kathleen (1994) *Eco Inquiry* Kendall Hunt

Holden, Peter (1995) *Environmental Games Guide* RSPB

Hoult, Charles (1991) *Living Green: A Summer's Cycle around Green Britain* Green Books

Houriet, Robert (1971) *Getting Back Together* Abacus

Howson, John (1995) *Young Person's Guide to the Environment* Souvenir Press

Huckle, J. and Sterling, S. (ND) *Education for Sustainability* Earthscan

Ingram, Mrill (1993) *Bottle Biology* Kendall Hunt

Institute of Earth Education (ND) *Earthwalks* Institute of Earth Education

James, Barbara (1992) *The Young Person's Guide to Animal Rights* Virago

Jenkins, Sid (1992) *Animal Rights and Human Wrongs* Lennard Publishing

Johnston, Jackie and Newton, John (ND) *Building Green* London Ecology Unit

Justice! (1995) *SchNEWS Reader* Justice! Brighton

Justice! (1996) *SchNEWS Round* Justice! Brighton

Khan, Lloyd ed. (1973) *Shelter* Shelter Publications

Khan, Lloyd *et al.* (1970 and 1990) *Shelter* Shelter Publications, USA

Lang, Peter (1994) *LETS Work: Rebuilding the Local Economy* Grover Books

Lewis, Martyn (1993 annual publication) *Go For it!* Lennard Publishing

Litvinoff, Miles (ND) *The Earthscan Action Handbook* Earthscan

Lovelock, James (1991) *Gaia: the Practical Science of Planetary Medicine* Gaia Books

Mabey, Richard (1989 2nd edition) *Food for Free* Collins

MacLellan, Gordon (ND) *Talking to the Earth* Capall Bann

Matthews, Graham and Stephens, Derek (1992) *Environmental Education Needs in Schools and Youth Work* CEE

McCloy, Andrew (1996/1997) *Coastwalk: walking the coastline of England and Wales* Hodder and Stoughton/Coronet

McHarry, Jan (1993) *Reuse, Repair, Recycle* Gaia Books

McKay, George (1996) *Senseless Acts of Beauty* Verso

Merrick (1996) *Battle for the Trees* Godhaven ink

Meyer, Kathleen (1994) *How to Shit in the Woods* Ten Speed Press

Money, Mike ed. (1993) *Health and Community : Holism in Practice* Resurgence Books

Myers, Norman (1985) *The Gaia Atlas of Planet Management* Gaia Books

National Youth Agency(1996) *Young People and the Environment Information Pack* NYA

Norris, Isobel (ND) *The Chase Schools' Pack* The Wildlife Trusts, London

North East Water (1992) *Wonderful World of Water* North East Water

Parkin, Sara (1991) *Green Light on Europe* Heretic Books

Peace Child International (1994) *Rescue Mission Planet Earth: A Children's Edition of Agenda 21* Kingfisher
Peace Child International (1996) *Rescue Mission: Indicators Pack* Peace Child International
Penney, Tony (1995) *The Initial Training of Youth and Community Workers* CEE
Penrick, Nigel (1987) *Earth Harmony* Rider Books/Century
Petrash, Carol (1993) *Earthwise: Environmental Crafts and Activities with Young Children* Floris Books
Porritt, Jonathon (1991) *Save the Earth* Dorling Kindersley
Porritt, Jonathon ((1990) *Where on Earth are we going?* BBC Books
Quarrie, Joyce ed. (1992) *Earth Summit, Rio de Janeiro* Regency Press
Randle, Damian (1989) *Teaching Green* Merlin Press
Redfern, Patrick (1996) *The Tipi: Construction and Use* Fish-Mani
Rogers, Alan (1996) *The Ass Kickers Guide to the Galaxy* Youth Clubs UK
Rogers, Alan ed. (1990 and 1992) *EARTHworks: The Action Pack* CEE
Royal Society for the Protection of Birds (1995) *The Wildlife Action Awards Group Pack* RSPB/YOC
Royal Society for the Protection of Birds (ND) *New Wave Games* RSPB
Rural Resettlement Group (various editions) *Rural Resettlement Handbook* Prism Alpha
Sarre, Philip and Blunden, John eds. (1996) *Environment, Population and Development* Hodder and Stoughton/Open University
Seattle, Chief (1992) *Chief Seattle's Vision* The Book Publishing Company
Seymour, John and Girardet, Herbert (1987) *Blueprint for a Green Planet* Dorling Kindersley
Sinden, Neil (1990) *In a Nutshell: A Manifesto for Trees* Common Ground
Smith, Alan (1994) *Creative Outdoor Work with Young People* Russell House Publishing
Stary, Frantisek (1991) *The Natural Guide to Medicinal Herbs and Plants* Treasure Press
Stauffer, Julie (1996) *Safe to Drink? The Quality of Your Water* CAT
Stone, C J (1996) *Fierce Dancing* Faber and Faber
Timberlake, Lloyd and Thomas, Laura (1990) *When the Bough Breaks* Earthscan
Trevelyn, John and Riddall, John (2nd edition 1992) *Rights of Way: Guide to Law and Practice* Commons, Open Spaces and Footpath Preservation Society and the Ramblers' Association
Usborne Nature Trail Books (ND various) *Ponds and Streams, Birdwatching, Wild Flowers and Insect Watching* Usborne
Vallely, Bernadette *et al.* (1991) *Green Living: Practical Ways to Make Your Home Environment Friendly* Thorsons
Van Maitre, Steve (ND) *Acclimatization* Institute of Earth Education
Walker, Pauline (1994) *The Young Person's Guide to the Environment* NYA
Watkins, David (1993) *Urban Permaculture* Permanent Publications
Wells, Phil and Jeffer, Mandy (1991) *The Global Consumer: Best Buys to Help the Third World* Victor Gollancz
Whitefield, Patrick (ND) *How to Make a Forest Garden* Green Books
Wilkes, Angela (1996) *The Amazing Outdoor Activity Book* Dorling Kindersley
Williams, Heathcote (1988) *Whale Nation* Jonathon Cape

Williams, Jennifer (1996) *Across the Street Across the World: A Handbook for Cultural Exchange* British American Arts Association
Wiseman, John (1996) *The SAS Survival Manual* Harper Collins
Woodcraft Folk (Environmental Packs) (1996) *Let's Grasp the Nettle (9-13 year olds), Let's Take the World in Hand (13-16 year olds)* Woodcraft Folk
Wright, Patrick (1995) *The Village that Died for Britain* Vintage
Wright, Rose (1928) *A Book of Symbols for Camp Fire Girls* Camp Fire Outfitting

Workshops at the Big Green Gathering 96

MAGAZINES AND JOURNALS

ARKANGEL, for animal liberation, BCM 9240, London WC1N 3XX.
BIG ISSUE, Fleet House, 57-61 Clerkenwell Road, London EC1M 5NP.
BUSINESS, The, Richmond Youth Service, Regal House, London Road, Twickenham TW1 3QB.
CLEAN SLATE, Centre for Alternative Technology, Machynlleth, Wales.
CLIMAX, Reforesting Scotland, PO Box 1701, Edinburgh, Scotland EH1 1YB.
CONSCIOUS CINEMA, PO Box 2679, Brighton BN2 1UJ.
EARTH FIRST! ACTION UPDATE, PO Box 9656, London N4 4JY.
EARTH MATTERS, FOE, England.
EARTHLINES, Council For Environmental Education, Reading.
ECOLOGIST, The, Cissbury House, Furze View, Five Oaks Road, Slinfold, W. Sussex RH13 7RH.
FESTIVAL EYE, BCM Box 2002, London WC1 3XX.
FOREST SCHOOLS CAMP MAGAZINE Filton House, 42 Payne Avenue, Aldrington, Hove, E. Sussex BN3 5HD.
FRONTLINE, c/o 53 Edithna Street, Stockwell, London SW9 9JR.
GREEN ANARCHIST, BCM 9240, London WC1N 3XX.
GREEN WORLD, Green Party magazine, 49 York Road, Aldershot, Hants GU11 3JQ.

GREENLEAF, 96 Church Road, Redfield, Bristol 5.
GREENLINE, PO Box 5, Lostwithiel, Cornwall PL22 OYT.
INTERACTIVE, Shell Better Britain Campaign, Victoria Works, 21a Graham Street, Birmingham B1 3JR.
JOURNAL OF ADVENTURE EDUCATION, Adventure Education, 12 St. Andrew's Churchyard, Penrith, Cumbria CA11 7YE.
LIVING GREEN, 11 Harpes Road, Oxford OX2 7QJ.
PERMACULTURE, Permaculture Publications, Hyden House, Little Hyden Lane, Clanfield, Hants PO8 0RU.
PINE CONE, Order of Woodcraft Chivalry quarterly journal, 73 Willow Way, Luton, Beds LU3 2SA.
POSITIVE NEWS with PLANETARY CONNECTIONS, The Six Bells, Church Street, Bishops Castle, Shropshire,SY9 5AA.
RED PEPPER, 3 Gunthorpe Street, London E1 7RP.
RESURGENCE, Salem Cottage, Trelill, Bodmin, Cornwall PL30 3HZ.
RIGHTANGLE, Save the Children, 17 Grove Lane, London SE5 8RD.
ROAD ALERT!, PO Box 5544, Newbury RG14 5FB.
SACRED HOOP: ancient natural wisdom, 28 Cowl Street, Evesham, Worcs WR11 4P1.
SCHNEWS, Justice?, Prior House, 6 Tilbury Place, Brighton BN2 2GY.
SCOTTISH ENVIRONMENTAL EDUCATION NEWS, University of Stirling, Scotland.
SPOTLIGHT, Save the Children, 17 Grove Lane, London SE5 8RD.
SQUALL, PO Box 8959, London N19 5HW.
STONEHENGE CAMPAIGN NEWSLETTER, c/o 99 Toriano Avenue, London NW5 2RX.
UNDERCURRENTS videos,16b Cherwell Street, Oxford OX4 1BG.
VOLUNTEER ACTION, National Youth Agency, Leicester.
WINGBEAT, RSPB Phoenix, The Lodge, Sandy, Bedfordshire SG19 2DL
WHAT ON EARTH, FOE, Scotland.
YOUNG PEOPLE NOW, National Youth Agency, Leicester.
YOUTH ACTION, National Youth Agency, Leicester.
YOUTH CLUBS, Youth Clubs UK, London.
YOUTH WORK, 37 Elm Road, New Malden, Surrey KT3 3HB.

USEFUL ADDRESSES

Details of many other organisations are given in the relevant sections of the book.

Black Environment Network (BEN)
9 Llainwen Uchaf, Llanberis, Gwynedd, Wales LL55 4LL
Tel: 01286 870715
BEN is a multiracial organisation which works to enable the 'invisible contribution' of black and minority ethnic communities to become recognised in environmental work.

British Trust for Conservation Volunteers (BTCV)
36 St Mary's Street, Wallingford, Oxon OX10 0EU.
Tel: 01491 39766
Involves people of all ages in practical conservation projects in rural and urban environments. Also has regional offices.

Centre for Alternative Technology (CAT)
Machynlleth, Powys SY20 9AZ
Tel: 01654 703409
The national centre for information and examples on alternative technology ranging from solar systems to energy efficient building design and permaculture. A very interesting centre for youth group visits with lots of 'hands-on' exhibitions.

Common Ground
Seven Dials Warehouse, 44 Earlham Street, London WC2H 9LA
Tel: 0171 379 3109
Offer a range of publications and examples of work which help people value their own surroundings. Their work includes supporting the planting of new orchards, tree dressing and the making of parish maps.

Council for Environmental Education (CEE)
University of Reading, London Road, Reading RG1 5AQ
Tel: 0118 975 6061
The national body promoting and co-ordinating environmental education. CEE's Youth Unit produces information, resources and a regular newsletter (*EARTHlines*) supporting those involved in environmental youth work, as well as running its own national environmental youth work programme.

Friends of the Earth (FOE)
26-28 Underwood Street, London N1 7TQ
Tel: 0171 490 1555
Campaigning organisation promoting sustainable development and policies to protect the natural environment. Some campaigns are particularly for young people, such as *Fuming Mad*. Produces a wide selection of leaflets and publications giving information on different environmental issues and can advise on local contacts.

Gaia Foundation
18 Well Walk, Hampstead, London NW3 1LD
Their work highlights the importance of cultural and ecological diversity, and focuses attention on issues surrounding indigenous people, particularly in the rainforests.

Greenpeace UK
Canonbury Villas, London N1 2PN
Tel: 0171 865 8100
Active campaigning organisation across the whole range of environmental issues. They are also a major publisher of environmental books.

Groundwork Foundation
85-87 Cornwall Street, Birmingham B3 3BY
Tel: 0121 236 8565
The national office for the local **Groundwork Trusts**, which aim to promote environmental improvement through partnership with the public, private and voluntary sectors of society. Increasingly involved in youth work programmes. If there is a Groundwork Trust in your area, they may be able to offer projects that your group could become involved in or give advice, identify sources of funding, offer practical support or otherwise enable your group to develop its own ideas.

National Association for Outdoor Education (NAOE)
12 St. Andrew's Churchyard, Penrith, Cumbria CA11 7YE
Tel: 01768 65113
A membership organisation open to anyone who is involved in or interested in outdoor education. It organises training events and provides a useful network for new information in the fields of adventure and outdoor education.

National Council for Voluntary Youth Services (NCVYS)
The Peel Centre, Percy Circus, London WC1X 9EY
Tel 0171 833 3003
NCVYS is the National Council for Voluntary Youth Services in England. It comprises the networks of 48 National Voluntary Youth Organisations and 72 Local Councils of Voluntary Youth Services. NCVYS also has 16 observer members. NCVYS aims to inform, support and enable organisations working with young people to respond effectively to the changing needs of the voluntary youth work sector.

National Youth Agency (NYA)
17-23 Albion Street, Leicester LE1 6GD
Tel 0116 247 1043
NYA acts as a central focus for youth work in England. It gives practical support to all those involved in the informal, personal and social education of young people, aims to improve the content and organisation of youth work and youth work training, and produces a range of publications. NYA also co-ordinates National Youth Work Week, which in 1996 focused on the environment.

Reclaim the Streets (RTS)
PO Box 9656, London N4 4JY
Tel: 0171 281 4621
A direct action network campaigning against the damaging effects of cars.

Rescue Mission
The White House, Buntingford, Hertfordshire, SG9 9AH
Tel: 01763 274459
UK headquarters of international organisation empowering young people to take action on sustainable development. Produced *Rescue Mission Planet Earth* (a children's edition of Agenda 21), and an indicators pack enabling young people to find out about and monitor progress on sustainable development issues in their area.

Royal Society for the Prevention of Cruelty to Animals (RSPCA)
Causeway, Horsham, W. Sussex RH12 1HG
Tel: 01403 264181
National organisation dealing with incidents of cruelty and neglect of animals.

Royal Society for the Protection of Birds (RSPB)
The Lodge, Sandy, Bedfordshire SG19 2DL
Tel: 01767 680551
Responsible for the protection and preservation of wild birds and their habitat. Has an active junior wing (YOC) and in 1996 launched RSPB Phoenix for those aged 13-19. Produces education materials and information as well as regular magazines and newsletters for members.

Save the Children (SCF)
Education Unit, 17 Grove Lane, London SE5 8RD.
Tel: 0171 703 5400
SCF has an active youth education programme. Its publications include the 'Spotlight' series of activity packs for use with groups of young people, and a regular magazine *Right Angle. Spotlight on children's rights and the environment* is of particular interest.

Survival International
11-15 Emerald Street, London WC1N 3QL
International campaigning organisation for tribal people worldwide.

The Wildlife Trusts
The Green, Witham Park, Waterside South, Lincoln LN5 2JR
Tel: 01522 544400
The national umbrella organisation for the local wildlife trusts. WATCH, its junior wing, co-ordinates a range of national scientific projects which can be undertaken by groups of young people. These include Riverwatch, Rockwatch, and the latest project, Treewatch.

WWF UK
Panda House, Weyside Park, Godalming, Surrey GU7 1XR
Tel: 01483 426444
Raises money for the international conservation of wildlife, natural habitats and natural resources. Produces a wide variety of education and information materials, largely aimed at schools but much of which may also be of use to youth groups.

Youth Clubs UK (YCUK)
11 St Bride Street, London EC4A 4AS
Tel: 0171 353 2366
National co-ordinating body for voluntary youth clubs. Publishes *Youth Clubs* magazine.

Russell House Publishing Ltd

Some of the practical books available from the current RHP publications' list

New Youth Games Book by Alan Dearling and Howie Armstrong

"A compendium resource of the first order." Young People Now. With over 36,000 copies sold, this classic book offers over 200 practical games and sequences for use with groups of young people. It includes everything from relationship games to alternative uses of pool and darts. Ideal for youth and social workers, teachers, playleaders and parents. **1-898924-00-7. £9.95.**

Creative Outdoor Work with Young People by Alan Smith

"One of the most light-hearted but immensely practical books about outdoor education." Times Educational Supplement. Successfully tried and tested activities for young people making creative use of the outdoors. Includes extensive sections on finding the way; orienteering; camp activities; problem solving; planning and safety; other outdoor ideas and the relevance to National Curriculum. A 'must have' for youth leaders, teachers and instructors. **1-898924-25-2. Large format. £11.95.**

World Youth Games by Alan Dearling and Howie Armstrong

"...delightfully illustrated and contains easy-to-follow instructions on table games, board games, active games and exercises for use in groups where adults try to enhance the self confidence, social, linguistic and numeracy skills of young people....useful for those working in a multi-cultural setting." Scottish Child. With games and activities collected from around the world, this is an invaluable and informative resource for playworkers, youth workers, teachers; in fact anyone working with young people. **1-898924-50-3. Large format. £9.95.**

Social Action for Young People: Accounts of SCF Practice
edited by Howard Williamson

"A shortage of 'youth work stories' has prompted the publication of this new book documenting the development of Save the Children's social action youth work projects." Howard Williamson says, *"social action youth work is a restatement of the centrality of old agendas of youth work: creating space, providing opportunities, establishing challenge, broadening horizons."* Young People Now. It offers blow-by-blow, worker accounts of projects which have genuinely tried to empower young people to make their own choices and take action for themselves. An important book for youth workers, students and trainers. **1-898924-60-0. £11.95.**

Quicksilver: Adventure Games, Initiative Problems, Trust Activities and a Guide to Effective Leadership by Karl Rohnke and Steve Butler

"We recommend it very highly." Alan Dearling and Howie Armstrong.
This new American bestseller provides an extensive, unusual and fun-filled collection of games and activities, plus practical tips on how to develop 'adventure leadership.' The authors describe their approach as using *"the basics of communication, co-operation and trust in the milieu of fun."* A valuable resource for youth games enthusiasts.
0-7872-0032-8. Large format. £23.95.

The New Youth Arts and Crafts Book by Alan Dearling and Howie Armstrong
Packed brimful with a wide and diverse range of practical arts and crafts activities to use with young people, this book represents the best of the old and new . It includes simple crafts such as hair-braiding, face painting and mask making alongside cooking and baking as a cultural activity; eco-activities; story telling; carnival and circus skills, giant bubbles; hot air ballooning and much much more. Each entry includes: how to do it, advice on materials, suppliers, and commentary on important aspects such as space, time, safety, staffing, problems and pitfalls and how to avoid them. Aimed at youth and play workers and others involved in creative group work. **1-898924-75-9. Large format. £11.95.**

To order books from this list please phone or write to Russell House Publishing. All prices quoted in this list exclude postage and packing which is charged at £1.50 per book (UK) and £2.50 per book (Elsewhere). Cheques should be made payable to Russell House Publishing Ltd. More detailed catalogue information available on request.

Russell House Publishing, 4 St George's House, The Business Park, Uplyme Road, Lyme Regis, Dorset DT7 3LS.
Tel/Fax 01297 443948 (9am - 5pm Mon - Fri)